# FOOTNOTE TO HISTORY

From Hungary to America
The Memoir of a Holocaust Survivor

## BY ANDREW LASZLO

D1711395

Footnote to History
From Hungary to America, The Memoir of a Holocaust Survivor
All Rights Reserved.
Copyright © 2023 Andrew Laszlo Sr.
v2.0

Text and photographs © 1996 by Andrew Laszlo; 2002 by University Press of America, Inc.; 2023 by Andrew Laszlo, Jr. Foreword © 2023 by Andrew Laszlo, Jr.

The opinions expressed in this manuscript are solely the opinions of the author and do not represent the opinions or thoughts of the publisher. The author has represented and warranted full ownership and/or legal right to publish all the materials in this book.

This book may not be reproduced, transmitted, or stored in whole or in part by any means, including graphic, electronic, or mechanical without the express written consent of the publisher except in the case of brief quotations embodied in critical articles and reviews.

Outskirts Press, Inc.
http://www.outskirtspress.com

ISBN: 978-1-9772-6060-4

Library of Congress Control Number: 2023901822

FOOTNOTE TO HISTORY was originally self-published as a limited edition by the author in 1996. It was published by University Press of America, Inc. in 2002. This edition is published by Outskirts Press, Parker, Colorado, in 2023.

The original photographs, letters, and postcards in this book now reside at the United States Holocaust Memorial Museum, Washington, DC, and are available for scholars and researchers.

Front cover photo: Forced as a young Jewish man to join the Hungarian Labor Service camp at Kőszeg, Hungary, Andrew Laszlo wears the camp uniform with the mandatory yellow armband on his left arm. Photo courtesy of the Laszlo family.

Back cover photo: Photo used with the permission of the United States Holocaust Memorial Museum.

Outskirts Press and the "OP" logo are trademarks belonging to Outskirts Press, Inc.

PRINTED IN THE UNITED STATES OF AMERICA

Nem tudom hol alusztok,

Nem tudom hol haltatok meg,

Tudom menyit szenvedtetek,

Emlékeid örökre szivemben van.

*To my wife and children*

# Contents

# FOREWORD

## by Andrew Laszlo, Jr.

My father told me of his secret when I was in my early forties. Until then, my mother, my three siblings, and I knew only that he had survived World War II and escaped Hungary under Soviet occupation. There was more to this story, much more. It was not something he cared to discuss, though occasionally there were anecdotes of happy memories and descriptions of his childhood. We did not know that he, his mother, father, and brother were all victims of the Holocaust and that only he survived.

On the date of the fiftieth anniversary of his arrival in New York Harbor, leather-bound copies of this book (he bound them himself) arrived at our doorsteps. He had made a conscious decision to keep this secret to himself so that his past would not be a defining influence in our lives. Though revisiting nightmarish memories and traumatic experiences must have been extremely difficult, he wrote of them in stunning detail. Remarkably, he had stored them away in a part of his mind where they could be retrieved but would not overwhelm his ability to go forward.

When my father arrived in New York, having turned twenty-one in transit, he had two dollars and sixty-three cents in his pocket. He wore clothes that he had sewn out of US Army blankets. He did not speak the English language. He had no college degree or formal profession. What he did have was the will to start again and leave a terrible past behind. He learned English by sitting in movie theaters watching continuous double features.

He was drafted into the US Army where he was assigned to the Signal Corps and learned to use modern motion picture equipment. He obtained his first job in the movie business on the *Phil Silvers Show* by claiming to be an expert on a new piece of camera equipment that no one on the set (including himself) had ever seen. After being told to come to work the following week, he hid in the studio over the weekend and practiced taking the camera apart and putting it back together. By the time the crew returned on Monday, he operated the camera perfectly.

My father went on to have a distinguished career. He was the director of photography for over fifty movies and television series. His credits include *Shogun* and *Rambo: First Blood*. He was nominated for two Emmy Awards. He traveled the world making films and teaching the next generation of filmmakers.

In 2004, he was an honoree along with Elie Wiesel at the annual Days of Remembrance ceremony in the Capitol Rotunda. Two years later, while accepting a lifetime achievement award from the Hungarian National Film Institute, he reminded the audience of Hungary's role in the Holocaust, admonishing them to never allow such horrors to happen again.

After reading his book, we traveled with him to Pápa, his hometown, where we retraced his odyssey from the family home to the ghetto, to the railroad station that led to the concentration camp. We visited his mother's burial place in the graveyard of the Pápa synagogue, once one of the largest in Europe, but now in disrepair with few remaining members. It was Holocaust Remembrance Week in Hungary. I remarked to my father that I was glad the Hungarian people were trying to make amends, but upon leaving the ceremony, we walked around a street corner and noticed a fresh swastika drawn on a wall, a reminder that hatred still existed.

Since my father's death on October 7, 2011, I discovered that he was in the Bergen-Belsen concentration camp at the same time as Anne Frank. As much as I mourn that period in history, I recognize that there were also many heroes, like his friend Rosa who risked his own life to bring my father water and cheese when he was starving on the train to Belsen. It is with that spirit that I republish *Footnote to History*. It is a monument to a great man and a reminder of a dark time in history. I hope that keeping the story alive might in some way prevent it from happening again.

# PREFACE

The following autobiographical account of my early years took almost ten years to complete—close to forty years after it probably should have been written. I have often wondered why it took so long. Though I have more than a few explanations that might be acceptable, I'm not absolutely convinced that the real reason for this delay may not be buried—hidden somewhere in the unreachable crevasses of my mind. I also wonder if an explanation is really important. As the reader will soon realize, when this book was written, it was not intended for general publication. Why did I take all those years to write it then? And once I wrote it, why was I still reluctant to publish it? The answer, I believe, is simple. I wrote about my early life and experiences, not just because I considered them unique and interesting, but because the events depicted in this book dramatically affected me and my family. Yet my wife and children knew practically nothing about the events and circumstances of my early life.

The book was written for my wife and children. I wanted to inform them, and thought that it would be easier and better to put the swirling mass of my thoughts on paper, than to tell the story orally, which at best would have been fragmented and disconnected. Writing about my memories in a more or less structured, coherent fashion, I sensed, would add continuity, and make the overall picture easier to understand.

I had also hoped that writing the book would lift the pressure I was living under for many years as I kept most details of my former life a closely guarded secret, and would help the reader understand the reasons behind that secrecy.

Because the book was intended only for my family, it contains certain elements that my wife and children are familiar with. But now that the book has been published, some explanations of those elements are necessary.

For instance, the opening page of the prologue makes reference to my daughter, as she "…waited for Vice President Quayle's plane in Shannon, Ireland…" without offering any further explanation. Everyone in my family knows that Liz—Lizzo, as we still call her—worked for the White House at that time in what is called the "advance section." The advance section is composed of Secret Service people, communications specialists, aides, and so on. Lizzo, in spite of her young age, was in what we thought was an important position, going all over the world helping to arrange and set up trips for the president, or the vice president, and their families and staff. That is why she was in Ireland.

Similarly, the caption under the first two photographs in the photo section of the book reads: *Your Grandparents*. Had the book been written for the general public, this caption would read: *My Mother and Father*. The book is full of similar, at times unexplained, references. But once the general theme and intent of the account—as it was written for my family—become obvious, I hope that this exclusivity, the familiarity of language as one talks with one's family, will become acceptable to the reader.

I invite the reader to try to fill in, disregard, or simply wonder about gaps that remain unexplained; or, in view of the obviously larger aspects of this account, dismiss them as unimportant. Reading about my early life and how I grew up in a war-torn country during an era of madness I hope will also suggest the underlying reasons that kept me from telling this story for such a long time.

I made no attempt at a literary style in telling my story. Instead, I opted for the way I normally speak with my family, as I describe the incidents and circumstances that surrounded and shaped my early days. Here, then, is my personal footnote to history, as the memories, good and bad, came out of the shadows.

# ACKNOWLEDGMENTS

## by Andrew Laszlo

As my children grew, asking more and more questions regarding past portions of my life they knew very little about, their insistence and desire to know reinforced my feeling that I should not—and must not—keep secrets from them. They urged me to tell the story and talk about secrets that could have died with me, or could have been revealed to them by other sources with possible traumatic effects. But it was my wife of over fifty years who, after learning about my life prior to our marriage in 1952, persuaded me to write the book, and assured me that revealing my past would not upset the equilibrium of our family. I am convinced that without her support, insistence, and patient understanding of my fifty years of pent-up turmoil, this book would never have been possible. The lion's share of the credit for making this account happen goes to her.

I received much encouragement from many others to publish this book. They believed that the information it contained would be of interest outside my family. To mention just a few, friends such as Leonard Leiman and his wife, Joan, and my onetime classmate Alex Jokay, who witnessed some of the events described in the book, and his wife, Sharon, were very supportive.

So were my friends whose names are mentioned in the book, some of whom are alive today. This book is dedicated to them, and to the memory of those who, along with my family, perished during the terrible events I describe in my account.

# ACKNOWLEDGMENTS

## by Andrew Laszlo, Jr.

The task of publishing a new edition of *Footnote to History* from an old PDF file turned out to be an enormous undertaking. The goal was to improve the readability and design without changing my father's words or thoughts.

I could not have even started without the guidance of semi-retired book publisher, Doug Pfeiffer and his company, Douglas Pfeiffer Consulting. He had the expertise to find a solution for every roadblock we encountered. He never let me get discouraged and kept the project moving to completion.

I thank Donald Gura of Don Gura Design Group for his inspired work and meticulous process. Don used powerful software to translate the old PDF into a usable file. The newly designed version is easier to read and enjoy.

I thank Olivia Ngai. She proofread and edited the book with enthusiasm and attention to detail. Her work was above and beyond what I could have expected.

I thank Tina Ruvalcaba of Outskirts Press for understanding the importance of putting this book back into print for the next generation to understand and never forget.

I thank Lisa Buckley of Outskirts Press for her help in pre-production constantly dealing with my questions and concerns.

I thank Jeff, Jim, and Liz Laszlo for their support and sharing their ideas, and Carol Michaud for her sound advice and help with the photo editing.

They certainly were the A-team. Thanks to their expertise and caring, the new edition of *Footnote to History* is a work that my father would have been proud of.

# PROLOGUE

Should auld acquaintance be forgot
And never brought to mind? —*Robert Burns*

*Happy New Year!*

For the first time in many, many years, Mom and I decided not to stay up till midnight to watch television and see the ball descend from atop the old *New York Times* building. Guy Lombardo had been dead for many years and the prospect of looking at Dick Clark's ever-young face again, and the crowds at Times Square replaying last year's madness, didn't appeal to us. Jeff, visiting from Los Angeles, and Jim were anxious to get to bed, having planned an early start the following morning to go skiing in Vermont. It really didn't make any sense to stay up. Instead, at ten minutes past ten, we opened a bottle of champagne and drank a toast to Lizzo, who, as you know, was born at that moment, twenty-seven years ago. As we drank, she was in Shannon, Ireland, waiting for Vice President Quayle's plane, which never came. Midnight was still a couple of hours away, and Times Square was already overflowing with brave tourists, drunks, and hopeful pickpockets. We drank another toast to the coming year, and went to bed.

It is almost 1991. Another year was gone, and in twelve days I will be sixty-five years old. I don't feel sixty-five—actually I don't know how sixty-five is supposed to feel—but it does bring one thing to mind: I am not getting any younger! God willing, I do expect to be here a year from now—actually, I hope to be around for some time yet—but I think it's time to carry out the promise I made to all of you exactly one year ago, to finally tell you who I am, where I came from, talk about my parents, my old family, the places of my youth, my life before you knew me, everything I never talked about until now.

I am not sure it wouldn't be better to let sleeping dogs lie. What follows in some ways might cause discomfort. If it does, I apologize and assure you it is done only in the interest of truth and because, like you, I also believe you should know all about me. There are many reasons why I did not talk about myself or certain parts of my life for so long. When you read this account, I hope you will understand. A long time ago I made a conscious decision to keep some aspects of my past tucked away in a strong box, out of sight, out of mind. The reason, or rationale, behind this decision was, I suppose, that I don't like to talk about things unpleasant, nor do I want aspects of my life that were painful to me to hurt you. I also believed that in the larger scheme of things, they were inconsequential, unimportant, and would have little, if any, significance in our lives and future. In fact, I was convinced that the future would definitely be better without the influence of the past. In other words, particularly as it concerned things unpleasant or unhappy, I made up my mind never to look back, cry over spilled milk, or feel sorry for myself. As you'll see, there were more than a few incidents in my past sixty-five years, which were unhappy and unpleasant, to say the least, but there are also many, which are now fond and pleasant memories.

In fact, now that you started me thinking about those years and my previous life is beginning to take shape again, I must admit there might be more than a few instances in my former life that, most probably, will be of interest to you. This is somewhat of a reversal in my thinking until now, in that I never believed I was anybody special. I still don't think so, nor did I ever believe that anyone would give a hoot hearing about who I was, where I came from, what I did at various stages of my life, and why. I am convinced the world would function equally well, or equally badly, with or without me. Yet, as I was mentally preparing this account during the past year, a thought crept into my mind that my life, though it may not be outstanding in any way, might nevertheless be a bit different in some of its aspects from what one might consider average or normal. I began to feel that in a sense, I was not "the fellow next door," born and raised in the same town, taking the traditional, predictable steps in life with equally predictable "normal" results, living an average, "normal" life. Please don't misunderstand me. I don't consider myself better, nor do I want to give the impression that I demean in any way the life of "the fellow next door." But I now believe that indeed I am, or perhaps my life is, in some respects, different. I do not apologize, nor do I want to take credit for this difference. I cannot claim that I consciously, or willfully, created it. It just happened, or was forced on me by circumstances, which in most instances were beyond my control. My sole claim can therefore be that I was at the right or wrong place, at the right or wrong time.

To start with, I was born in a faraway place—it's not clear where—

which I'll try to explain in the proper part of this account. Grew up, and survived some of the most turbulent and dramatic years and events in recent history while my entire family perished, and all material holdings my family and I ever had were lost forever. These are hints of what's coming in this account of my life, almost from infancy and as a young fellow. The war with its devastating consequences, coping with the aftermath of that tragedy, was perhaps the most influential factor during my early life. The war, which you fortunately didn't know, and few still remember in its full impact and significance, disrupted and changed my life completely. Yet you, my new family, are a consequence and a reward of that war. Without it, I might never have come to the United States and have providence provide you, my new family.

While the war and the turbulence it created, upsetting the equilibrium of my life, might have been, and most probably was, most significant, it was by no means the only important event influencing the years that, until now, I never talked about. Other, "normal" experiences of growing up, far less notable or interesting, round out the overall picture of my past, which might be difficult to understand without them.

Looking back, I now know that the war was the event that forced me to the next critical and most consequential crossroad of my life. Shortly after the war, I decided to lick my wounds, believing they would heal, chuck my past, and take every measure within my means to avoid facing anything like it ever again. I knew that The Past, Volume One of my life, had to be deliberately and decisively finished. The book had to be closed so as not to allow the devastating past affect Volume Two, The Future. It was a most important and very difficult decision to make by a young fellow just twenty. In fact, as it affected my life from that point on, it was probably the most momentous and consequential decision I have ever made. I had to break ties with everything, material, spiritual, and emotional. I had hoped my resolve would be strong and that my brain and willpower could overcome all obstacles so that the past, hopefully, would be erased, forgotten. I placed the past in a strongbox, locked it out of my future, and threw away the key. I made up my mind the past was forgotten. But it wasn't. It couldn't be. In fact, hardly a day goes by when in some manner I am not reminded of it. One thing I still believe is that it would not have been fair, or served any purpose, to burden you or anyone else with the weight of those events.

So liberated from past—or so I thought—with very little in my pockets and with a heavy heart, but with boundless, blind hope, and great expectations for the future, I pulled up stakes and struck out on a journey most of my friends and relatives considered foolhardy, even dangerous. The journey did turn out to be long, and at times arduous, but it landed me in America, the land of my dreams.

From this point on my life is not shrouded in as much mystery. Leaving some of the horrors and tragedies of the first half of the twentieth century behind, it was time to forget, look to the future, be born again, and start building a new life. A life I can look back on a half a century later, fondly with pride and with a sense of accomplishment.

My new family, the only thing of true importance in my new life in the new world, was started just five years after I got off the boat in New York, a homeless refugee, on the seventeenth of January 1947. In the years which followed, you—my family—grew. I want you to know that I consider my new family my greatest compensation for the past.

Somehow, I was also fortunate to land in an industry that is unique and interesting and that, with all its ups and downs, was good to me, offering unusual and at times exciting and fascinating opportunities. It rewarded me with a modest success professionally and with the ability to provide a lifestyle, which I had hoped for, for all of us. But let me get on with it, starting at the very beginning, uncovering the void, revealing the unknown portions of my life, which, until now, I have discussed only in disconnected and very brief snatches, and, in some of its aspects, not at all.

To recall and write about a lifetime in all of its aspects, experiences, highlights, as well as the low points, I know would be impossible. But I will try to describe all the events that I know are significant or that I think will round out the picture and might be of interest to you. Good and bad, important or not, reading what follows, you will for the first time know all about me as I try to recall and relate the events of so long ago, before the memories fade.

# Chapter 1

# 1926 –
# BEFORE SCHOOL

The earliest recollections of my life go back to the late 1920s and come to me in brief, vague, and fragmented snatches. At times, almost like still photographs or short vignettes, they are without sound or color. These early remembrances are most of the time pleasant and fond. Over the years some have been etched into my memory with the crystal-clear definition and sharpness of a fine photograph.

Others are hazy. Whenever my brain tries to produce them, I am aware that parts are missing, and in some cases they seem like unfinished puzzles to which pieces have been lost long ago. There are times when I am no longer able to say how accurate some of these memories are. Did my imagination, I ask myself, or the passing of time alter them? Did fantasy or wishful thinking take over where the ability of a young brain failed to accurately store images on a day-to-day basis, particularly when the events were routine or without particular significance? Likewise, did the horror of certain moments affect these images so that portions would be locked out, or altered to a more acceptable level? Were some parts simply erased or unrecorded, lost forever? At times one recollection conjures up another, and even though pieces are missing, somehow they still seem to add up to a whole.

I probably wasn't more than three years old in one of the earliest images I can recall. Strangely, every time I think of it, the image appears to have a yellowish, faded appearance, not unlike an old photograph, and the motion within the image is slowed down.

My cousin Gyuri, who occupied the other bed in a room I was sharing with him while he was spending his summer vacation with us, was awakening me. He was much older and, having come from Budapest, much more sophisticated than I. At least I thought so then, and for some time to come. While my heavy oak bed was in a dark corner of the room, his bed seemed to be in the pleasant light of the dawn coming through the lace curtains. He was sitting on the edge of his bed, pulling on his socks, and urging me to get up quickly as there was a fire in the house. Indeed, there was a smell of smoke in the room, but I was very sleepy, and instead of getting out of bed, I asked him where the fire was. This is where the memory abruptly ends and the image disappears, as though waking from a dream. Years later I found out that, indeed, there was a fire, but it could not have been anything important, as no other detail of it stayed with me. For some reason or other, this is a very fond memory, possibly because it is amongst the first ones, if not the first one, I am able to recall. It took place at our country place, Bikolypuszta, which I loved, about forty or so miles west of Budapest, in Hungary.

Bikolypuszta, or Bikoly, as it was called at times, was owned by my father. I was never able to learn what the name Bikoly meant, if indeed it had a meaning, but I knew, though not then, that puszta meant a barren tract of land or an isolated farm on barren land, such as the ones on the great Lowlands of Hungary, the Hortobágy.

In our case the land was not barren. In fact, it was lush, hilly, and wooded, and our house, according to my limited memory, was very large. Quite by coincidence, years later, living in America, I found out that the villagers of Bikoly referred to it as the Kastély, a word probably derived from "castle," really meaning "Manor House."

In other fragmented recollections, the outbuildings, barns, stables, sheds, and the nearby village, Bikoly, come back to me. While at that time I had no conception of wealth, we lived well. The puszta, or farm, was basically an agricultural enterprise, as farms are all over the world, with fields that were plowed, planted, and harvested. There were woods and forests, where, I learned later, my father sometimes hunted. We had lots of animals: horses, cows, oxen, pigs, ducks, geese, chickens, even ewes and lambs, which were my favorites.

There were people around us always. Guests, or family visiting us from Budapest and other parts of the country, mostly in the summer. Somehow, I always seemed to be the youngest, left out of most of the fun, spending my time with my mother or with one of the people working for us in the house. Amongst these, my favorite was a young girl, Fáni. She worked for us as a maid and always had time to play with me, let me follow her around, and tell me stories.

One of the other people I remember who worked for us was our coachman. On some Sundays he would wear his formal driving outfit, a tight-fitting black velvet jacket with lots of braids and braided buttons. Matching pants with shiny boots, and a cocky little hat resembling a small black bowler with a ribbon, which flapped and fluttered in the wind as he set erect on the carriage, driving a matching pair of horses.

I recall one tableau, in disconnected snatches, when we went to picnic by the nearby Danube. This is another image which appears to me in the form of still pictures, without sound, and while I vaguely sense the whole event, only certain snapshots of it come back with clarity. One of these snapshots is of us, my mother, and one other woman I can't identify, sitting on a blanket under a large tree by the river. My brother and some other kids who joined us from the nearby village Süttő were playing on the pebble beach alongside the river. In my memory, I can see our coachman unhitching the horses from the yellow carriage, which he had driven into shallow water. I remember him washing the carriage, his trouser legs rolled up, his boots neatly placed in the back of the carriage, and my mother giving him a plate of the picnic food after he finished.

This memory, just as the one about my cousin waking me with the news of the fire, is the clearest of all recollections about Bikolypuszta. All memories of that place, as vague as they are, fill me with warmth and fondness for that carefree portion of my early life spent there with my family.

Bikolypuszta vanished early from my life for reasons which I didn't understand until years later. We moved to our town house in Pápa because, as I was told, my brother, Sándor, was about to start school. That event would indicate that I must have been almost four years old then, as schooling in Hungary at that time started when one became six years old, and my brother was fourteen months older than I. The explanation made perfect sense. As a matter of fact, I probably accepted it as just one of those events without significance that a child deals with on a daily basis. I didn't find out until much later that my father had to give up Bikolypuszta for financial reasons.

But even if I had been told the real reason for our leaving Bikolypuszta, at my age I probably would not have understood nor cared, as no other aspect of our lifestyle had changed. Our house in Pápa was also big and comfortable. As at Bikoly, guests, mostly cousins, would still be brought or picked up by their parents who would seldom stay longer than a day or two. Fáni and some of the other people from Bikoly were still with us, and geese would be fed every day. We had a carriage, sled, and horses, although the stable and the outbuildings were much smaller than the ones we left behind. I even had a pet lamb, which we brought with us from Bikoly.

We lived well, and I never suspected that things were not going well for us financially. Our house was comfortable. Servants in and around the house surrounded us, and I had no measure at that phase of my life to gauge our standards or where our station in life was on a social or financial level. My clothes and shoes, for example, were custom made by tailors and shoemakers who came to the house to measure us for new clothes and shoes, and brought the half-finished clothing back for fitting. It never occurred to me at this time in my life that this was not the norm for everybody.

As I figure it, the year was around 1930. I was growing up and my world was expanding. My only brother, Sándor, started elementary school. Until then I had taken him for granted; he was there, as were my parents, as was the house, the trees, Fáni, all the things which surrounded me every day. As he left for school for the first time, his absence created a void in my daily routine. I was alone. He would occasionally bring new friends home from school, or tell me about the outside world that existed beyond the wrought-iron fence and gates surrounding our house. I was not allowed to venture beyond, but spent more and more time at the gate looking out at the world, people, the occasional carriages, and other traffic which passed in front of our house. I learned to do turns and some other gymnastic tricks on the slanted iron bar, which braced and kept the carriage gate closed. At times people stopped to talk to me after I showed off some of my tricks and told me how good I was. It made me feel proud, even though I was, I now believe, very timid at that time of my childhood.

A new phase of my life had started, much different from life at Bikoly in some respects, while in others, such as our family life, there seemed to be no change at all.

# Chapter 2

# 1930 –
# MORE BEFORE SCHOOL

The world was slowly coming into focus. I became increasingly aware of my surroundings and whatever else I could see from behind our fence. As I learned to explore secretly on my own, one of my great discoveries was our attic. I could look out from the high vantage point of our attic through the small vents in the roof onto a world which went beyond my imagination.

I found exploration exciting and adventurous without really knowing what excitement or adventure was. Occasionally, when my mother was occupied and no one was paying attention to me, I would climb the curving stairs from the entrance hall of the house. It took me to the top floor with guestrooms and a door at the end of the hall, beyond which lay the unknown. I remember going through this door for the first time with great trepidation. My heart was pounding, as I had been told not to go up there. It was supposed to be a dangerous place. From the point of view of a parent, I suppose, the attic could have been a dangerous place for a little kid of my age. It had heavy beams all over, and it was large. I could have been hurt without any one knowing where I was, but to me the attic turned out to be a world full of wonders. Sharp shafts of sunlight came through the vents with a never-ending show of dust particles curling in the shafts, as my feet churned up dust and created a hazy atmosphere in the dark attic. Unlike the rest of the house, the floor was a layer of sand. I still don't know why, other than to guess that it was simply the way they built houses at that time, or perhaps because the sand might have had good insulating qualities. The attic was full of treasures; old furniture—probably from Bikoly—lamps, enormous trunks with heavy leather straps, old beds, and all sorts of other interesting stuff. By far the most wonderful thing about the attic was that I could build platforms from the old furniture under the vents, climb up, and be able to look out on a world I could not see from the gate. I would spend hours in the attic, wondering if I would be punished if I were caught, not understanding, why I wasn't supposed to be up there.

It was on one of these occasions I was exploring the world through one of the vents that I heard music coming from some place below me. It grew louder and soon I saw a marching band coming down the street towards our house. I never saw anything like that before. In front of the band a man was carrying a flag of red, white, and green colors, which I later learned were the Hungarian national colors. I ran out of the attic, leaving the door open in my excitement, and down the stairs as fast as I could, out of the house to the front gate. The band was now stopped in the middle of the street in front of our house and a man with a fancy stick in his hand was shouting orders. On his command the band was executing all sorts of maneuvers while playing a stirring kind of music. Some of the people who worked for us came from the outbuildings behind the house, and Fáni came out of the house to watch the band with me from behind our gate. I saw my father watching also, smoking his pipe in the window behind me.

The band was now facing the house on the opposite side of the street, and a very important-looking man, dressed in a strange black suit, came out. He talked with the man holding the baton, but they were too far for me to hear what they were saying. The bandleader saluted him and the band started playing again. After about three or four numbers, on a command from the man with the baton, the band turned and marched away.

I still don't understand why this made such an impression on me. The tunes and the beat stayed in my head, echoing over and over again, and I wished I could have been one of those people marching in the band.

My father was in the hall when I went back into the house and I had a feeling he was waiting for me. I don't suppose I was aware at that time of what the concept of love was—I am not even sure if I had ever heard the word until then—but I felt a very special attachment towards my father, even though I was afraid of him. He was a very handsome, powerful, big man, certainly so from the vantage point of a four- or five-year-old. Most of the time he seemed very stern and only talked to me, as I can best recall, on few occasions. This was one of those occasions. He asked me what I thought of the band. When I shrugged my shoulders, not really knowing how to express what I thought, he explained that they were leventék. As far as I know, the translation for the word means "knight," but the leventék, or levente, then were synonymous with a nationwide paramilitary youth organization for young men of pre-draft age. Naturally I had no idea what this meant at that time, but I remember I was very impressed. He further explained that they came to express their thanks to the man in black I saw talking with their leader, whose brother sent the uniforms the band was wearing from America. The small colorful shoulder patches on the shirts, my father told me, were the American flag. The whole event, or his explanation, didn't make much sense to me. I couldn't grasp the meaning of the leventék, uniforms, shoulder patches, and I certainly had no idea what, or where, America was. But I loved the music, the color, and the excitement created by the band.

As my father towered over me, he asked if I knew who had left the attic door open. I knew I was found out and might be punished, and my first impulse was to deny all knowledge of the attic door, but I also remembered my father telling my brother and me time and again how wrong it was to lie, and what a manly virtue it was to tell the truth. I don't believe any child of my age then has a clear understanding of the concept of truth, but as best as I could figure it, it was telling about something as it was, or as it happened. Fearing the worse and mustering all my courage, willpower, resolve, whatever that moment called for, I told my father that I must have left the attic door open. The feared retribution didn't come. Instead, my father told me to be very careful next time I went into the attic. He warned not to get splinters under my skin as I climbed over the beams or onto the platforms I had built to look out of the vents. I figured he must have known about my trips to the attic, otherwise how could he have known about the platforms? He also told me that there may be wasps in the attic, and suggested I let someone know whenever I went up there in case they were looking for me. Somehow, I sensed this was a grant of permission to go to the attic whenever I chose to; in fact, it felt like his admonition amounted to encouragement, perhaps even a certain pride he might have felt for my initiative. At the same time I sensed that the mystery of secretly going up to the attic had been somehow dented. Nevertheless, I was pleased as much for not being punished as getting his permission. He told me to wait for him in the entrance hall, and a few minutes later he came back with one of his old army caps from World War I. He then took me by my hand and the two of us went to one of the sheds near the stables in the back area of the house, where he picked out a piece of scrap wood and with his pocketknife fashioned a sword for me. Next, he taught me how to salute. He gave me marching commands, and as the people who worked for us watched from a distance, he and I played soldier. After a while he relit his pipe and went back into the house. I stayed outside for quite a while, marching around the riding circle, shouting my own commands, as the people who watched me laughed.

* * *

I recall these preschool times as a most wonderful period in my life. I had no cares, very few responsibilities, and even though I was isolated from the outside world, every day brought new discoveries, new excitement. Then tragedy struck. For the first time in my life I was confused about how things which were unpleasant could happen so unexpectedly without my father being able to avert it.

It was early morning when I woke to the loud report of a gunshot. Dogs were barking, and there was lots of commotion in the house. I heard feet shuffling as people scurried around and I climbed out of bed. My brother's bed was empty. The noises seemed to have come from the outside, and I walked out of the house towards them. The sun wasn't up yet. There was gray dampness in the air when I saw a group of people standing near the riding circle. I saw my father standing there with a shotgun and I heard the bleating of my pet lamb. My mother grabbed me just as I got to the group of people, but before she could drag me away, I saw my pet lamb lying on the ground, her belly torn open, bleating as she slowly bled to death. Some of our people tried to help, but it was useless. I didn't understand what had happened and let my mother walk me back into the house. She let me crawl into bed with her, held me close, and I went to sleep. I loved sleeping in my mother's bed and was allowed to do so only on special occasions, which reinforced my feeling that something terrible had happened. But I was too scared to ask questions. When I woke, my mother was still in the room, almost as if she were waiting for me to wake up. She came over to the bed, stroked my hair, and in a gentle way, which was so much part of her nature, she explained what had happened the night before. A pack of stray dogs had somehow gotten into the back area of the house and attacked the lamb. By the time my father heard the noise and scared the dogs away with a shot, the lamb was beyond help. I thought I could see tears in my mother's eyes. She told me she would get me another lamb, but I said I didn't want one. I felt strangely helpless. The shock of losing my pet lamb filled me with anger at the world, which permitted such a terrible thing to happen. I was disappointed in my father, because until that morning I thought he was in control of everything.

I didn't have a lot in common with my mother then, but I loved her and knew that she loved me very much. She was a quiet, sensitive, gentle person, who understood me and everyone else around her. She was shy and extremely self-conscious about her weight. Her face was beautiful, but she was short and stocky, and as a result, she was very withdrawn. At that time, in Hungary, it wasn't customary for parents to spend a lot of time with their children. Children were usually taken care of by people hired for that purpose, but I knew I could always go to my mother, day or night, when I had a problem, if something was disturbing me, a nightmare for instance, and she would understand and comfort me.

We had lots of people in the house, so I was seldom alone. In fact, the solitude of my own world, such as the attic, might have been a reaction to all the attention my brother and I were constantly subjected to. And that is what conjures up the next memory, our French governess. I never had a chance to get to know her. I have no idea what her name was or what she looked like. What I do recall very vividly is an image of my brother standing on her bed, in the Mansard room on the top floor of our house, peeing into her open trunk full of her clothes. As I heard it told years later, this happened about a day after she arrived at our house. Needless to say, my brother and I were severely punished; but the French governess left within a day, and up to this day I have not learned to say anything beyond "oui" in French. This incident was recalled and retold in our family for many years afterwards, every time with more glee than before.

Many other funny events took place during those early years, the beginning of a new decade, some of which, I believe, are worth telling. I have no way of remembering where I was or what I was doing when I heard my father calling for me one day. I do know I was alone, as my brother was in school and I had no one else to play with. When I came into the house, my father, with his ever-present pipe in his hand, introduced me to a man I had never seen before. He was Mr. Turner, a retired or unemployed schoolteacher who, it was explained to me, was going to teach me mathematics. From the very first moment I met Mr. Turner, I knew I was heading into disaster. Mr. Turner was short and skinny, and had a most irritating, patronizing manner about him. I had a feeling of foreboding the instant I shook his clammy hand and saw his condescending smile. My first lesson was to start immediately, and I couldn't believe my father would so easily disregard what I was doing for the sake of a math lesson. Mr. Turner and I were ushered into our library, and then my father left and closed the door. I sat there as Mr. Turner was smiling at me for what seemed a very long time, and felt that now with my father gone, the smile on Mr. Turner's face had a mean twitch to it.

After a while, Mr. Turner produced a pad, a bunch of pencils, and a box of large kitchen matches. He opened the pad. On the first page, across the top were large hand-drawn numbers, from one to fifteen. "Have you ever seen numbers before?" were Mr. Turner's first words to me. I nodded, being somewhat intimidated, and Mr. Turner asked me where I'd seen numbers before. I had to think quickly and told him there was a number on our gatepost. He smiled again and told me this was very good, then asked what the number was. It was the number six, I told him. I knew it was the number six, as I heard most everybody in our house mention it at times, but I don't believe I knew what it meant or why it was on the gate post. Mr. Turner told me I was very smart to know the number of our house and that I probably knew so much, he wouldn't have to teach me. I don't remember replying but mentally agreed that that would be all right with me. In his next sentence, still with a smile, which I thought was definitely mean, he proceeded to prove how little I really did know. He pointed to the first number with his pencil and told me it was the number one. He told me the number one was the only number that was a single number, meaning that it was alone, and that is why it was so skinny. This logic went straight over my head, but he smiled at his immense mathematical wisdom, and pointed to the next number, which he told me was the number two, worth two number ones. We went all the way up to fifteen. He then pointed to the first number and asked me what it was. I had no idea. He pointed to the number two; I shook my head. We went all the way to fifteen, Mr. Turner pointing, and I shaking my head, except at the number six, which I knew from our gatepost. He told me he didn't expect me to learn fast and explained that mathematics was a very difficult science to master. As time went by, he said, I would learn a lot from him. I sensed he thought I was stupid, and the way he talked and smiled at me, he certainly made me feel stupid. He assigned homework for me. I was to memorize the numbers from one to fifteen before my next lesson the following day. As a parting note, perhaps to impress me, or himself, he once again pointed to the pad and asked me if I saw anything unusual. I shook my head. He put a match in front of the number one and another between the two and the three on the pad. The two numbers together, between the matches, he explained, read twelve. He smiled with obvious self-satisfaction for a long time. After a while he moved the second match between the three and the four and told me that the first three numbers written together meant one hundred and twenty-three. He smiled, moved the match again, and continued. The first four numbers, read together. I was thoroughly confused, but the lesson was over and Mr. Turner told me the following day he was going to show me some more wonderful things with the numbers and the matches. We then left the library, and on his way out I heard him tell my father what a bright, young lad I was and how much he liked me. I, on the other hand, instinctively and immensely disliked Mr. Turner. I didn't understand the point of the math lessons and saw them as an interference with and a threat to everything I liked to do on my own. Fortunately the lessons didn't go on for long. During the third or fourth lesson, I lit one of Mr. Turner's kitchen matches—an accident on purpose—and burned a hole in the pad. Mr. Turner slapped my face, which incidentally was a teacher's prerogative and an accepted practice at that time in Hungary; but when the lesson was over and Mr. Turner was saying goodbye, my father saw the tears in my eye and asked why I was crying. I was too scared to say anything, but Mr. Turner volunteered the information to the effect that I misbehaved and needed to be disciplined. The next thing I knew, my father had Mr. Turner by the collar of his jacket and his feet almost off the ground. He carried Mr. Turner through the front door, down the steps of the veranda, towards the front gate. I was delighted, but when he came back into the house he lectured me about not being respectful and attentive enough to a teacher. He told me I must learn authority and sent me to my room. I don't believe I understood any of this then, except that my face still smarted and I knew very little more about math than before. But I was grateful to sense that this was to be the last math lesson for the time being. Actually I did learn one thing. Not being a psychologist, I can only suspect that this incident might have been the turning point in my life when I learned to hate mathematics forever. Years later in school, math was my worst subject, and to this day I shy away from most things which have to do with numbers.

* * *

Then there was the haircut incident. I don't know exactly when, but probably during my early days in high school I recall listening to a lecture about a famous philosopher or orator, maybe Cicero, Plato, perhaps one of the Caesars—I no longer remember who—but as the lecture pointed out, he was a stickler for expressing the full meaning of one's thoughts. The point was a matter of definition, with clarity and unmistakable meaning. In other words, the precise, to-the-point delivery of the message. As I was listening to this lecture I recalled an incident, years before, around the time of the math lessons, when my father walked my brother and me into town to the barbershop for a haircut. On the way he told us that summer was coming and that we should get a very short haircut. While his words might have been precise, something went wrong with our interpretation of his meaning. By the time we got to the barber, my brother and I figured that "very short" meant bald. After all, how could you get shorter than bald? We thought this would please our father and insisted the barber cut all our hair. He didn't want to do it and looked miserable when my father came for us, but after my father assessed the irreversible damage, he took us home without comment. My mother, on the other hand, was speechless for quite a while when she saw us. We stood in front of her, like two grinning little Buddhist monks, and watched her become hysterical. Crying or laughing, I knew she was not pleased. That afternoon we were going to visit our grandmother. It was her birthday. Sprouting a new crop of hair was impossible, but we were dressed to the hilt for the inevitable yearly birthday photograph of the assembled family. These birthdays played such importance in our family's life that even my Uncle Mátyás (Matthew), his wife, Margit (Margaret), and their son, Gyuri, drove down from Budapest in an immense, gleaming, chauffeur-driven car. He was an important man, Margit, his wife, was a pain in the back, and I'll surely be talking about them later in this account. For

12

now, let's get back to my brother and me dressed in our new sailor suits. The matching suits had a blue-and-white piped flap around the neck and at the back of the blouse, and a ribbon in front tied in an oversized bow. We had short pants, and I clearly remember the white socks, and brand-new patent leather shoes. Even then, I unconsciously must have known it was a sissy outfit and wasn't too happy about wearing it. But I had no choice. When we were fully dressed, we were told to go outside to play or go down to the stables and ride up to the house in the carriage, which was to take all of us to my grandmother's house. As we hung around the tack room watching our coachman harness the horses, my brother found a magazine, which must have belonged to one of the people who worked for us. It was a sports magazine. On its cover was a picture of a Black boxer, who, as the coachman explained, was a great champion. The picture showed him in the classic stance of a pugilist, legs spread apart, one arm and fist extended and the other held in front of the boxer's face. My brother and I were very impressed. Never having seen a Black person, neither of us understood why this boxer was black. I, for one, thought that all boxers or great champions were black, and if that is what it took, it was okay with me.

Next to the tack room, in the same building, was what we called our "wash-kitchen" laundry, where our clothes, towels, and bedding were washed, it seemed, constantly. Behind this wash-kitchen was a small room where hogs were butchered and the meat was prepared to be smoked. In other words, it was a smokehouse with a big, closet-like cavity with iron doors, the smoker built into the wall. The furnace part of this smoker was open, and with magazine in hand, my brother and I calmly proceeded to apply generous amounts of soot from the inside of the furnace, magically transforming each other into black champion boxers. As best as I can recall, we did a fine job. By the time our parents found us, the only thing about us that was still white was our souls. My mother shrieked and almost fainted. My father turned around and left without a word, but I thought I saw a smile on his face, though he tried to look very severe. Minutes later my brother and I were sitting in sudsy hot water in one of the huge wooden tubs used for washing bedsheets as Fáni and one of the other girls scrubbed us with lye soap and bristle brushes, trying to remove the soot. The sailor suits were beyond redemption, total write-offs, and the family photograph taken later that afternoon at my grandmother's house clearly shows two bald-headed little kids, scrubbed to within one layer of skin, wearing ordinary playclothes.

* * *

You might be interested in knowing something about the house my family and I lived in. It was located in Pápa, at 6 Eszterházy utca, or Eszterházy Street, named after the Eszterházy family, who had a beautiful estate near us at the end of the street. All of you have seen the photograph I keep in my den, one of a few I was able to salvage, showing the front view of our house, with my father, mother, brother, and me barely visible in the window, taken through the gates from the street. The house is still there, at least it was in 1988, when Mom and I visited Lizzo in Hungary and took a side trip to Pápa. Incidentally, our town's name, Pápa, goes back, I've been told, a thousand years. It was named after the pope by his emissaries, who settled at the present location of the city, sent to convert the pagan nomadic Magyar tribes to Christianity. Eszterházy utca is a pleasant street with a double row of linden trees on one side and a single row of trees on the other. A relatively short section of Eszterházy Street is lined with houses much like ours.

The house had a spired tower on one side, the inside of which was a smoking room. Alongside the carriage gate in front of the house was a pedestrian gate and a paved path leading to stairs at the side of the house to a veranda and the main entrance of the house. Inside this entrance was a fairly spacious entrance hall. Double doors opened into the library, and another set of double doors to what we called the formal room. These doors were painted white with gold trim. The circular smoking room inside the spire was connected to the formal room at one end. One thing worth noting was the pleasant smell of this smoking room. It is interesting how one can hold onto a smell and recall it. The smell was a combination of wood, leather, and the aromatic scent of my father's tobacco, which, together with his cigars in a humidor, was specially blended and made for him by a tobacconist in town. From the formal room at the far end of the entrance hall was the door, which led into our living quarters, bedrooms, dining room, bathroom, etc. The entrance hall also had the curving staircase, the one I climbed to get to the attic. It even had what we in Hungarian called a Vay-Tzay. Vay-Tzay, WC, really, a derivation of "water closet" reduced to the letters *W* and *C*, which appeared on toilets in public places, pronounced in Hungarian as

Vay-Tzay. Consequently, all toilets in Hungary became known as Vay-Tzay. I might also mention here, as a further introduction to local color, that some public toilets were identified by a double zero, OO. But I suppose double zeros couldn't be pronounced, so we stuck with calling toilets Vay-Tzay. Of course our toilets in the house were not identified by double zeros, or WC, as in public places, but we still referred to them as Vay-Tzay. The noteworthy thing about our toilets, particularly the one in the hallway, was that very few private homes had modern indoor facilities at that time and a toilet in an entrance hall was thought to be superfluous. Most homes with indoor plumbing, built at that time or before, would have possibly had one toilet for all to use. I frankly don't remember how many toilets we had altogether, but I do remember the one in the entrance hall. Besides this toilet in the hall, we had our toilet and bath near the bedrooms, and I think I remember at least one other complete bath and toilet on the Mansard (top) floor of the house, and a very basic, minimal toilet and bath on the kitchen floor for the people who worked and lived in our house. Incidentally, in all cases the toilets were a separate room from the bath. As I write and think about this, long-forgotten details, such as the bathrooms, come to the surface again. Our bathroom, for instance, was red marble. The tub had four legs, and it was very large, but I suppose once again the perspective of a small child has to be taken into consideration. All the fixtures, the faucets, the flexible shower hose, were fancy and chrome plated, considered modern at that time. Water for the bath had to be heated by a hot water heater, which stood at the end of the tub, and was wood fired. One of the girls working for us was assigned bath fire duty once a week. The bathrooms had ornate sinks, towel racks, and a large, wardrobe-type cabinet with bath supplies. Oh, yes. We bathed once a week and the washbasins in the bathrooms, as well as in the kitchen, had a single, cold-water faucet only. In the winter, the girls would heat water in the kitchen and we would pour a pitcherful into the washbasins for our morning wash-up.

There was another interesting feature in our house, a dumbwaiter, or lift, as we called it. It was behind a panel in a small pantry adjoining the formal room, also opened to the dining room on the other side of the wall. It went down to the kitchen floor, where it had to be hand cranked with a large wheel to raise and lower it. The lift in the formal room also went up to the Mansard floor. Incidentally, the Mansard floor was so called because of the architectural style and features of its outside appearance and the characteristic shape of its windows, perhaps originated by someone called Mansard. Back to the lift. It was small, designed to carry food and dishes only, to and from the kitchen. But I learned to climb into it and raise or lower myself between the floors. I no longer remember how this was accomplished, the mechanics of propulsion I used, but it was great fun. In between floors I would be in darkness. The rope smelled like dry hemp and the lift made creaking sounds as I raised and lowered it. Fantasy helped turn these rides into adventures of escaping from formidable dungeons, or descending to the depths of the earth. Fáni knew about this, and I knew she was afraid that my father would find out that she knew and would be angry with her, but bless her heart, she didn't tell on me. When my mother found out about this innovative use of the lift, my father ended the practice.

The inside appointments of the house were very beautiful. In the formal room, for instance, the floor was inlaid parquetry, and the walls had gilded trim and panels. This, incidentally, was not unusual for that type of a house at that time in Hungary. The furniture was heavy, hand-carved original pieces made for us. There were tapestries, oil paintings, a large chandelier, and probably a lot of other furnishings I can no longer remember. The house had certain other features which might be considered unusual and unnecessary by today's standards, such as a sick room, where my brother or I would be isolated when we were sick.

The bottom floor, which had to be entered through a separate entrance in the rear of the house, is where the kitchen, pantry, storage rooms, and maids' rooms were located. I used to love to go down there with Fáni. On days when we baked bread, she would keep some of the dough out till the following morning, pound it into thick pancakes, and toasted them on the top of the stove for my brother and me. The pancakes were called lángos, which, loosely translated, means "flaming." I don't know why this was so, as there was no flame involved, but I loved them and looked forward to bread-baking days. Fáni would rub garlic on the pancakes after she toasted and buttered them with a brush made from goose feathers. It was my favorite breakfast.

My mother also liked to spend a lot of her time in the kitchen. She was a marvelous cook who genuinely liked cooking and canning the best pears, peaches, jams, pickles I have ever had. She also liked to do the shopping in town at the open market called piac, pronounced pee-utz, adapted from the Italian word "piazza." I liked to go with her. Fáni, or at times one of the other girls, would come with us to carry the baskets, which would be filled with fresh vegetables such as enormous green peppers, fresh home-churned butter, and all sorts of other things the villagers brought to the market twice a week.

Rare items could be bought at the piac during certain seasons. Morels, a form of a wild mushroom, which looked like miniature Cossack fur hats made out of sponge, fried in batter, as my mother prepared it, were amongst my favorites.

On days when we made strudel, I liked to spend my morning in the kitchen, watching my mother and the girls stretch the dough. They walked around a table covered with a flowered cloth, slowly pulling the dough from the center of the table. The idea was to stretch the dough so thin that it would become transparent. When this thin dough covered the entire table, the heavy portion around the edge was cut off; the filling was spread at one edge. By lifting the cloth along this edge, the strudel was rolled into its familiar shape and then baked. I would be allowed to clean the bowl with some filling purposely left in it for me. The food in our house was very good, and as the story moves along, I will probably talk about it time and again. While my mother spent a lot of her time in the kitchen, my father never came down to this floor. I shouldn't say never; there were a few occasions I recall he did come down when some work had to be done in one of the rooms, to tell the people doing the work what he wanted done. There was another floor, a cellar, underneath the kitchen, for firewood, potatoes, turnips, and beets, but for some reason I can't recall too much about it other than the fact that it had compartments separated by walls made from wooden slats.

The grounds around the house were pretty, but as a child I never really thought of them as pretty or anything else for that matter. I never consciously concentrated on it. The grounds were just there for me to play in as I saw fit. During those years I explored and got to know every inch. As I recall the grounds now, the front was landscaped. It had flower beds bordered with low hedges and rose trees my father worked on occasionally. In the winter, the slender rose trees would be bent over, and their crowns, covered with a paper sack, would be buried in mulch to insulate them against the severe cold of the Hungarian winter. Alongside the house bordering the carriage path, just outside our bedroom windows, were large linden trees, which, along with the ones on the street, gave off a most marvelous scent in the spring and the fall. There were pine trees near the entrance to the house. More pine trees were arranged in a circle behind the house. We called this the riding circle, which is what it was. I have heard that my father used to ride, but I must have been too young to remember. I vaguely remember my father giving a riding lesson to one of my aunts. She rode around the circle while my father controlled the horse on a long lead from the center of the circle. On one side, beyond the riding circle were some sheds where we kept firewood to age and to be split later for the bathroom and the kitchen stoves, and the big ceramic stoves we had in each room for heating the house. Sled runners, which replaced the wheels on the carriage during the winter, transforming it into a sled, were also kept in this shed. I don't know why I recall certain things, but one thing which stands out in my mind with crystal clarity is how we used to dry fresh vegetables on the low roof of this shed during the summer months. Aside from the enormous amount of canning, we also dried vegetables and fruits for use during the winter. Sliced green beans, mushrooms, apricots, peaches, apples, and so on were dried under cheesecloth on the roof of this shed, perhaps because it was low enough to get to easily, or because it slanted in the right direction to get most of the sun's rays.

The stable, tack room, wash-kitchen, and smokehouse were at the very end of the property, and to the left of them was a small vegetable garden, which as far as I can recall was mostly untended. There were some coops for chickens and geese, but in later years we abandoned raising them, because, as I understood, they were very smelly. A broken-down fence bordered this area of the back. There isn't much else I can recall about this part of our property, except that years later, in the wooded, overgrown section along this fence, I had my first encounter with one of our neighbor's daughter.

# Chapter 3

# PICKING UP WHERE I LEFT OFF...

This year I made only one New Year's resolution. Unlike other years in the past, I did not resolve to lose weight, start a strenuous exercise program, learn Japanese, and so on. This year I simply resolved to go back to writing this account. I thought about this resolution for most of the past year, prompted by Mom, as well as other events, which I'll explain in their proper place in the account. But most importantly because time is flying by and the more I think of it, the more convinced I become that I owe this to all of you.

Well, here we are—January 1, 1996. A new year is starting and in eleven days I'll be seventy years of age. As I sat down to my computer this morning to pick up where I left off, it came home to me that the last time I saved material for this account was on January 31, 1991, one month shy of five years ago. Where did five years go? How fast will the next five go? I better get to work!

# Chapter 4

# TO 1932
# GOD'S BIG BOOK...

Looking backwards over sixty-odd years, it is almost impossible to pinpoint the time or location of certain events. The private math lessons with Mr. Turner were not that hard. I knew it happened the year before I was to start school, and I believe it was in the spring. Likewise, the levente marching band had to take place at about the same time or perhaps a year earlier, but the haircut, the black champion boxer incidents are harder to place. They could have happened a year later, but most likely a year earlier. The time frame is really not very important. When one is very young, time has a different perspective. Passing years aren't noticed. Night follows day, and tomorrow is always a day away. Many things, going back so far in one's past, flow together.

I remember learning to skate, for example, sometime during those early years. With skates dangling from our hands, I remember my father, my brother, and myself walking along the Tapolca River, towards the PFC Clubhouse. I remember hearing the music even before we saw the place. In the years which followed, walking the banks of that river after the early frosts of the winter was always an exciting experience for me. If I heard music coming from the distance, I knew there would be ice and skaters, friends to meet, to have fun with.

On that first occasion, the wonders of the Pápai Football Club opened up for me. The Pápai Football Club, or PFC, as it was called in Hungarian, pronounced Pay-Eff-Tcay, had nothing whatever to do with football. The PFC was started as a soccer club. Football in Hungary meant soccer, and for a short time the club sponsored a local amateur team, which disbanded after a couple of unsuccessful seasons. But the clubhouse, such as it was, remained. It stood in front of four tennis courts, which were flooded in the winter for skating. The usually severe winters in Hungary permitted the making of ice without any modern ice-making equipment as early as November at times well into March. The shack, affectionately referred to as the Club, or PFC, was a relatively small, undistinguished wooden building. It contained two large rooms, one for women, one for men, separated by a smaller entrance hall. It is not clear to me how, but my father had some part in organizing the Club, and as a result we didn't have to pay. Tóni, the caretaker and chief ice maker, made a fuss over us, put on our skates, and took my father's coat. My brother and I knew Tóni. He was a big, rough-looking man in tattered, hand-me-down clothes who occasionally did some odd jobs around our house, chopping firewood or doing carpentry repairs around the back buildings. In the winter, he worked at the Club.

Tóni was a proud professional. He would bring his own saws and hatchets with him when he worked at our house splitting firewood, and at the Club he had keys to fit almost any kind of skate. My brother and I had our own keys, but as Tóni was squatting before us putting on our skates, we didn't have to use our own keys. Tóni also tightened our shoelaces and produced a jumbled mass of small leather straps from one of his pockets. He picked out what seemed like the best ones and strapped the skates to our shoes, explaining that the straps would help keep the skates on even if the jaws of the clamps would come loose.

As I looked at Tóni, I distinctly remember wondering if God created Tóni. I mean he was very rough looking, unshaven, and wore old, torn clothes. This was the time period in my life when the fairy tales, the bedtime stories, slowly gave way to some other topics and I was becoming aware of concepts such as God. I used to love to listen to my mother talk about God. How God created the Heaven and the earth and everything and everybody on earth. One image which stands out in my memory is of my mother knitting or doing needlepoint near one of the windows of her bedroom. I would sit on a small stool in front of her, listening to her at times talking about God. As I sat on that small stool holding loops of yarn, which she wound into a tight ball for her knitting, I remember her telling me that there was only one God and we—all of us—were God's children. God was good and, like a parent, would always help us in need, but would punish us when we did something wrong. He would also grant our wishes if we followed his commands. She told me that God had a very large book and that all our names were in the book with good and bad marks for everything we did in life. If there were more good marks than bad ones, God would erase some, or all, of the bad marks. She also told me that God knew everything. He knew what we did, even our innermost thoughts, and could see everything and everybody at all times. We could never see God, but one could always pray to God and his decisions would always be final without appeal. In God's book all our lives were preordained, written down to the minutest detail, which was unchangeable.

I looked forward to these periods of sitting on the little stool holding the yarn, listening to my mother talking to me in her sweet, quiet voice. I loved it and could not get enough of listening to her talk. I adored her. I didn't know it then, but thinking about these moments years later, I sort of suspected that there was a certain sadness in her voice whenever she talked about God. Over the period of my early years, this concept of God was instilled in me. Even today, perhaps even more so now, I strongly believe in this concept, as some events in my later life would not have worked out the way they did without this Heavenly guidance. I also hope that her strong convictions gave her strength years later, during those events which I will talk about in subsequent portions of this account.

But I vividly remember sitting in the Clubhouse, amongst heaps of overcoats, which Tóni pushed aside on the benches to make room for us, watching him and wondering if he, like my brother and me, was also created by God. How could he be so ugly and so different and still be a child of God? Why did he not wear the same kind of clothes we wore? Why did he not ask God to give him things God gave us? I had no answers. I didn't understand, and when I asked my mother, her explanation didn't satisfy me. She told me that even though we were all God's children, for reasons known only to God, he assigned different stations and conditions, different lifestyles to all of us, and it was only in his power to change these conditions. All of our lives, every passing moment of our lives, were dependent on God's will. God could change everything for the better or the worse, and we had to accept our lives as it was administered for us by God and were not allowed to question God's decisions. For the time, and for some time to come, I accepted all of this, but as I was looking at Tóni then, the first doubt, I should say question, crept into my mind. Later, Tóni became a focal point of my doubts, a personification of my conflict with a beautiful theory. I recall being one of the very last ones to leave the ice one evening, years later, as a session ended watching Tóni drag heavy water hoses, getting ready to remake the ice. He wore no gloves, and his shoes were wrapped in burlap against the cold. As he sprayed water, the mist, carried by the wind, covered him with ice, and as I watched him shiver in the cold I wondered how God could permit such suffering. The only explanation I could come up with was that Tóni must have done something terribly wrong.

Learning to skate was not hard at all. At first my father held our hands, holding us up, but in what seemed like a very short time, he was pulling us with a piece of rope and later on had us push a chair sled around on the ice. Before we went home that day, we were able to slide a few feet on the ice by ourselves. Even falling down was fun. I got the grasp of skating a little faster and better than my brother, and was sorry to leave and couldn't wait to get back to the club the following day.

Tony took our skates off and wiped them dry with a dirty-looking rag he kept in his hip pocket. When we were ready to leave, he brought my father's overcoat and tipped his cap when my father gave him some money. I might note it here that my father also seemed to have a good time teaching us to skate, but I cannot recall any conversation with him. In fact, this whole incident, as vivid as it still is in my memory, has the quality of a silent movie. I hear the music, the festive noise created by the whooshing of skates cutting into the ice, and the carefree, happy squeals of other skaters. I see my father's smiling face, but I don't hear his voice. I know he encouraged us, told us what to do and how to do it, but I don't remember hearing his voice. I tried very hard to skate well and please him, and was delighted noticing that he was pleased with me. Years later, I instinctively knew whenever he was pleased. Unlike my mother, I was a little afraid of my father. Most of the time there was an air of authority about him.

The Hungarian language provides for a formal way of speaking, as a form of respect usually with one's seniors and superiors. There is also a familiar way of addressing others. He used this familiar form of speaking with us, as well as with all the men and woman who worked for us. He spoke to Tóni in this manner, though Tóni always used the formal manner of speech, calling my father uram, "sir." I believe Tóni was my father's putzer during World War I. The word "putzer" derives from the German, and used in the Austro-Hungarian army of World War I; it denoted a person who served as a personal servant assigned to one of higher rank. In the English army, I believe they were called batboys or batmen. Their role, as close as I can surmise, was to clean and care for their superior. Shining shoes and boots, cleaning military equipment, clothes, and so on. In the military, ranking people used the familiar form of the language to address the lower ranks, and as in the case of my father and Tóni, this carried over to civilian life after the war. Incidentally, in the Hungarian army, even if one were discharged from service, everyone would remain on reserve status. I didn't know this until later years and events.

As far as I can recall, my father never appeased or in any way gave verbal indications of his expectations of us. Instead, our tasks were clearly defined. He told us what we, my brother and I, were to do or not to do. When we didn't measure up, there would be a quick and definite and, from his point of view, appropriate response. He did not pull up short of whacking me on the bottom or sending me to the room I shared with my brother. Strangely enough, I learned to like this sort of discipline , perhaps because when I did things well, I could tell he was pleased with me. He had a way of challenging me to do things and when I did, I sensed that he was pleased and proud of me. While my mother in her gentle manner talked about God, my father instilled other values in me. Virtues of manliness, the ability to take command of our lives, deal with problems as well as successes, control our destinies. I don't want to give the impression here that my father never talked to me or my brother. He wasn't very talkative, particularly with us children at a very young age, but on a few occasions when we had some moments together, more and more as we were getting older, I particularly liked to hear him talk about the nobility of sacrifice one is called upon to make at times for one's family and one's country. The endurance of hardship, for instance, illustrated by some references to Spartan life or his personal experiences while serving in the Hungarian army during World War I, self sacrifice, dealing with pain were all important factors in a man's life. All things one could look back on proudly. I had no idea at that time who or what the Spartans were, but the stories as my father related them were uplifting and wonderful to listen to. At that early age I could not reconcile some of the differences between his points of view and those of my mother.

I didn't know who was right or wrong, but looking back on it years later, I know they were both right.

* * *

One of the highlights of those years, perhaps the best remembered one, occurred during the summers when we went to visit my grandmother in the country. I don't know why we called it "the country." She lived in a small town, Celldömölk, exactly twenty-seven kilometers, less than twenty miles by train, from Pápa. Her house was big, though very different from ours in Pápa. It was also on a wide street, but all the houses were connected to one another along both sides of the street. There was a row of trees on both sides of the street between the paved roadway in the middle and the sidewalks. The house had massive gates, which led into an arched passageway. My brother and I looked forward to entering these gates. Our footsteps echoed in the tunnel and our voices took on a different, reverberating quality. It was almost like arriving in a much-anticipated fairyland. The courtyard the tunnel led into was covered with flowers, neatly trimmed hedges, some trees and rows of buildings on both sides of the garden. These were the outbuildings most homes of this type had, housing the food storage rooms—wash kitchens so called, as laundry was done there—and the outhouses at the end of the row of buildings. My grandmother's house had no inside plumbing. As big and comfortable as it was, there were no bathrooms nor toilets in the house. Even the water used in the kitchen and for drinking had to be carried in. There was a well in the garden. It had a large wheel on the outside of the barred, aboveground portion with a peaked roof. The wheel was attached to a roller on the inside of this barred portion. A length of chain was coiled over this roller, at the end of which was a very heavy, iron-strapped wooden bucket. It was fun to unhook the large iron hook, which held the wheel, and let the heavy bucket plummet to the bottom of the well. The wheel would spin fast and screech as the chain unraveled and whipped around inside the cage before the bucket hit the water at the bottom of the well. It took all the strength of my brother and me to wind up the chain on the roller again, hoisting the water-filled bucket. When the bucket was visible we would reattach the iron hook to one of the spokes of the wheel but usually did not dare to dump the bucket of water in the trough, as should have been done. We were warned about doing this. One had to open a door on the barred upper portion of the well housing, reach in to empty the bucket into a trough, which discharged the water to the outside of the well. The length of our young arms would not have permitted us to reach the bucket, nor would we have had the strength to lift and dump the heavy, water-filled bucket. We could have easily fallen into the well with possibly disastrous consequences. The well was fascinating, but we weren't supposed to play around it. This prohibition made it even more intriguing, and we played with the wheel and the bucket whenever we thought the coast was clear to do so. The well was a delightful part of our earlier summer visits. We didn't have a well at our house in Pápa, which is what may have made it such a novelty. There were big frogs in the well. Though we never saw one close up, we heard them croak and saw their eyes peer up at us. As we peered down at them, the reflections of our faces broke up when the frogs dove into the still, mirror-smooth water at the bottom of the well. Mári (Mary), my grandmother's maid, told us that it was a good well, otherwise there would have been no frogs in it. I found the idea revolting. I thought everybody else did, as we were told not to drink the water from the well. The well water was to be used for washing and bathing only. Our drinking water was brought to the house and into the kitchen by one of the men who worked for my grandmother. He would carry two covered buckets hanging from a crossbar over his shoulders. The water came from an artesian well in the center of town. It was Celldömölk's entry into the twentieth century to have a deep town well, producing good, safe drinking water in abundance. In many parts of the country ordinary well water caused goiters, which became very obvious to me later on as I visited some of the villages with my father on his business trips.

We talked about and prepared for our annual summer vacation in the country weeks in advance. When we saw my mother start packing, which was sometimes a week before we actually left, we knew that the exciting trip was not far away. Then the day finally came, when we were dressed in new clothes and watched the suitcases being loaded into our carriage, which then went ahead to the railroad station. The station was a short distance from our house; in fact, I could see it as soon as we turned out of our gate, and the walk to the station took only a few minutes. Just seeing the train pull into the station, belching black smoke and steam, blowing its ear-shattering whistle, was exciting. We said goodbye to my father, who helped us aboard and saw to it that we had our own compartment. He made all the arrangements, as he was an experienced traveler. We waved to him as the train pulled out. He stayed on the platform, standing erect with his waking cane in hand, waving at us until the train rolled into the long curve out of the station. As a very young child it didn't occur to me to wonder why my father never came with us. As a child, one takes things for granted, but as the years went by, the reasons which explained his not coming with us came together in my mind. More about that later.

The trip on the train was fascinating. After we managed to lower the heavy window by pulling up on a wide leather strap, unhooking it and then lowering the window with it, we stuck our heads out into the wind. I watched the engine and the cars ahead of us curve and speed along the tracks with what at that time seemed like breakneck speed. My mother didn't want us to stick our heads out and look forward in the direction the train was traveling for fear of getting cinders from the locomotive's smokestack in our eyes. Indeed, on more than a few occasions we did get cinders in our eyes and bellowed as she gingerly fished them out with the moistened tip of her lace handkerchief.

We even brought a snack along for these trips. It was usually cold chicken or goose, or some other meat, pickles, hard-boiled eggs, potato salad, and so on. We had cold, overly sweet coffee to drink, which incidentally wasn't coffee at all. It was a dark brown–colored liquid brewed from roasted oats, chicory root, and some so-called coffee preparation we bought at the grocery store. A small amount of this brew was mixed with milk and sweetened with lots of sugar. At times in the mornings at our house when we had this kind of coffee for breakfast, I wouldn't stir the sugar, letting it settle to the bottom of my glass and spooning it out after drinking all the coffee. While snacking in the train, we watched the telephone and telegraph wires on the poles along the track sink and rise gracefully to the crossbars on the poles, rapidly and rhythmically sinking and rising again, and again. The train chugged and lurched along as the lush countryside slid past us. It was interesting that whatever we looked at from the speeding train's window would seem to stop, and the rest of the countryside would revolve around it. It was also fun to watch the village people wave at the train as they waited for it to pass at road crossings, and to see the local stationmasters salute the train as it zipped through some of the smaller stations. Coming into stations along the way was always fun. People would get on and off the train in front of the yellow-painted station buildings. At times our train would sit in the station, waiting for another train coming from the other directions to pass, which is why a short trip, twenty-seven kilometers, less than twenty miles, took such a long time.

We gathered our things before pulling into the station at Celldömölk. When the train stopped, our mother ushered us off, and the conductor usually helped us with luggage. My father had tipped him before we left Pápa, but my mother also gave him money at Celldömölk. My grandmother's carriage was waiting for us at the station. As at Pápa, only the suitcases got to ride. Holding our mother's hands, we walked to my grandmother's house, which was also very close to the station. Although I didn't realize it then, nothing really was as far in those little towns as it seemed to me at that time.

Just outside the station, the first attraction of our summer vacation waited for us. We always looked forward to seeing a very large Saint Bernard dog harnessed to a small cart which was loaded with candy. I've never since seen such a large dog. To us at that time, it looked enormous. Its owner and his wife made their living selling candy in front of the station. The dog pulled the cart to its regular spot in the morning and home in the evening. My mother always bought us candy at the cart, which she knew we looked forward to at the conclusion of our train ride. We also had a dog in Pápa, which I never knew, as I hadn't been born yet, but heard many stories about later. He was a large German shepherd called Vitéz ("Hero"). One of these stories related to an incident I heard tell many times. Next to the large iron carriage gates at our house on Eszterházy Street was a smaller pedestrian gate coming into our grounds. A walk from this gate led up to the stairs and main entrance on the side of the building, as well as going around to the back entrance of the house. This back entrance was used for deliveries and service people. My brother, Sándor, pronounced Shahn-dohr, Alexander in English, would be asleep in his baby carriage in the mornings in the back of the building at a point where the walk turned towards the service entrance. Vitéz would lie next to the carriage and place a paw on the spokes of one of the wheels. When my brother cried, Vitéz, I was told, would rock the carriage until the crying stopped. This was a beautiful story, but as I've heard,

Vitéz had a protective side to him also. On one occasion the mailman came to our house and headed for the back entrance. I'm told the dog would not have bothered him if he had gone to the front door, but when he passed the front door and kept advancing towards the back entrance with the carriage blocking the way, Vitéz sprung into action with disastrous results. The man was bitten, and his clothes were torn. The following morning my father took Vitéz to my grandmother's place in the country. The next train back to Pápa was in the afternoon, and by the time my father arrived home Vitéz greeted him. According to the story, Vitéz, following the railroad tracks, came home from Celldömölk.

My grandmother, who seemed very old during those early visits, never came to the station. She waited for us at her house, usually working hard in her kitchen cooking a feast for us. She was a heavyset woman with a round, reddish face, always wearing an apron and a kerchief around her hair. She was obsessed with cleanliness. We found that out as soon as we arrived. After she hugged and kissed us, we had to wash our hands and face at the washstand in a small alcove next to the kitchen. The next thing on our list of musts was going into her bedroom to look at a large oil painting above her bed. The painting was of a Russian troika, a sleigh pulled by three horses, with the middle horse having a large, horseshoe-shaped harness with bells on it. The sleigh in the picture almost seemed to move. The driver was whipping the horses, hoping to outrun a pack of wolves, fangs bared, with glowing yellow eyes. I don't know the history of this painting, but I remember the nightmares of being chased by hungry wolves. Another thing I remember about her bedroom was how it smelled. The heavy odor of carved wood furniture, the massive beds, chairs, and lamps with silk shades over them and clothes wardrobes mixed with scents of furniture wax and starched linen and, I suppose, the smells of old age. The room had heavy oak shutters on the inside of the windows, the same as all the other bedrooms in the house. In the bedroom where my brother and I slept, the roll-up shades on the outside of the windows were lowered in the evening as we went to sleep to keep the light and the street noise out. My grandmother always wanted us to sleep late, and was bent on putting some extra pounds on our skinny bodies. She usually accomplished this by the end of the summer with her abundant wonderful food.

In some ways, I thought then, she was a strange person. The house had electricity, yet in the evening, particularly after the evening meal, the electric lights were turned off and replaced by a few kerosene lights. I won't ever forget the warm glow of these lights, particularly the sight of my grandmother sitting at the dining room table with my mother, talking in hushed tones till far into the night. The kerosene light on the table warmed their faces while quietly keeping the walls and other parts of the room dark and mysterious. I couldn't make out what they were talking about, as the door was kept open a crack only, I suppose, so they could hear us if we called to them. But they talked for hours, at times joined by Mári néni. This was before there were telephones and the communications between my mother and grandmother were by long, handwritten letters only. But even if my grandmother had a telephone, she wouldn't have used it. She was extremely frugal. She didn't need to be, it was just her nature. One thing I still do, having learned it from her, is to use my tea bag twice. We had no tea bags in those days of course, as tea was brewed from tea leaves one bought in beautiful tin cans. The dry tea leaves were placed in a silver egg-shaped holder with holes in it, which was suspended on a small silver chain from the edge of the pot to steep. At other times a strainer was placed on the lip of teacups and hot water was poured over the tea leaves in the strainer. In either case the tea leaves were discarded afterwards, except in my grandmother's house. She or Mári would collect the used tea leaves and dry them in the sunlight on the windowsill in the kitchen for a second use. She must have been right, as then and now I can't tell the difference in the taste of tea the first or the second time around.

One of the rooms in the side buildings had all sorts of canned food in it. It wasn't the pantry—the real pantry was next to the kitchen in the house—but this room stored canned food as it was curing, or whatever it was doing prior to being brought into the house. There were canned fruits, pickles, peppers in large glass jars on shelves, as well as a very large wooden barrel sitting on bricks on the floor, filled with sauerkraut. On top of the sauerkraut was a round wooden lid held down with a heavy stone cube, pressing the juice out of the kraut. Though we weren't supposed to do it, my brother and I would sneak into this room when we thought no one was watching us, and helped ourselves to several handfuls of this wonderful-tasting sauerkraut.

We were too young to go anywhere by ourselves, outside and away from the house during those early visits. My brother and I played or fought with one another, or played with cousins and the cousins' friends who were brought to play with us. Sometimes my mother or Mári néni would walk us over to our cousin's house and leave us with my aunt Ilona néni.

Mári néni, I'll call her Mári, as I did in later years, was one of my all-time favorites. She was my grandmother's maid. It was years before I had the whole story put together about who she really was. To understand it, you should know something about an aspect of life then in Hungary. Some of the peasant families living in small villages were very large. Ten or more children were not unusual. I don't know why they had such large families, as in almost all the cases they were unable to support all the children. The male children, as they grew up, were needed to work in the fields, but girls, though they also worked, became an unneeded, unwanted burden on the families. When they reached the age of twelve or thirteen, their families would bring them into town hoping to find work for them as domestic servants. There were agents who specialized placing these girls as domestics with families such as ours. These girls and their families were, in all cases, very poor. The girls my mother hired, accompanied by their parents, sisters, and brothers, would be brought over to our house by the agent who made the deal with my mother. After the families left amidst lots of tears, and the young girl, like a frightened puppy, remained at our house, my mother would show her where she was to sleep and tell her when she was to get up in the morning and what was expected of her. Each of these girls had a book of employment. In it were her personal statistics, usually with a photograph taken the day she was brought into town, and lots of blank pages an employer was to fill out whenever her employment ended. As some of the girls went from one domestic position to another, a single bad comment could seriously affect their future. But as far as I can remember, I've never heard of problems with any of the girls who worked for us. In a short time, their only possession, the one shift they wore when they came to us, would be replaced by new or altered hand-me-down garments. Some of the girls never had shoes until they first came to work for us. Their pay at the start of their employment was minimal, perhaps the equivalent of one dollar a month. But the chances are that was a dollar more than they ever had until then. The quality of their life, their food and board from that day on, was far better than anything they had left behind at home in the village. After the shock of being abandoned by one's family wore off, as they got to know us and the other girls working at our house with similar backgrounds, the girls became cheerful and happy. They also worked very hard doing all the chores in the house, starting with cleaning. Feeding geese, helping with the cooking, firing and cleaning the wood-burning stoves, waxing the parquet floors, polishing furniture, washing windows were amongst their many chores. Their families would come to visit on some Sunday afternoons. They would sit and talk with their daughter, and at times leave with whatever cash their daughter accumulated. Most of these girls stayed with us for years. By the time they were ready to leave, they would have a bit of money, a trousseau, a hope chest full of good clothes, some of which were gifts from us and some of which they had made and embroidered in their free time. My mother even taught some of them to knit and bought them yarn and needles. Mári, as I learned later, came to work for my grandmother when she was ten years old. I have no information about her real family. My grandmother became her family. By the time I met her she was no longer thought of as a maid. We called her Mári néni, or Aunt Mary, as we regarded her the way we regarded our grandmother. Though she was at least ten, maybe more, years younger than my grandmother, to us then she seemed almost as old. Just like my grandmother, Mári also wore a kerchief over her head all the time. It became obvious to me later on that she had very little education. I know she could read and write, but her reading matter was almost exclusively restricted to books about dream interpretations. Educated or not, we loved her as much as we loved my grandmother. I watched her clean the house, or work on canning fruits and vegetables and cook. She and my grandmother would argue and fight constantly, becoming loving sisters again just minutes after those arguments.

I don't know how old Mári was when I first met her. To me, she never changed. She looked and behaved the same the last time I saw her as she did when I first met her. Aside from her first ten years, she had no family besides my grandmother and our family. She must have been older than my mother and aunts, whom she grew up with. It was obvious that the relationship between my mother and Mári was very close. My grandmother had five children, four daughters and one son. The four daughters were all married.

When one of the daughters got married, Mári went with her to help set up their new household. Then she would go back to my grandmother.

\* \* \*

The first couple of summers at my grandmother's house passed slowly. After the novelty of the train trip and her house wore off, the time started to lag between the hide-and-seek games with my cousins and friends. When the last big event of the summer, the annual grape harvest, was announced, we knew summer was almost over. I won't go into a detailed account of the grape harvest now—perhaps it'll come up again—other than to tell you how much I looked forward to it. We packed again, not as extensively as for our summer vacation, but small suitcases were packed with such items as rubber raincoats, galoshes for the mud, an extra sweater, and of course the usual extensive picnic lunch. We would only be gone for the day, but it would be a long one. Our destination was Sághegy, pronounced Shaaghedj, meaning "Shaag-mountain," where my grandmother's vineyard was. We got up at what seemed like the crack of dawn and half asleep, got into the carriage we called a fiacre for the trip to the vineyard.

The carriage could take us only so far. When we arrived at the bottom of the vineyard, we got off and walked uphill to the press house. By the time we got there, the picking was well in progress. What seemed like an army of people were walking up and down the hillside with wooden buckets called puttony strapped to their backs, loaded with freshly picked grapes. At the press house the puttony would be emptied into vats, and the men would start up the hill again for the next load. The man in charge greeted my grandmother and mother, while Mári, my brother, and I hiked to our small house halfway up the mountain. Though I don't remember spending any nights in this house, I always think of it fondly. Because it was built on the steep side of the hill, the front of it had two stories, while in the back it had only the upstairs floor. It had a small kitchen, but I don't remember it ever being used. The two small bedrooms in the back, in fact, the whole house, smelled like decay. When we first got to it, Mári opened all the doors and windows to air it out. Even then it smelled and felt damp and murky. The windows stuck and were hard to open. The house had a large porch on the second floor overlooking the hillside. There were some simple wooden benches and a rocking chair I liked to sit on watching the activities below.

34

I heard that years before, my grandfather, whom I never met, sat in this rocking chair, watching the picking. I sat there one day crying, as somehow I didn't realize that I was alone in the house. When I discovered it and couldn't find anyone, I just sat down on the porch and cried. Mári found me there. She must have just gone outside the house with my brother for a minute, but to me it seemed like I was abandoned. She picked me up and quieted me down as I sat on her lap, and she wiped my tears. She and my grandmother always pampered me. They called me all kinds of names of endearment: nicknames, one of which was Káposzta Salátac, loosely translated to "Cabbage Salad." If I ever knew what was behind this nickname, I've long forgotten it. But at this time Mári, I distinctly recall, called me by that name and told me a story, which I still remember.

She told me that if I'd listened to the quiet, I would have heard her and would not have become frightened. She told me the story of a young boy in a village who herded his family's cows every morning into the hills, away from the village. He would listen to the quiet and after a while he would hear all sorts of sounds from the distance. In the evening the little boy's mother would call out to him from the village to bring the cows home and the little boy would hear her. As we sat on the porch, Mári told me to listen to the quiet. "Listen hard," she said. "Do you hear the dogs barking at the press house?" Indeed, as I did listen hard, I heard the dogs. I also began to hear some of the people talking in the distance below me on the hillside, though I couldn't make out what they were saying. "If you listen to the quiet," Mári told me, "you will never be alone again." She was right. I've listened to the quiet many times, since that day, but... more about that later.

* * *

The years went by. Winters followed summers, and the summers faded into winters again. The cycles were repeating themselves with pretty much the same regularity of routine, year after year. Yet, as far as I can remember, none of it was boring. I looked forward to the winters for all the excitement of skating, building snowmen, snowball fights, and the usual things kids do in winter. One thing, which very few children have the pleasure of experiencing anymore, was riding in the sleigh. It was fun watching our coachman remove the wheels from our carriage with the first heavy snowfall and hoist the body over to runners. The carriage metamorphosed into a sleigh and the horses had spikes screwed into their shoes so they wouldn't slip on the ice. But the most fun was hearing the bells on the horses' harnesses. They had a soft, rhythmic chime to give a pleasant warning of the silent, approaching sleigh. As the sleigh had an open body, all of us slipped into sheepskin sacks to keep ourselves warm during the ride. Even so, by the time the sleigh turned into our gate, our faces were pretty well frozen. I only recall a few of these rides. As a very young child, the image of my grandmother's oil painting and the fear of wolves chasing the sleigh were always on my mind.

* * *

Our visits to my grandmother in the country got shorter as we got older. With our world expanding, there were more and more new things for us to do. During our summers in Pápa, most of our time was spent swimming. Baron Eszterházy built a fairly modern (for Hungary at that time) pool complex in town, called Strand, completed during the early thirties. A large, blue *E*, Eszterházy's initial, was placed prominently over the entrance to the Strand, with a five-pointed crown above the *E*, denoting his rank. The powerful and wealthy Eszterházy family had large and beautiful castles on big, manicured estates all over Hungary and Austria. Baron Eszterházy Tamas (Thomas) had an estate in the center of Pápa, a large U-shaped building painted "Hapsburg yellow," sitting behind huge, wrought-iron gates, surrounded by outbuildings, stone fences, and a well-kept private park, the size of the city. My father did business with Eszterházy's estate, actually quite a lot of it, particularly in the early forties, but more about that later. The pools were built over the Tapolca River. The river flowed into the smaller of the two basins on the upstream end and flowed out of the bigger basin at the furthest downstream corner. The water was not chlorinated or treated in any way. The Tapolca River was said to be clean and safe enough to swim in. Its headwaters provided drinking water for the city, and because it was flowing through the pools and didn't stagnate, it was considered to be safe. Some time later, I actually swam in other sections of the Tapolca. There were two pools with a cement footbridge between them at the Strand. The smaller of the two pools was twenty-five by twenty-five meters, the bigger twenty-five by fifty meters, large enough to have swimming meets, in which I participated in later years. In 1936, after the Berlin Olympics where a

Hungarian, Dr. Csik, won a gold medal for the 100 m freestyle event, I was assigned as one of a bunch of students who greeted and assisted Dr. Csik, and swam with him when he visited Pápa for a swimming demonstration.

Our first visit to the pool was, to say the least, interesting. As with skating, my father took us swimming the first time. By this time I must have been four, five, maybe even six years old. After we paid the admission, we were given keys to a changing room with lockers in it. We put on our full-body bathing suits—the fashion of the day—walked down the steps along a snack bar to the small pool for our first swimming lesson. The swimming instructor was a muscular, suntanned man. We watched him finish the lesson he was giving to a young girl who was dangling from a rope attached to a belt around her waist and to the end of a long pole the swimming instructor was balancing over a rail in front of him. I think his name was Mr. Pulitzer, or something like that. My father knew him and after he introduced us, my brother, being the older, had the belt put around his waist and was lowered into the water. For the next fifteen minutes he bobbed up and down, swallowing and spitting water, gagging. Then it was my turn, and I didn't fare any better. As we were walking away from the swimming lesson across the cement bridge between the pools, my father explained to us that the best teacher of just about anything was necessity. With that explanation, he threw both of us into the deep pool. As we splashed around, about to drown, he jumped in and scooped us up. But he insisted we continue taking lessons from Mr. Pulitzer and learn to swim properly, which, over the summer, we did.

* * *

Otherwise, the days, the seasons, and years went by slowly. I was getting older and had more freedom to explore, sneak away from the house now and then, finding new excitement. A most memorable experience was standing on the footbridge over the tracks at one end of the railroad station. It wasn't very far from our house, and even though I was scolded for it, every now and then I would sneak out and head for the bridge. From the bridge I could see the tracks coming from the distance and dividing into many branches before reaching the station. There was a lot to see all around me: repair sheds, freight trains on sidings, people getting on and off the trains; but the most exciting thing was to spot a train in the distance coming towards the station. As it got closer it would be switched onto one of the sidings. As soon as I saw which tracks it was on, I would run to the portion of the bridge that was directly over those tracks. As the train, I should say the locomotive, went under me, I'd be engulfed in a thick, wet cloud of hot steam and smoke. The steam had a strange smell to it, which I learned to like.

Beyond the bridge and the tracks, the city abruptly gave way to pristine countryside. No houses, just green fields as far as I could see from the bridge, with dirt roads and occasional large trees. I explored these fields, which at a certain part of the year were covered with wild flowers. That is why I headed for them one day during the summer. I found out that it was my mother's birthday. I wish I could still remember her birthday, but like so many other things, that date also faded into oblivion. I had no present to give her, and even though we had flowers around our house, I thought she would like a bouquet of wildflowers. I guess it must have been after the wildflower season, as there were no wildflowers in the field when I got there. They were all gone, except for some very small yellow flowers, which I collected into a pitiful little bunch and took home to her. I wasn't prepared for her emotional reaction to the flowers. There were tears in her eyes as she smiled and took the flowers. Her image at that moment is etched into my memory. I shall never forget it. She put the little bunch of flowers in between the pages of a beautiful prayer book she had. The book was small, slightly larger than a standard paperback book today, but it was bound in ivory and bordered with gold. It had a star, also made out of gold, on the cover, and a snap holding the covers together. I know that years later, the flattened, faded, dry bunch of little yellow wild flowers was still in her book.

* * *

One day, our harness maker followed my father into the entrance hall of our house. My father gave him a small leather case, which he explained was his map case during the war. He instructed the harness maker to remove the long shoulder strap from the case and put on back straps that would fit me. When the case was brought back, my father told me to try it on. It fit perfectly. It was a handsome case with, my father explained, a proud military history. I was delighted to have it.

A new chapter in my life was about to start. I was six years old. The year was, I believe, 1932, and it was time for me to start school.

# Chapter 5

# 1932 – 1936
# ELEMENTARY SCHOOL

At about this time, perhaps a bit earlier or later, I began to wonder about my father's name. He was the only one I knew then, or now, with the same last name as his first name. His name was László László. László is a strange name. I know lots of people whose first name is László, I even know some whose last name is László. But the only László I ever knew with the same first name as his last was my father. Some Hungarian names can be translated. Kovács in English means Smith. Szabó means Tailor, Fehér means White, Fekete means Black, and so on. As a given name, László has been translated into English as Lester, or Leslie. As far as I know, it has no literal translation. I wasn't bothered by the lack of meaning of the name. At that time, I wasn't even conscious of a name having to have a meaning. I just couldn't understand why one should have the same name twice. I had heard my father's friends call him Laci (Lutzy), a nickname, while younger people, cousins, for example, referred to him or called him Laci bácsi, Uncle Laci. This was quite common in the Hungarian language. Addressing one's seniors in a familiar but respectful manner, depending on the gender, even if they weren't relations such as uncles or aunts, called for the "bácsi" (uncle) or "néni" (aunt) addition to one's name.

I didn't learn till a number of years later that my father changed his name shortly after, or perhaps during, World War I. His original family name was Kluger, which in its original German means clever, wise, prudent, judicious, or something like that.

As best as I was able to put it together years later, shortly after World War I, or perhaps even before or during the war, my father and his brothers decided to change their names to ones with a more distinct Hungarian ring to it. This was a common practice just about then, as scores of people gave up their family name stemming from another ethnic background for a more Hungarian-sounding name. There were a number of reasons for this.

Hungary, as other Middle European and Balkan countries, had a mixture of population whose history went back hundreds, in some cases thousands, of years. Nationalism swept the countries of Middle Europe, and in some cases a Hungarian name meant easier fitting into and acceptance by a native population. It also meant better opportunities for advancement in society, in business, even in private life. The same held concerning religion. Hungary was a predominantly Roman Catholic country. The second largest religious bloc was the Reformed Church of Hungary. Almost all other religions of the world were represented, but in minority. After World War I many individuals as well as entire families converted from one of the minority religions to one of the two main religions of Hungary. This was the case, I believe, in my father's family. The Klugers were German Jews.

My grandfather and grandmother, I understood later, did not convert but didn't oppose their sons' conversion to Catholicism. Whether they were too old to care or just bent under the pressure, I do not know. As I put it together over the ensuing years, on the basis of overheard conversations, information gathered from friends and relatives, most of this pressure originated from my Aunt Margit. She, a born Catholic, and her husband, Mátyás, were social climbers. Conversion to a more popular religion was part of their scheme. Uncle Mátyás—I'll call him Matthew, the name you met him with—was also persuasive enough to influence his brothers to do likewise. Such was the power of the firstborn of brothers at that time in Hungary. His logic was not altogether unreasonable from any of a number of perspectives, though ideologically all his reasons might have been wrong. My father, for instance, became a large landholder after World War I. His landholdings were Bikolypuszta, described in the first chapter. Bikolypuszta came to my father as a wedding present from my mother's family, who also owned and controlled large landholdings. My father's family also owned land near the towns of Zalaszentivány, Zalaegerszeg, and Nagykanizsa. I never saw any of these, but as I have been able to figure out, their land was much smaller than Bikolypuszta. You should know that prior to World War I, people of the Jewish faith could not own large tracts of land in Hungary. In fact, they were excluded from many other professions, businesses, and activities. When these laws were changed or done away with altogether and land became available for Jews, some, like my maternal grandfather and his brothers, prospered. Owning land was very typically a Christian Hungarian privilege. To some extent, it denoted the aristocracy of the country and, under the feudal system, which goes back centuries, separated landholders from the peasant and merchant class. Though some of the peasants owned small parcels of land, most worked for the large landowners. There were small landholders also, some steps above the peasant class. I never believed that in my father 's case, becoming a landowner was the only reason for converting. To be certain, I've never been able to totally substantiate when or where, or if, indeed, this conversion did take place, but if it did, I suspect it happened under the pressure of Uncle Matthew, the oldest of the brothers, and Uncle George (Gyuri), the second oldest. I did make an admittedly halfhearted effort to research this after WWII, but most of the records were destroyed or unavailable, and most importantly, at that time the issue seemed academic and unimportant. Prior to that, as I was growing up, very little information was passed on to or discussed with us children. Whatever I do know, or think I know, came together over years of gathering snatches of overheard conversations, arguments, fights, and whatever information came from outside sources. One of these outside sources was Uncle Matthew. His wife, Margaret, whom you've also met, was a born Roman Catholic. Uncle Matthew was heavily into his new religion. It was he who told us that my brother and I were born into the Catholic faith, and as we grew older we were going to have to make our own decision about which faith we were going to follow. At that time, still being preschool age, I had no idea what he was talking about. Years later, when I first arrived in New York as a refugee, Uncle George advised me to continue in the Catholic faith and even introduced me to his priest. Frankly, particularly at that early age, I found the entire concept of religion confusing. What added to the confusion was the fact that my mother, with whom I could discuss almost anything, pulled back whenever I approached the subject. Rather than dogma, her explanations were conceptual, philosophical, idealistic, and almost naive descriptions of faith within one's self, as opposed to rules one was expected to adhere to in following a religion. I can't say that this confusion totally cleared up even after I was able to reach my own conclusions and set my own course to follow. I arrived at certain conclusions in later years, but then, as a six-year-old, it was confusing and unimportant.

I'll be talking more about this, as it'll be cropping up, I know, again and again. For now it will get you a bit closer to understanding my confusion at that time as I started school.

I won't dwell too much on my first day in school. The experience was probably not unlike yours, but there are a few things that stand out in my memory, which I'd like to mention. The anticipation of school grew, as it was talked up by all in our household. Everybody, except my father and my brother, made quite an event out of it. When the time came to go, I was very anxious, I could say frightened. The morning of the first day I was dressed in new clothes. Some days before, my father or somebody showed me my new notebook, some textbooks, and a pen and pencil case, which was made out of wood. It had a slide-out cover, and in it were a pen with some spare points. There were several sharply pointed pencils, an eraser, and a pencil sharpener. One memory indelibly etched into my mind is the way this pen and pencil box smelled. Whenever I sharpen pencils even now, I recall this smell fondly. The other thing was my mother's admonition never to hold a pen or pencil with the tip pointing straight up. It seems that a distant relative of mine held his pencil that way when the kid sitting behind him in class pushed my relative's head forward, poking one of his eyes out with the pencil. I still shudder when I think about this and, needless to say, never hold my pencil or any other sharp instrument pointing towards my face.

On the way to school, my brother, who by this time was a class ahead of me, and I would try hard to keep pace with my father, who never simply walked but marched in military cadence. We always had fun whenever we walked with him, and he taught us how to walk erect, shoulders back, chest out, looking straightforward. He even taught us how to change step if and when we got out of step, which, considering our size compared to his, happened often.

I loved his stories about teaching some young village kids, fresh recruits during WWI, to march. Some of these young men didn't know their right from their left, and as the drill instructors called cadence, "Left-right, left-right," the young men got confused and got out of step. He told me he ordered some strands of straw tied onto the right ankles and some hay onto the left ankles of the recruits, and the drill instructors called out, "Széna-szalma, széna-szalma," *Straw-hay, straw-hay,* teaching the recruits to march in step. On rare occasions when he talked about them, I could never get enough of my father's war stories.

On the way to school he told us that we must always look out for one another. Brothers, he told us, should stick together no matter what. He also told me that I must be respectful to my teachers and do whatever they tell me to do. Some people greeted us on the way to school, my father tipping his hat and explaining that it was my first day in school. I was congratulated, though I didn't understand why. My father was also greeted with great respect as we arrived at the school and met some of the teachers. My first grade teacher was a Mrs. Bihari, Renee néni, as we were to call her. I know I was a bit teary-eyed as my father left and I sat scared in a strange room next to a kid I didn't know. But I got used to school pretty fast. The school was in an old building, but then almost everything in Pápa was in an old building. It was two stories high with a rather small yard to play in between classes. There was a gymnasium on the ground floor. Its floor was raked sand, which, I suppose, was intended to cushion one's fall if one did fall. Along one wall was some strange equipment called the Swedish Ladder. The same piece of equipment was in a very state-of-the-art gym in my high school also, but I still don't know what the purpose of this equipment really was. We did some exercises on them, which I thought were contrived and didn't like. Dirt floor or not, I loved this room. In a very short time I learned to climb up the poles and ropes to the ceiling and do turns on the low bars. But we didn't get to the gym often enough, which I regretted. The rest of the first year in school, as the next three, went fast. I learned to read and write by the end of the first grade, as well as count to twenty and do simple arithmetic. At times I liked chanting my multiplication tables, but most of the time it bored me: 1x1 is 1, 1x2 is 2, 1x3 is 3, 1x…We usually did this while waiting for the teacher to enter the classroom. The only time it had an element of fun was when I could punch the leg of the kid sitting next to me under the desk, or the back of the kid sitting in front of me, to the cadence of the chanting. As I'm sure you can surmise, I wasn't a model student. Even Renee néni, a kind and lovable person whom I liked very much, would make me stand in a corner at times for various minor and major offenses.

The breaks between classes, no overworked joke intended, were my favorite times at school. I had some real favorites amongst the games we played. One was King of the Hill, or Capture the Flag. One team would be atop a mound of dirt while the other team would try to force them off and take control of the mound. The other game was a bit more complicated, if just as dumb. I don't remember what we called it—the word probably wouldn't have a translation anyhow—but one kid would stand with his back braced against a wall, his fingers laced in front of his belly, cradling the forehead of a bent-over kid who, with his legs spread for stability, would be the first in line of about three or four other kids, each holding onto the waist of the bent-over kid in front of them. This chain of bent-over kids in a line represented one team, the "defenders." The "attackers" were an equal number of kids lined up some distance from the last bent-over kid, and one by one, taking a good run, they would leap onto the backs of the bent-over kids. The second kid in the attackers' line would follow likewise, trying to land on the back of the first jumper. One after the other, the attackers would pile up on the backs of the defenders. The objective was to collapse the line of bent-over kids. If the line held and the attackers were unable to collapse it, the attackers would then become the defenders and form up, bent over, trying to prevent the former defenders from collapsing their line. There were many techniques for collapsing a line. One was to hang over the side of the kid under you, pulling him to the ground. The problem was that if one fell off him without the defender falling to the ground and breaking the chain, you were out of the game. Good teams, made up of mostly older, bigger, and stronger kids, almost never had to defend. Very few other teams wanted to go up against them.

Breaking the Chain was another game. Two teams would form lines, facing each other a few yards—I should say meters—apart. We would lock hands in what we called the fireman's grip, holding onto the wrists of the kids on both sides, forming the chain. When the lines were formed and ready, the captain of one team would call the name of a kid on the other team, who then had to run against the opposing line and try to break through the opposing players by breaking the grip of two of the players. If he couldn't break through, he was considered captured and had to join the capturing team, lining up with them. If he did break the line, he could take the two opposing players he broke through back to his own team as prisoners. These prisoners were now new members of the team. Naturally, one always tried to break through at the weakest part of the opposing chain, but the problem was that these weak players became members and the new weak points in one's own line. When the bell rang, signaling the end of the break period, the team with the most players was the winner. Incidentally, the bell was a handheld brass bell, the kind one sees in American movies about frontier schools. It was usually one of the honor students who got the bell duty and the responsibility to make sure that the break periods started and finished on time. I never had bell duty.

But I was a dead eye at marbles. Not the ordinary game of marbles you know, but "shooting" for marbles, as we called it. There were several types of marbles. Small, baked clay-colored marbles were the most common and the cheapest. Glass marbles with beautiful designs on their insides, depending on their size and quality, were considered valuable. But the most valuable marbles were steel balls. As you couldn't buy these, particularly the bigger ones were sought after possessions. At times, those who had them or the glass marbles would put them up as targets. This meant that they would allow someone to shoot at them. The shooting, actually pitching, was done with ordinary marbles. The more valuable the target was, the longer the negotiated distance was to shoot from. The target would be placed on the ground; the distance would be measured from it and a line scratched into the dirt. The shooter had to remain behind this line, and even leaning in over the line at times was heavily contested. The objective was to hit the target with ordinary marbles. Whatever marbles missed became the property of the owner of the target marble. Most of the time shooters would loose all their marbles trying to hit a valuable. If, on the other hand, the shooter hit the valuable marble, it would become his property. As I said, I was a deadeye and had many valuables. Marbles followed me into the lower grades of high school.

There were other games also, some pretty rough, and there were injuries during just about every break. But we had no infirmary. If one was hurt or injured, he would go up to the teachers' room where the teachers congregated for their smoke breaks between classes. One of the teachers would take care of the injury by administering the only remedy offered, a large dabbing of iodine, for a cut or a scraped knee, or a wet cloth on one's forehead for a bump. In all the four years I spent in this school, I don't recall any serious injury to anyone during our wild, unsupervised play periods. I do recall getting hurt often, particularly while in the younger grades. I was a small child, but as time went on and I grew, I became what I believe could be classified a hell-raiser. I didn't mind the sting of the iodine. In fact, I sort of liked the smell of it, and even today, if and when I use iodine, I remember the rough games, the smoke-filled teachers' room, and the smell of iodine. I never cried. Crying, according to my father, was a waste of time. As a child, I never saw him cry, and every time I cried, he seemed less than sympathetic, even scornful. Many years later, I saw him cry once. I'll tell you about that later in this account.

One other teacher I remember was Mr. Winkler. He was a tall, dignified-looking man, gentle in nature, but also a stern disciplinarian. I liked him and I know he liked me. He was extremely knowledgeable. The teachers then didn't just teach one subject. They taught whatever the curriculum of the particular grade was. Under him my grades improved, though I still wasn't what I would call a top student. The four years of my elementary education went very quickly.

* * *

It would serve little purpose trying to cover all events of those four years spent in school. They are not unlike anyone's experience in grade school, but some other events of my first decade are worth mentioning. As in the case of Tóni at the skating rink, I discovered in school that not everyone lived the way my family and I lived. For instance, my clothes, shoes, and so on were different from some of the others in school. As I mentioned earlier, my shoes and clothes were custom made for me. Our old clothes were usually given away. It was a surprise to spot one of my favorite sweaters on a kid in my class. His name was Rót. That was his last name; I don't believe I ever knew his first name, as until later on kids called each other by their last names. I was just László and Rót was just Rót. Rót, meaning "Red" in German, was an orphan. He and several other kids in school wore roughly made, ill-fitting gray garments, sort of like prison uniforms given to them by the orphanage. By this time I no longer questioned why some of us lived differently from others. I accepted our privileged position in life without wasting too much of my time thinking about it.

Every now and then, as part of our education, the school or just our class went on excursions. These were usually three- to five-mile day hikes to places of interest in or near Pápa. The trips were always fun. It broke the monotony of classroom life and the places we visited were interesting.

Picnicking under trees, sitting on rocks, and eating lunches we carried in our backpacks were always fun. I always loved salt, and the fun part of these picnics was not to have my mother or Fáni tell me how much salt I could put on my hard-boiled eggs. I remember touring a brick factory with my class, about three or four miles out of town. We were shown how clay was mined, processed, and baked into all kinds of bricks and shingles. Another place of interest was the headwaters of the Tapolca River, which you might recall I had mentioned earlier flowed through town, and which supplied Pápa with water. The springs were in a small town called Tapolcafő, meaning "Tapolca headwaters." This town might have been five or six miles from Pápa. It took us the better part of the morning to get to the large limestone springs, which were truly amazing. Immense amounts of water was gushing out of holes in the rocks, forming a pool and the river. The water was ice cold, pure, and tasted wonderful. We went there several times during my four years at grade school.

As my mother packed my backpack for one of these trips, she showed me several packages similar to mine marked with Rót's name. She told me the food was for Rót and I was to give him the packages when we stopped for lunch. On the way to Tapolcafő I noticed that Rót was one of the few kids who didn't carry a backpack. I didn't realize then that being an orphan, he had nothing to carry. It occurred to me that I was carrying his food for him and I didn't think this was right. Halfway to Tapolcafő, as we were taking a break sitting under some large trees along the road, I told Rót that I had food for him, but he would have to help carry my pack if he wanted me to give him the food. He carried the pack the rest of the way to the springs. As we unpacked our lunches, I handed him his packages, which were identical to mine, yet his food was gone long before I finished my lunch. He ate ravenously, attacking his food. When I mentioned this to my mother, she explained that Rót, being an orphan, was probably hungry all the time, as orphans very seldom got good food or enough to eat. My mother also explained that in the orphanage bigger kids probably took the food away from the young ones, which may have been another reason why Rót ate his food fast. I thought then that this was clearly another case of God slipping up. I let it slip out that I had Rót carry my bag in exchange for his food. That was the only time I remember my mother losing her temper with me. I didn't hear the end of it for I don't know how long. It came under the heading, I

47

guess, of being (or not being) my brother's keeper. To make up for my lack of sensitivity, on subsequent trips I didn't let Rót carry my backpack and sat next to him during lunch to make sure no one would take the food away from him.

There were many other excursions and trips during my first ten years. Some I was too young to remember, and even the ones I do recall, fully or partially, at that time did not have special significance for me. For example, one trip I went on but really don't remember in any of its detail was with my parents to Vienna. I vaguely recall the Prater, an amusement park with the world's largest Ferris wheel. I heard them talk about it later on, which is how I know we stayed at the famous old hotel, the Hotel Sacher. It was best known for its restaurant and the famous Sacher-Torte (a cake). In 1987, Mom and I visited the Hotel Sacher in Vienna, had dinner in the restaurant, and had a piece of Sacher-Torte. The one notable thing about this trip with my parents, as I heard tell later, was our visit to the zoo in Vienna. My father told us the story many times when we were very young, how an Embden goose, or perhaps an emu or ostrich, had reached through the bars of its enclosure, grabbed and swallowed my father's burning cigar. This and some other similar stories he told were the few occasions when I would see my father smile. It had to be a special reason for him to smile. He even resented being told to smile when somebody took his photograph.

I remember staying at the Gellért Hotel, which at that time was the best in Budapest. I remember the green marble indoor pool where compressed air bubbles were forced through holes in the bottom of the pool. It was like swimming if not in champagne, in seltzer water. The glass roof of the pool would be open during the summer. At the far end, one could swim out of the pool into an adjoining free-shaped outdoor pool with bridges and terraces overhead, above the water. In the afternoons a band played dance music and while some were swimming, others were dancing on the terraces. A long, white marble slide would drop one into the biggest pool way below and in the back of the hotel. This pool had artificially created waves, which, once one got used to them, were lots of fun. Though I was pretty young, I do recall watching fireworks over the Danube from our window at the Gellért. It was August 20, I don't know what year, but it was Saint Stephen's Day, the Hungarian national holiday, which was traditionally celebrated with fireworks. Hungary's first Christian King, Saint Stephen, was later canonized and became Hungary's patron saint. The fireworks reflected in the water and lit up the beautiful bridges and buildings over and along the Danube. The many-spired Parliament building and the Var, an ancient fortress and royal palace, faced each other on opposing sides of the river. The Gellért and its once magnificent pools are still standing. When Mom and I visited Budapest while Liz was going to school there, we went to look at the hotel. It was run-down, seedy, and in bad repair, then serving as a people's recreational facility, catering to a few overweight and out-of-shape women, probably wives of party favorites and commissars. I've heard that it has since been renovated, now that the Soviet regime has given way to a free-market economy in Hungary.

As the years went by, we traveled less and less for pleasure, I now know, for financial reasons. In those later years when we went to Budapest, we stayed with my Aunt Manci and her husband, Uncle Jancsi, Dr. Zala János. He was a dentist and she had a beauty parlor next to his office, both of which were part of an apartment on the top floor of an apartment building in the central section of the city. As small as the apartment seemed to me, they managed to put us up in relative comfort. My aunt and uncle were both lovely, wonderful people. I stayed with them many times later on and will be talking about those visits in detail.

Manci néni, my aunt, a beautiful, slender woman, was my mother's youngest sister, and this brings me to tell you a bit about some of my relatives. Manci néni was one of four sisters. The oldest of the sisters, Ilonka néni, was married for the second time, also to a dentist, who also practiced as an MD, which was a common practice at that time in small towns in Hungary. They lived within walking distance from my grandmother's house in Celldömölk. Another sister, Jolán néni, was the second oldest, also married to a physician, Dr. Weisz Gyula, who was Archduke Somebody-or-Other's personal doctor. They were very wealthy and lived in a huge house near the Austrian border, in a town called Magyaróvár. Loosely translated, Magyaróvár means "Old Hungarian Fort." I'll also talk about them in more detail later. My mother was the third of the sisters, followed by Manci néni. My grandmother also had a son, Márton, who was the youngest of the five Klein offspring. Klein, "Little," as translated from German, was my mother's maiden name. In my opinion, Uncle Márton, Marci bácsi, as we called him, was, with the greatest of generosity, a loser. While I never disliked him, in later years I thought very little of him. He never worked a day in his entire life, lived at my grandmother's, was demanding, and, with the greatest of respect, I considered him obnoxious. He thought of himself as a great opera singer, a tenor, I believe. On one occasion he gave a concert in Pápa, and for about a week prior to the concert he stayed with us and every day practiced with some musicians in what we called the Mansard room, on the top floor of our house. A much younger man, cousin Zoli also lived at my grandmother's house. He was Aunt Ilonka's son from her first marriage, and when she married for the second time, Zoli went to live with my grandmother. He and Uncle Marci were a pair, both obnoxious and demanding, but at least Zoli worked occasionally.

There were many more relatives, and I will be talking about them as they fit into the scenario. For now, I want to mention one of my favorites, my father's youngest brother, Uncle Miklós. He and his wife, Aunt Alice, lived in Pápa in a modern apartment on the second floor of a new building. They had a young son, my cousin Jancsi, who was three or four years younger than I. Uncle Miklós was also a decorated veteran of WWI. His knee was shot up during the war and he walked with a very noticeable limp, as he couldn't bend his right leg. Many years later, I think in the late thirties or early forties, his leg developed an infection and had to be amputated above the knee. I remember lying in a hospital bed next to his, giving him a blood transfusion. The medical arts were not quite up to today's standards then, particularly not in Pápa. The jury-rigged transfusion apparatus and process, tubes running out of my arm into his, transferring blood, I thought even then was primitive. Within hours after this transfusion, he went into shock. I suppose doctors at that time had no idea about cross-matching blood. He recovered, and in a couple of weeks, though on crutches, was his cheerful old self again. I found out later that he was in almost constant pain with his leg since his injury in WWI and even after the amputation. Yet I never heard him complain. In fact, unlike my father, he was always in good humor, laughing and telling jokes. He and his wife frequently took my brother and me to Lake Balaton during the summers. Lake Balaton, Europe's largest lake, had several beautiful resort towns around it. Some of these were old, some were newer, but we loved all of them, particularly when we went with Uncle Miklós.

In earlier years we would go in our car. Uncle Miklós couldn't drive because of his stiff leg, and in later years when we no longer owned a car, he would hire a car to take us to the lake. He, as his wife, were wonderful to be with. He had a special rapport with my brother and me. Though I respected and looked up to him, somehow I didn't feel the same way about being with him as I did with my father. There was closeness, perhaps on a bit more equal level. I'll be telling you a lot more about Uncle Miklós, as well as other relatives. But as long as I am talking about our car, I want to tell you about it and about Zöld János, Zöld bácsi.

I remember him vaguely. As I mentioned, he was our coachman turned chauffeur. He was the one I talked about washing our yellow carriage in the Danube while we picnicked at Süttő, near Bikolypuszta. I don't know where or how he learned to drive; there were very few cars around at that time. I also remember his son, Jani. In later years he became one of the first pilots in Hungary. On one occasion we heard his plane fly very low over our house with tremendous noise that rattled the windows. All of us ran outside to see the plane, which was an extremely rare occurrence at that time. It was the most exciting thing to hear the plane's engine in the distance, rapidly approaching our house and disappearing in a flash over the trees. Zöld bácsi's son, Jani, came to our house to visit his father later that day, after he landed his plane in a field just outside of town. The plane was, I later found out, a Hungarian-manufactured biplane called, what else, *Hungaria*. It was made of orange-colored plywood and had silvery fabric wings. Under the bottom wing the plane had an electric sign, which Jani turned on at night. It spelled out "Schmall Paszta." Schmall Paszta in translation means "Schmall Paste," the most popular shoe polish at that time in Hungary. This was a new and unique way of advertising a product then. Hearing the plane, everyone would run out of their houses as the plane flew from town to town at night with "Schmall Paszta" blazing in the sky. People would talk about the unusual event for days. Zöld Jani told us that he was going to fly over our house again that evening and would wave to us. He did. The pink glare of the "Schmall Paszta" sign in beautiful calligraphy, just as it appeared on the cans of shoe polish, looked sensational in the crimson-blue evening sky. He made several very low passes over our house, missing the tower by what seemed like inches. It was still light enough to see his face as he waved to us from his open cockpit. Zöld Jani in his lace-up boots, riding britches, short leather coat, scarf, and leather pilot's cap with goggles made a big impression on me. I made up my mind then that one day I was going to be a pilot. From that day on, whenever possible, my friends and I, or just myself, played pilot at times for hours. My imagination easily turned childish fantasies into reality. A round outdoor table, similar to the one we now have by the pool, turned over on its side became the fuselage. A board of lumber appropriated from a back fence and inserted into the legs of the table was the wing/pilot's seat. A push broom, handle pushed through the hole in the top of table where an umbrella would normally fit, was the propeller, and a short stick served as the joystick to control the "plane" with. I had authentic goggles, probably from our carriage days in the country, and a cap worn backwards completed the illusion and allowed my imagination to soar. I flew this "plane" for hours on end, at times being scolded for doing too much of it at the expense of more important ways I could have spent my time.

* * *

Aside from a few minor incidents, I don't remember too much about our car. In fact, at this point I'm not even sure we had a car. We did use one often, and I remember it being kept in what used to be our carriage and tack room. The carriage, the sleigh, and the horses were gone by this time (the time frame is hazy), and I remember the shiny front bumper of the car protruding from the relatively small room. But at this point I can't swear that the car was ours. It might have been, or it might just have been kept there by whoever owned it. I know it was a Daimler-Benz, as I recall hearing conversations about it while growing up, and I remember that it was very big and shiny. What makes me think that we did own the car is that Zöld János, Zöld bácsi, our onetime coachman, was the driver. On one occasion, as he would let me do at times, I was sitting on his lap holding onto the steering wheel. We were driving through a small village, probably on one of my father's business trips. In the middle of the village the road curved around a church. Zöld bácsi told me that just past the church, I was to make a left turn. He knew the road, but he didn't know that the road was under construction and just beyond the corner of the church was a large pile of granite blocks that the road was going to be surfaced with. As I turned the wheel, passing the church, the left front wheel of the car ran up on this mound of rocks. If Zöld bácsi didn't yank the wheel back to the right, we could possibly have turned over. I didn't drive for a while after that.

On another occasion we were parked somewhere in Pápa along a sidewalk, which made a right angle turn in front of the car. In other words, the car was nosed up to this ninety-degree portion of the curb. On the inner edge of the sidewalk in front of the car was a high stone fence. Zöld bácsi let me sit behind the wheel as we were parked, waiting for I don't remember who or what. The engine was on, I suppose so it wouldn't have to be hand crank–started, which was a backbreaking, difficult job. I must have hit some lever, and the car just about jumped off the ground over the curb and the sidewalk, smashing into the stonewall. It bounced off and, like a charging ram, smashed into the fence again. I was petrified. Eventually Zöld bácsi managed to stop the engine and the car. There was minimal damage to the stone fence, but the front end of the car was pretty well smashed.

On a trip to Budapest we had a flat tire near a town called Veszprém. It was in the fall on a cold, bleak rainy day. Zöld bácsi had to jack up the car while everybody was still sitting in the backseat. Besides the regular seats, the car also had folding jump seats in the back. He took the wheel off the car. We had no spare. There were extra tires, but for some reason, which is not clear, we had no spare. Zöld bácsi removed the tire from the wheel, found the hole in the inner tube, and proceeded to fix it. I watched the whole procedure from the window sitting on my mother's lap. First, the inner tube had to be cleaned around the puncture. This was accomplished by rubbing it with gasoline, or benzin, as we called it, and then he roughened up the surface with a rasplike tool, which was the cover of the tire-patching kit. Rubber cement was applied, and the patch was placed over the hole. A metal disk was clamped over the patch and some substance on this disk was lit. Zöld bácsi had a lot of trouble trying to light it in the rain, but when he finally succeeded the substance on the disk burned with a lot of dense smoke, bubbling, spitting reddish sparks before finally going out. I thought the whole process was fascinating. The inner tube was placed back into the tire and the tire was reinstalled onto the wheel with lots of tools and grunting. He then pumped up the tire with a hand pump and put it back on the car. We were on our way. As far as I can recall, this may have been the last trip we took in that car. If indeed we did own this car, it must have been sold shortly after the tire incident. At that time, I'm guessing Zöld bácsi left us and we were without a car or carriage for the first time. I didn't miss them. I could walk every place I wanted to go, and whenever we needed a carriage or a car, we hired one.

* * *

There were many other isolated memories, incidents, experiences during those first ten or so years, too numerous to try to list all of them here. Lots of them have faded beyond recollection, but there are a few which are still vivid and come to mind frequently. Others I'll be backing up to as they are brought to the surface in the course of putting this account together.

One aspect of my early life, which never occurred to me to think about then but which is so amazing to me now, is that everything we had, most of the things which surrounded me and dominated my daily life, were handmade. I already told you about my clothes and shoes. Handmade things were the norm in those days at our level of lifestyle; in fact, certain store-bought items which are commonplace today were the novelty then. To start with, in almost every family there was someone who would do embroidery, needlepoint, sewing, and knitting. My mother was extremely good at those things and loved to do them. My brother and I, my father, uncles, cousins, and nieces had more hand-knit gloves, socks, scarves, sweaters, and caps than we could use. My mother could turn out a pair of gloves in a matter of a couple of hours, and a pair of socks in less time than that. She was also a very good cook. The variety of good dishes never ended. She would spend most of her mornings in the kitchen assisted by Fáni and some of the other girls. In the afternoons she would knit, at times getting together with some of her friends, also knitters, teaching each other new stitches and exchanging food recipes. There was only a minimal amount of store-bought food at our house. Coffee (the ersatz variety), cocoa, sardines, prepared food stuff such as mustard or yeast for baking bread, and so on would of course be bought in stores. We baked our bread. Every week, three or four huge loaves in big baskets covered with linen clothes were taken to the local bakery to be baked in the ovens. As far as I was concerned there was nothing better than the warm, fresh-baked bread, especially where the crust was broken open, with lots of fresh butter on it. I already told you about the lángos, which was the byproduct and the bonus of bread-baking days.

All our other foods were hand prepared, starting with the most basic peasant dishes such as noodles with cottage cheese to the most elaborate strudels. I'd watch with fascination as the strudel dough was stretched, with infinite patience, so thin that one could see through it to the size of our kitchen table. I liked watching my mother cook. There were always tidbits, some pots, pans, and dishes to clean up with more than the normal amount of residue, chocolate or whipped cream or something equally good, left in them for me.

One of the main delicacies in our house was roast goose. It was a dish on the level of frequency and importance that roast beef used to be at our house in Roslyn as you guys were growing up. We fattened our own geese. Every afternoon one of the younger girls who worked at our house would sit on a small, low stool near the stable, two geese tucked under her legs, with a tub of corn soaking in salty water next to her. She would stretch the geese's necks upwards and stuff hands full of corn down the birds' throats. After weeks of this kind of feeding the geese became very fat, producing huge livers, ready for the roaster. The liver was a great delicacy. It would be cooked and preserved in its own fat, which is different from ordinary goose fat. It never occurred to me then to give any consideration to how expensive goose liver would have been in restaurants around the world. I would slice huge slabs of it, particularly later on in life when my friends and I would come in from skating on a cold winter day, and eat it for a snack on a slice of bread spread with liver fat. Even the feathers of these birds ended up being used for various purposes. The small, soft breast feathers, or down, were carefully washed, sorted, and ended up in pillows, quilts, and comforters. Bigger feathers, such as the wing feathers with their stems stripped almost to the tip ends, would be braided together into attractive brushes to be used in the kitchen for basting.

Even our furniture was handmade. Most of the bigger, more ornate pieces, such as our carved and sculpted dining room set, were made by a master furniture maker in Pápa, Mr. Császár, pronounced Tzah-ssahr, meaning "Kaiser." Someone else made our bedroom furniture, matching beds, wardrobes, dressers, and so on. Even the kitchen chairs were handmade. In the dining room was a very beautiful hand-carved wood-and-glass cabinet with many pieces of fine Meissen and Dresden china, cut lead crystal, and on the center shelf in a frame were my father's military decorations from WWI. Even the large clay and china stoves in every room were disassembled once a year, cleaned and reassembled in preparation for winter. These stoves were fired up early every morning by one of the girls using the wood Tóni cut and chopped for us.

Off to the side of the dining room, the inside of the tower at this corner of the house was a small circular smoking room. Once again, what I remember most about this place was the smell of it. All my life I had a keen sense of smell. I mentioned this in connection with the steam of the locomotives, my grandmother's house, the railroad station, my pencil box, and so on. There was a heavy but very aromatic, pleasant smell in this small circular room. It was a combination of smells of tapestry, leather furniture, floor wax, but predominantly the smell of cigars and pipe tobacco in beautiful hand-carved wooden boxes called humidors. The boxes were the work of Russian prisoners of war who worked on my grandparents' farm during the First World War. Because of male labor shortage during the war, the government assigned Russian prisoners of war to landowners for farm work. Some of these Russian prisoners, I was told, were talented carvers and woodworkers. There were many other items in our house that they made for us. My grandmother, my father's mother, talked about these prisoners often. She told me the Russians were hardworking peasant people who appreciated the good treatment and comforts they received at my grandparents' place, as opposed to the misery they would have had to endure in prisoner-of-war camps. One of my father's brothers, Sándor (Alexander in translation, also my brother's name), was killed in WWI. My grandmother, I was told, did not accept this for years. Even after the war was over, she believed that her son was alive, maybe a prisoner somewhere in Russia, and she hoped that as she treated Russian prisoners, someone in Russia would treat her son kindly.

\* \* \*

My exposure to the world grew rapidly towards the end of that first decade. My brother and I grew apart somewhat. Being almost a year and a half his junior created quite a gap between us. Before he started school, the two of us were very close, being confined to our house and grounds and most of the time isolated from others of our age. I was left by myself when he started school, with only an occasional visit by some other kids my age, mostly kids I didn't know well, nor did I see them frequently enough to have much in common with and enjoy their company. When my brother came home from school, he had homework to do. His whole orientation seemed to have changed. He was no longer interested in some of the games we used to play. At times I felt he was looking down at me, now that he was a student and I continued being the same, stupid little kid. I didn't understand this until I started school and branched out into things other than the games we used to play around our house. I still piloted the overturned table on occasion, but not as frequently or for as long as before. I made new friends. At times I was allowed to return to school by myself in the afternoons and meet up with friends, spending the afternoon playing soccer and other games. Being allowed to walk around town more and more by myself was a huge step forward in my life. After my father took me to school the first day, I would walk to school with my brother in the morning and be picked up by my mother or Fáni as school finished for the day. By the following spring I was allowed to come home by myself, but with strict limitations. I had to come directly home without lingering anywhere, always following the same route. When I was finally allowed to go back to school in the afternoons, I no longer thought that the previous restrictions applied. At times on the way to or from school, I would stop off in the Liget, the City Park, play by myself, watch a soccer game, or practice at the soccer field from outside the fence, and at other times stop off at my Uncle Miklós's store on the Fő tér (the Main Square) in the center of town. He had a small farm-machinery parts store. Later on, he also sold bicycles. He had a bicycle at the store, which was used for deliveries by a young fellow, his one employee. Every once in a while I'd work up enough courage to ask him to let me use the bike. He knew I wasn't big enough to ride the bike sitting on the saddle, but I think he got a kick out of watching me ride with my right leg sticking through the frame, working the pedal. On one occasion I spotted him and my father watching me. I made as though I didn't see them as I executed some fancy maneuvers, and was very proud to notice their approving smiles when I glanced at them.

The Main Square in Pápa was a large area surrounded on one side by business and residential buildings. In the middle was the Big Templom, a large Roman Catholic Church with tall bell towers. Behind the church dominating the square were the massive ornamental iron gates of Baron Eszterházy's castle and estate. Between the gates and the back of the church was a large, flat area of dirt, which is where I rode Uncle Miklós's bicycle. Other times, instead of going to school in the afternoons, or if there weren't enough good friends there to play with, I would walk around town, exploring. Pápa was an interesting town with surprises beyond just about every corner.

* * *

All of us congregated one day in the entrance hall of our house as two workmen installed our first radio. There were two long wooden boxes on a table in the hall, each resembling a small coffin with large black knobs and little windows with dials. The workmen poured water mixed with some white powder into a row of glass jars, about the size and shape of pitchers, under the table. Heavy copper wires connected these glass jars, which were the power supply, the batteries for the radio. A long wire antenna was strung outside between the house and a pole. Another copper wire went through a hole drilled into the floor to the lower level of the house, where it was connected to a water pipe. Then the system was turned on and scared us all as loud noises, whistles, and crackles came out of the huge horn on top of one of the cases. When the installation was complete, the two workmen fiddled with the knobs, and the room was filled with varying intensity whistles and crackles, but finally some faint music and snatches of talk in a strange language came out of the speaker. It was a modern miracle. Even when a station came in strong, at times it would fade and come back, or just fade and disappear altogether. But it was fun fiddling with the radio. Though I was told to be very careful of the batteries, I played with the radio and listened, enchanted by some of the music coming from faraway places. Hungary had one radio station then, which only broadcasted on certain days, usually in the evenings.

* * *

Going to get fagylalt in the evening during the warm summer months with my father, mother, and brother was always fun. Fagylalt (pronounced fudjlult) is what ice cream was called in Hungary. Loosely translated, it means frozen something, but the word really applied only to ice cream. We would walk into the center of town in the evening to our favorite confectioner's shop, which had a garden with many tables. My brother and I would get a cone, or at times habos káve—that's coffee with whipped cream—and a nápoji szelet—which was a sugar wafer. My father always ordered a block of lemon ice cream, and both my mother and he would have jeges káve, which was iced coffee. My father also would get a glass of iced water, a big rarity in those days. As children, we weren't allowed to drink anything very cold. It was said to be bad for young stomachs. Going to get fagylalt in the evenings was one of the few and rare occasions when my mother came with us. Though we had an icebox at our house, keeping ice cream at home was not possible for any length of time.

During the hot summer months there were also ice cream vendors in the streets with pushcarts. For ten fillér (ten cents, though worth far less), one could buy a cone filled with a choice of vanilla, peach, cherry, and ices of other flavors. One had to eat it fast, as it would melt quickly and drip.

* * *

I became an avid reader in grammar school. As a birthday present, I believe, I was given a subscription to a publication called *Én Ujságom*, *My Newspaper*, which came in the mail once a week. It looked more or less like an actual newspaper with articles aimed at the very young. I loved the prestige of receiving my own newspaper, addressed to me, but I thought later that the contents were childish. After a while, as the subscription ran out, it wasn't renewed.

I also started collecting. In the box of ersatz-type coffee were beautiful color pictures of plants and flowers. On the back of each picture—one to a box—was a description of the particular plant or flower. It took a very long time and drinking a lot of coffee to collect the complete series. There was a lot of exchanging of these pictures with friends, as at times one got the same picture twice or even more often from the boxes of coffee. When all the pictures in a series were collected, we sent them in to the coffee company, which would return them mounted in a very beautiful album.

The pictures were mounted in such a way that they could be flipped up and the descriptions on the back of the pictures would be readable. It was a wonderful way of learning about trees and flowers. I thought of these pictures and albums many times as you were growing up, and wished that they could have been available for you.

Stamps also fascinated me. My stamp collection grew very large over the years into high school, helping to expand my understanding of geography and different people around the world. Just about that time I also started to read adventure and travel books.

* * *

Mom and I watched a program last night (January 17, 1996) on the Discovery Channel about zeppelins that reminded me of the day when the Graf Zeppelin flew over Pápa during its record flight around the world. It was quite a sight. The year must have been 1933–1935. A huge silver cigar, its engines humming, moved slowly over the city. When I asked him, my father, with his ever-present pipe (or was it his cigar?) in hand, explained that the markings on the zeppelin's tail were swastikas, the new national symbol of Germany. That was all he said and his expression told me not to ask any more questions.

* * *

The post office in town, a big, imposing, and very official-looking building, was another interesting place. It was part of the government, the same as post offices are here in the US, but there it seemed to have more importance, more stature. Actually, anything that had something to do with the government in Hungary was very important. The government owned a lot and substantially controlled just about all aspects of life. There were lots of government services, and every government service—not just the military—had uniforms. All railroad employees, not just conductors, had uniforms. There was an arm of the government that dealt with taxes, and the control of imported goods as well as government monopolies, such as tobacco, tobacco products, salt, and alcohol, even flints for cigarette lighters. The agency dealing with it, called the Financok, had, you guessed it, their own characteristic uniforms with swords. After watching the levente band from our attic, the post office was the next place where I became aware of uniforms. The most interesting aspect of the post office was that it had the only public telephone in Pápa at that time. Every town that had a post office had a telephone. This was a big step forward, particularly to someone such as my father, who occasionally had to talk with people in other towns. The procedure wasn't simple. When my father wanted to talk with someone in another town, he had to go to the post office, fill out a form with the name and address of the person he wished to speak with and specify a time for the call. Our post office in Pápa would then notify the post office in the town of the person called by telegram, which would be delivered by a uniformed mail carrier on a bicycle. If the person called was available and could go to the post office at the specified time, my father would be notified by telegram and would have to return to the post office a few minutes before the specified time to wait for the connection to be made. The phone would ring in a large, padded (for soundproofing) phone booth, and my father and I would step into it and close the door. The floor of the booth would give a bit, activating a light. But there was no ventilation and in a few minutes, particularly on hot summer days, one would be drenched with perspiration after even a short phone call, which, due to the primitive equipment, was usually a shouting match. A couple of years later private phones became available in Pápa, and we were amongst the first to get one.

* * *

Three important things happened towards the end of my first decade. As I was meeting more and more people, I began to notice that there were differences in their family lives from ours. There were lengthy periods, for instance, when my father and mother didn't talk to one another. On those occasions I could tell that both of them were upset, but had no idea what they were upset about. On the basis of what I could put together over the following several years, there might have been several reasons that caused a rift between my parents. Thinking about it today reinforces some of my earlier suspicions. My father's business wasn't doing well. While I was never told in so many words, right after WWI, when my father and mother married, the house at Pápa as well as Bikolypuszta were given to them as wedding presents from my maternal grandparents. Bikolypuszta must have been a part of my grandparents' landholdings. As I understand it, after my grandfather's death these landholdings, which were controlled by him and his brothers, fell apart. It seems that the brothers couldn't get along with one another, nor were they able to manage the large holdings without the leadership of the oldest brother, my grandfather. This seems to suggest that to some extent my father, and the management and running of Bikolypuszta, were also somehow dependent on my grandfather. For whatever reason, this support was lost or possibly withdrawn before I was born. The withdrawal of this support might have been prompted by another factor. My maternal grandparents' family, as was the case with my paternal grandparents, were religious Jews. Not the Hassidic, fundamentalist, overly religious variety, but what in today's circumstances may be defined as moderate, reformed. For all outward appearances, nothing distinguished them from anyone in the country. But they took their religion seriously, even to the extent of attending synagogue on important holidays. Whatever religious observance was practiced in our home was initiated by my mother. I accepted this as part of life at an early age without really knowing or caring enough to assign any special significance to it. When my father's brothers decided to convert, the Klein family, my mother's parents, I suspect, might have been alienated and withdrew their support. This could possibly have resulted not only in the loss of Bikolypuszta but also in the rift between my father and my mother's family. The anxiety caused by this rift, the resulting financial hardship it created, the conflict it caused on an ideological basis might all add up to obvious difficulties between my mother and my father. It is strange that I have never been able to fully ascertain the conversion to Catholicism in my father's case, though I knew it was a fact in the case of Uncle Matthew and Uncle George. Whether it took place or not at this stage bears very little significance. Then it caused a terrible rift between my mother and my father, which, like a heavy weight, was felt in our home and, I believe, strongly affected the lives of all of us. I know it was there, and the basis of it was probably religion. In later years I heard my mother say that she would not have been able to visit her father's grave had she converted. Conversion, I suspect, was also a major reason for my father not coming with us during our summer visits to my grandmother in Celldömölk. Who held a grudge against whom, I don't really know. Many years later, whatever the cause might have been behind this rift faded with the passage of time and became less and less obvious or important. The distance between my father and my mother's family, actually my grandmother, who by then was the only remaining grandparent on the Klein side of the family, narrowed and improved slowly, which, in turn, relaxed the tensions in our home. But looking back on it now, I know that a completely harmonious family life was never reestablished.

As my family moved to Pápa after the loss of Bikolypuszta, my father was without work. We must have had enough money to carry us or we might have been still subsidized by my mother's or my father's family, but financially at least, there seemed to be no problems. Not until later. There is no point trying to dwell on this in detail now, but I want to point out that the reason I liked my Uncle Miklós so much, and the reason it was so much fun to go on excursions with them, may have been their truly harmonious family life. As a child, and even now, as I think about those days and years with my family, I tend to or try to lock out those unpleasant aspects of our family life.

Sometime after leaving Bikolypuszta, I don't know when exactly, my father started a business of buying and selling livestock. He called his business Tenyészálat Kereskedés, which, as close as I can get to a translation, means "Dealership of Pedigreed Breeding Animals." He bought and sold on speculation or on orders the best bulls, oxen, and cows. As far as I can recall, there were no steers in Hungary. Cattle was not raised for beef as much as for dairy production and farm work. Of course lots of these animals were butchered for meat, but those were usually the odd, old, or unsalable, unwanted animals. We did have an abundance of veal. When the dairy animals calved, the calves were separated from their mothers as soon as possible for the cows' milk. The calves were sold to be butchered. It was good meat and we ate more of it than just about any other kind of meat. Later on my father branched out into trading in other types of animals, such as longhorn oxen, which particularly during the war years were very popular for farm work. Occasionally he bought and sold horses. I recall a pair of matched Lipizzaners, not the riding kind, which I believe were bought for Baron Eszterházy. As I put it together, this was a rough and unrewarding business at its start and for years to come. I suspect that during those lean years, my mother's family limited or held back their support. This could have been due to their own financial inability, or possibly because of their resentment caused by the conversion. Those lean years created anxieties, which must have contributed to the deterioration of our home life, and resulted in drastic changes in our lifestyle.

Next to our home life being affected by religious differences and the difficulties of my father's business, a most important other factor began to affect my life. I recall a rather strong image of my Uncle Márton and several of his friends listening raptly to the radio at my grandmother's house in Celldömölk. The voice, booming out of the radio speaking in German, interrupted by frequent applause, was that of Adolf Hitler. I must have been six, seven, perhaps eight years old as Adolf Hitler was gaining prominence in Germany and became a major, perhaps the most important, single influence affecting my life and future.

# Chapter 6

# 1936 – 1940
# STARTING DECADE TWO

By the end of my first decade I became a better-than-average skater, a good swimmer, and while was not the best runner or jumper, I managed to hold my own in field athletics. Later on I became a fair shot putter. The garden behind my grandmother's house in Pápa on Bástya utca, Bastion Street, had a rock wall fence maybe seven or eight feet high. The interesting thing about this wall/fence was that many years before, it was a section of the walled fortification that encircled Pápa, hence the name Bastion Street. The top of this massive fence was about eight feet thick, and on the outside it dropped about twenty-five feet to the ground. At its base the moat, though it no longer held water, was still visible. At one time when I was already in high school, I lowered myself on ropes about halfway down this wall and extricated an iron ball, probably a cannonball fired into the wall, perhaps by the Turks who occupied Hungary for about a hundred and fifty years in the fifteenth and sixteenth centuries. Getting the ball out of the wall and up and over the fence was not an easy operation, but after I did it I scraped the rust off the ball, filed and ground the rough surface smooth, and cleaned it up so it was shiny bright. It became my shot to practice shot putting with. I flew my outdoor table "plane" less and less, as other more important aspects crept into my life. For instance, I became absolutely gaga over a little girl two classes behind me, Vera Neumann. She was slender, had long, blond hair; without a doubt, the most beautiful little girl I had ever seen until then. Though girls and boys seldom interacted while in grade school, it was always fun to catch a glimpse of her during the breaks, show off when I thought she was looking, and ignore her on purpose in what today would be described as a very macho way. But I knew she liked me, and by the time I became thirteen or fourteen years old, we did spend a great deal of time together.

\* \* \*

About the time I finished grade school, we moved. The house on Eszterházy Street was sold and we moved to a house we referred to as the English House. The reason for this name, I believe, stems from having put some of my father's clients from England up there on occasion. Like so many other houses in Pápa, this house also had massive gates, which, as at both of my grandparents' houses, led into the garden through a tunnel. This was a two-family house. We had the front section, which was the corner of Assisi Street and a street the name of which I no longer remember. The back section was leased to a widow who later married a defrocked Roman Catholic priest.

My mother was devastated by the loss of our house on Eszterházy Street. My father had to be also, but he concealed his emotions better than my mother. I, as a child, as all children, took things for granted but was also sad to leave a lot of memories behind. My father's business continued to be bad and I am sure it was the reason for selling the house.

The location of our new home put us within minutes of my grandmother's house and closer to my new school, the Pápai Református Kollégium, the Reformed Church School of Pápa. I don't know how long we lived in this house; probably not very long, as I don't remember too much about it. What I mean is that there were few extraordinary experiences I think of often and associate with the English House. There was a Dominican (I believe) monastery diagonally across from the house, and every morning I saw the brown-robed, hooded monks leave in double file for the Catholic high school where they taught.

They would return in the afternoon, the same double file, hoods over their heads, wearing sandals without socks, winter or summer. Their heavy robes never changed. In the summer they even played tennis in the monastery gardens, wearing the same heavy robes. Their hair was cut in a style that looked like a large doughnut on a bald head.

I recall one incident which I believe I told you about. Sometime while living in this house, my brother and I were given a small violin—I don't know by whom. It was not a toy violin, but lessons, if that was what it was intended for, did not materialize. Somehow, the violin broke into what seemed like a million pieces. For some reason or other, my father kept the pieces in a cigar box. One day, how or why—the detail is no longer there—a very young Gypsy kid showed up at our house and wanted to buy the violin pieces. My father told the kid that he could have the pieces for one pengő, at that time perhaps twenty cents. Later that afternoon, the Gypsy kid returned with one hundred fillér, one pengő's worth of Hungarian pennies, and my father gave him the pieces of the violin. A couple of weeks later, the same kid came back to our house with the violin, reassembled, refinished, and looking brand new. He even played it for us and my father gave him a couple of pengős, as he really never intended to take money from the little kid. My father didn't have much money at that time, but one would never have known it. In spite of the shortage of money he was a very generous man by nature.

Within the next five years, we moved three more times.

* * *

At about this time my cousin Klári, a very beautiful young woman, got married. She was the daughter of my father's only sister, Józsa, who was the second oldest amongst the Kluger offspring. She was a widow, having lost her husband many years before I was born. Besides Klári, she had two sons, Imre, the older, and János, the younger. Imre was an attorney, János a young doctor in research. While in research, János contracted some disease he was studying, which killed him in a very short time. Klári married a wealthy young man, Saudek József, who later Hungarianized his name, changing Saudek to Sas, meaning "Eagle." He and his brother owned and operated the largest yard goods store in Pápa, which in the era of the tailor-made suit was a prosperous business. He and Klári had a beautiful little daughter, Ágnes. When Klári and her husband first married, they lived at my grandmother's house on Bástya utca, later moving to their own place, a beautiful, large, and modern apartment house, which they built over their store on Kossuth utca, one of Pápa's busiest shopping streets.

Józsa néni, Aunt Józsa, was a headstrong cripple who kept going on sheer willpower and iron determination. Her entire body was racked by rheumatoid arthritis to the extent that she could hardly move. She owned a notions store on Main Street in Pápa, where she spent most of her life sitting behind the counter at the cash drawer. Every morning she was carried into the store and placed on her specially constructed chair, which gave her body support. In the evenings when the store closed, she was carried to a waiting carriage, which took her home to Bástya utca. In later years, to spare the agony of the carriage ride over bumpy roads, she and my grandmother moved to an apartment on the top floor of the building her store was in. She was carried up and down the stairs twice a day to and from her chair in the store. Her hair was done for her every morning by my grandmother, who also bathed, dressed, and fed her. Her hands looked like dried-up snarled twigs, huge bumps over every joint, and fingers bent by the disease in every direction. I guess it was a family trait not to buckle under pain. She never talked about her agonies, nor did she tolerate anybody trying to make her feel better by expressing sympathy. I don't know, though I believe, she converted to Christianity with her brothers, and I do recall her voicing strong opinions, condemning the old Orthodox Jews for their ancient, archaic, and separatist practices from local customs and communities. To my knowledge she practiced no religion of any denomination, which of course might have been at least partially due to her physical disabilities. Before her marriage, Klári had many suitors, amongst them young army officers, some of whom hung around the shop every chance they had hoping to see her.

* * *

There was one memory connected with living in the English House, which I talked about in the past, but this account wouldn't be complete if I did not include it. This was the silkworm experience. By this time I was perhaps in the first or second class at the Kollégium, and during one of our natural history classes our teacher showed us a movie about silk production. It was fascinating. The entire process was described on the film, starting with the initial step of picking up all the necessary items of silk farming from one of the governmental agencies in town. That meant any and every town in the country. Hungary was bent on developing all sorts of cottage industries at that time and silk production was one of them. The necessities—the tiny worms, instruction booklet, perforated paper, and so on—were given free for the asking, and at the end of the summer, after the fully grown worms formed their cocoons, the same government agency would buy the cocoons for what the film claimed a considerable sum of money. The money, as well as the whole process of raising worms, seemed interesting and easy. Adding to the attraction, our natural history teacher explained that aside from everything else, raising silkworms was a patriotic activity. The silk, he pointed out, was going to be used in the making of parachutes for our troops. The aspect of doing something patriotic appealed to me. Within days I picked up one family of worms. They were in a small box, smaller than a cigar box, a glob of black dirt–like mess, which, when I looked closely, appeared to move. There were thousands of tiny worms, none bigger than the point of a pin. I also carried home a generous supply of perforated paper, books, and all sorts of other things necessary for the raising of silkworms. Everybody who picked up worms was also given a handful of elderberry leaves for the worms' first meal. I set up my worms on a table at home, probably in a room that wasn't much used, cut up the elderberry leaves with a pair of scissors as the book instructed, and watched it disappear, absorbed by the swirling, mysterious mass of microscopic little worms. Then, with my backpack on I got on my bike and went to pick more leaves. The highways, most of them dirt roads at that time in Hungary, were lined on both sides with elderberry trees. Along with the worms and the supplies, everybody was also given a very impressive-looking official document attesting to the fact that as a bona fide silkworm raiser, the holder, in this case me, had permission from the government to pick elderberry leaves. In a country of all-powerful government, this was a clear indication of being in a privileged position. I mean, how many people could have just walked up to any elderberry tree anywhere and pick leaves? I know this sounds ludicrous, but such was the mentality at that time in Hungary. I arrived home just in time for the next feeding with my backpack stuffed with elderberry leaves. It looked to me as though the worms had grown a bit while I was picking leaves. The following morning, I took a bigger sack with me to collect more leaves. By about the end of the first week, it seemed I did nothing but pick leaves and feed the worms. Shortly, I was doing it twice a day. The worms grew awfully fast. I would cover them with the sheets of perforated paper and spread fresh leaves on top of the sheets. Within seconds worms would be coming up through the perforations to get at the fresh leaves. When they were all on top of the sheet, I would lift the whole bunch to another clean portion on the table and clean off the area where they had just been removed. This turned into an increasingly bigger, more difficult and dirty job, but it had to be done with unfailing, monotonous regularity. It definitely looked a lot easier in the movie in natural history class. Then I would go pick more leaves. I had to set up more tables as the worms grew and required more space. It was fascinating to watch the now inch-long little critters as so many tiny automated monsters relentlessly gnawing away, chewing up the leaves in a curious, never-stopping, arcing motion. They never stopped eating. The more leaves I brought home, the more they ate and the faster they grew. As they did, I found myself in the trees along the road to Celldömölk at the crack of down, making as many as four runs during the day. Thank God I was a good tree climber. I constructed a clever rack for my bike to carry as many as six sacks jammed full of elderberry leaves. The routine kept intensifying and repeating itself. I picked, fed, cleaned, created more space for the growing worms, and went to pick again. But I kept telling myself that by the end of the summer I'd make a bundle of money. It was not to be. As the worms grew, I had to transfer them to our attic, spread out on wide, triple-tiered shelves with just enough space in between them to hold the straw tents in which the worms were to form their cocoons. There were so many of them that I had to spread some of them out on the floor on cardboard sheets. My young cousin Jancsi came to see the worms one day about a week before the worms were ready to form their cocoons. He didn't realize there were worms on the floor and, without knowing it, killed some by walking on them. The result was that some sort of disease spread amongst the worms decimating the bunch. Even the ones that survived formed inferior-quality cocoons. The total take for my summerlong patriotic work was probably less than ten dollars.

* * *

Leaving the English House, I'm certain, was due to further financial difficulties. We moved into a relatively small apartment. All our large and beautiful furniture was jammed into small rooms, but fortunately not for long. My father's business started to pick up, and as money was once again available we moved to a much larger home, to 28 Jókai ut (street). This house, massive wooden gates on the street, tunnel leading into gardens, also had a very large vegetable garden in the back with the Tapolca River flowing through it. This was where I used to swim in the river and at times used one of our large, wooden washtubs as a canoe, propelling it with ping-pong paddle–shaped oars of my own making. We also had a very large roofed-over wooden terrace overlooking the gardens in the back. It had stairs on both sides leading down into the gardens and the river. We left this house also as business continued to improve, and moved to a very nice home in an area called the Tókert, Lake Gardens. Hundreds of years ago there was a lake at this location, which was drained for farmland as Pápa grew was developed for residential use. Our house was at 12 Pozsonyi ut. Once again we had an ornamental iron fence, but no carriage gate, no stables, nor outbuildings behind the house. There was a small wooden shed to keep potatoes and firewood in. But we did have a wonderful vegetable garden and orchard. My favorites were the pear trees, the sweet, sour, and white cherry trees, peaches and apricots, plums of all shapes and sizes, and a row of raspberry bushes at the back fence along a small stream, the Bakonyér, Bakony Stream. I would literally eat myself sick when the fruit was ripe. One who hasn't done it can have no idea how ripe fruit fresh off the tree tastes. There was also a large walnut tree behind the house. It was relatively easy to climb, and because of its massive branches and smooth bark, there were several spots in the tree where I could get comfortable and read for hours. When my mother first saw me way up in the tree, she was very scared, but after a while got used to the idea that I was all right in the tree. There was a terrace in the back of this house also, but not as big as at Eszterházy ut. We had our supper out there often, shaded by the old walnut tree in the cool breeze, which seemed to prevail in this part of town in the evenings. Through all the bad years Fáni stayed with us. It would be misleading if I allowed the impression that we were impoverished. We were not. We still wore tailor-made clothes, though by the time we moved to our house in Tókert, more and more store-bought items became available. By then good quality shoes, for instance, were almost all store-bought. It was also a fairly common practice to have an old suit turned inside out. By this I mean the tailor would take the old suit completely apart, remove all stitches, and reassemble the suit with the inside of the fabric now on the outside. The suit or garment would look completely new, except for the handkerchief pocket and the buttonhole in the left lapel, both of which were now on the right side of the jacket. One could always tell who was wearing a turned-out jacket by those telltale signs. But this was not degrading; in fact, it was almost a badge of distinction to have a turned-out jacket, which proved how good the fabric was in the first place.

It would be difficult and probably pointless to try to list in chronological order all that happened during these years, as we moved from place to place. While very important things were happening during this decade, the account of my personal life from here on will be told as the events and episodes come to mind, in no special sequence or order of importance.

For instance, Uncle George, or Gyuri bácsi, as we called him, came to visit us in Pápa for the first time since he left Hungary shortly after WWI. He was considered somewhat of a black sheep of the family. Though he graduated from a university with an engineering degree and served during WWI as an artillery officer, he left the country shortly after the war to live in Paris and work as an artist. As I understand it, he also lived in London for a while before going to America. I heard he wouldn't write to us at times for years, which was much resented by everybody in the family, but in a way, many years later, I learned to understand it. After coming to America, I also found it difficult to correspond with friends and relatives in Hungary. I had heard lots of talk about Uncle George, who by 1936 achieved some recognition in the US as a well-known artist. A very popular Hungarian magazine, *Szinházi Élet* (*Theatrical Life*), ran his picture as he was painting an oil landscape, his easel set up in the backseat of his large American convertible touring car. I was very proud of him and looked forward to his visit. The year was 1936, and I was ten years old. All of us went to meet his train at the railroad station. I recognized him instantly when the train came in. Like my father, he was a big man and had a wonderful smile. He had lots of luggage, including some easels. I was hoping to watch him paint and wasn't disappointed. After the second or third day, he set up his easel and paints and started to paint my grandmother's portrait. It was amazing to see how a charcoal line drawing of my grandmother materialized on the canvas within minutes. He worked fast, but not for very long. He said something about painting a portrait in six sittings, as he put away his things after the first short session. He told me that I could come and watch him again the next day. I couldn't wait. The portrait was finished in about a week and the canvas was taken to a picture-framing shop on the Main Square of Pápa. It was beautifully framed and exhibited in the store's window for about a week. Lots of my time every day was spent standing in front of this store window, admiring the portrait, hoping to hear good comments from those who stopped to look at it. I was dying to have the opportunity to tell people that the lady in the picture was my grandmother and the picture was painted by my uncle, a famous artist from America.

About this time I think I started to develop an interest in America. Just about everything I heard or read indicated that it was truly a land of milk and honey, a large, rich, and beautiful country of extraordinary opportunities where people lived well.

Uncle George left almost as suddenly as he arrived. He made a big impression on me then and I hoped I would have a chance to see him again. I did, exactly twelve years later, as you know, in America.

* * *

Perhaps the most important event that happened to me going into my decade number two was starting high school. At that time we did not separate junior high from high school. We referred to the school simply as "the school" or the "Kollégium," and once enrolled, one was expected to spend the next eight years at the school. I was enrolled in Class One. The atmosphere in the Kollégium was very different from the grade school I graduated from. To start with, the school was much larger, more imposing, and almost overbearing. I felt intimidated by large groups of older and bigger kids, all of whom seemed and acted very confident and superior. You might find it hard to believe that students entering the school for the first time were referred to and called szecskák, which, believe it or not, translates as "grasshoppers." I often wondered if the writer of the popular kung fu TV series in which young students of martial arts are called grasshoppers might have gone to my school. Szecskák—I won't even try to give a phonetic equivalent—were all the upperclassmen's patsies. Lots of upperclassmen, though maybe only one class above, tried and did exert their superiority. I no longer remember who it was, but an upperclassman and I got into an altercation shortly after I started the school. Although he was bigger, I managed to push him down the stairs. Nothing would have happened beyond this, except that he had to have a band-aid put on his elbow, which was done by our phys ed teacher, Kovács ur. He had a small office next to the dressing area in the gym and he called me in to tell him what happened. He listened and said very little. Though he hardly looked at me, somehow I felt that I liked him. In later years, he turned out to be a great influence on my life. His name was Vitéz Kovács Lajos. "Vitéz" in front of one's name denoted an honored status as a decorated hero of WWI.

Becoming a student at the Kollégium (Coal-lay-ghioum, as close as I can get to an acceptable pronunciation) signified a direction in one's life towards a privileged future. At that time, Hungary was determined to wipe out illiteracy, and elementary education was compulsory and free. But most children of less educated or lower-income families would stop attending school after four years of elementary school, though some went for an additional two years, which was available but not compulsory. Some went on to four years of trade school, after which around the age of fourteen they would go into a trade. Many students dropped out of the Kollégium by or before the end of the fourth year. Some went on to military schools or other private schools, while most just could not deal with the academic life at the Kollégium. Some dropped out for financial reasons and went into a trade or business. The school had a long and distinguished history. It was founded in 1531, and with some short and longer interruptions remained as one of the great schools of Hungary. Throughout the centuries of the school's existence, many graduates achieved fame and worldwide recognition in just about all fields. Throughout all the years I attended the school, the idea of future leadership was constantly hammered into the students. In the past, some students of the school led or were involved in the most important events of Hungary's turbulent history during the hundreds of years of the school's existence. As intimidating as it was to be a szecská, I was proud to be a student at this school and hardly ever went anywhere without wearing my school cap. It was a handsome, military-style cap made from burgundy velvet and braided with gold. On the front of it, in baked enamel on brass, was the official coat of arms of the school, a tree (of learning) in a white field, bordered by red, blue, and gold. Surrounding the tree on the shield, below the name of the school, was Pápa and the year 1531, the year the school got its start. On certain important occasions, the celebration of a national holiday for example, it was customary to stick a long goose feather behind the shield. Higher education, such as attending a university, would have been out of the question without completing a school such as the Pápai Református Kollégium. Completing it meant automatic advantages and privileges, and higher social positions in a feudal militaristic society such as Hungary still was at that time. My class was very large. Over a hundred kids entered from all over the country. This group was broken into two classes, A and B. I ended up in B being constantly reminded that the B class was for dummies. There might have been something to this as I also thought that there were an awful lot of simple kids in my class. Not so much in their academic skills or their native intelligence, but in their obvious lack of sophistication. Most of them have never been away from their villages till the first day of school at the Kollégium. We had day students, such as my brother and me, as well as those who came every morning by train from neighboring towns. Students from points too far to commute from lived in a dormitory, the old school building built with six-foot-thick walls in the 1500s. They ate their meals at the school's dining hall, which was available only to them. Some students from distant parts of the country lived with families in town.

All the classrooms were in what at that time appeared to be an enormous building. There were classrooms on three floors, and unlike elementary school, we went to specific classrooms for certain subjects. Each class also had a homeroom with small desks for two large windows, an elevated teacher's platform, a blackboard, and a large wood-burning iron stove. Each homeroom had a class library of hundreds of volumes of reading material. It contained not only the books that were compulsory reading, but also popular books of interest to the age group, approved by the school. I think I read most of the books in the library of every class I attended. I always liked to read, but there were periods in my life when I devoured books, particularly of the travel, adventure, and patriotic variety. We also had a library at home, some of which by this time was relegated to boxes in storage, but the best books were still kept in a very beautiful, large cherrywood cabinet in a room with leather furniture. Amongst these books I found a volume on Hungary's WWI heroes and their deeds. My father and my Uncle Miklós were both in the book. The account of my father's battery continuing to fire until their ammunition ran out and as he rescued the cannon harnessed to six horses, before the area was encircled by whoever the enemy was, was uplifting to read. I read it over and over, etching in my mind the words and the ink drawing of galloping horses pulling a cannon. In the picture the cannon was bumped into the air over the rough road and the horses were all lathered up. This image is still vivid in my memory. The particular decoration my father was given for this was called the Nagy Ezust, the Large Silver. It was a beautiful medal, as I mentioned, displayed alongside his other medals in a glass cabinet in our home.

Looking back on it, life at school was conducted in an archaic, almost militaristic manner. Every moment, every action of a student, was clearly defined and regulated. We jumped to attention as our teachers entered the classroom, and stood until we were told to be seated. Most of our teachers were old, or appeared to be old, stern, and dignified. Some, on the other hand, were bordering on or were downright pompous. Aspects of even our private, off-campus lives were regulated. There was a strict curfew imposed by the school, beyond which a student could not be on the street without a parent or guardian. These curfew hours varied during the seasons and were stricter for students of the lower classes. We even had to petition permission to go to the movies. By this time there were two motion picture theaters in town, but going to the movies on a weekday was out of the question. On weekends, if the movie was listed on the school's bulletin board as approved, one had to petition the homeroom teacher on a handwritten sheet of paper of a certain size and even folded in a special way. If permission was granted, the teacher signed the slip. At times permission was denied on the basis of the student's academic performance, record, behavior, or even if the petition contained mistakes or was incorrectly executed. Whether the teacher liked the student or not also played an important part in getting permission.

The older of the two motion picture theaters in town, the Jókai Mór Theater, named after Hungary's most famous and revered author and one of the important players of Hungary's independence, was located near the electric plant in an out-of-the-way area behind the outdoor marketplace. It was a large theater with a presidium stage, where plays would also be performed on occasion. Next to the auditorium was a very large lobby with a small candy booth. During intermission, we were allowed to buy candy. My favorite was a soft, gumlike taffy called Tutti-Frutti. It was always fun to go to see a mozi, the Hungarian name for a movie, abbreviating the name of "something which moves"—in other words, moving pictures. American movies were the most popular. You might get a kick out of knowing how movies were presented. Before every performance, there were commercials advertising local businesses, grocery stores, undertakers, and so on. These commercials were projected slides, hand drawn or painted on glass by some local artists, including my art teacher Tóth Sándor. As these slides were silent, music, usually Gypsy music, was played without voice announcements. Then came the newsreels, occasionally American but mostly German and Hungarian, followed by everybody's favorite, American cartoons. There were some Hungarian cartoons also, a Felix the Cat-type cartoon character called Sicc Ur, pronounced Shitz Uhr. Every time this cartoon was shown, a comic book dealing with the same character would be available in the lobby. I loved them. A ten-minute intermission followed, time-out for Tutti-Frutti, and then the bell rang, announcing the feature. On summer nights, as the theater was not air-conditioned—nothing at that time was—the side doors of the auditorium would be opened as it got dark. Within minutes there would be flies in the theater. Ushers would walk up and down the aisles pumping a scented fly spray into the air over the heads of the audience. I don't know who fared worse, the flies or the audience. Fortunately, during the summer months there was an outdoor movie theater in town also. It was at the football (soccer) stadium, where a small projection booth would be added onto the front of the grandstand, and on movie nights a screen on tracks would be rolled in front of this projection booth. At the end of the feature, as the lights would come on, the Rákóczi March by Liszt would be played. It was the custom in Hungary to play this march at all public events and gatherings, signifying the end of the event. I loved going to the movies, and even after all these years I vividly remember some of the movies I saw then in most of their detail. I walked or bicycled to school every day, six days a week. Classes started at eight a.m. and lasted until one or two in the afternoon. Extracurricular activities, sports, lab, music lessons, and so on met in the afternoon. Each regular class was fifty minutes long, with a ten-minute break between classes. The beginning or the end of a period was signaled by a shrill bell on every floor, triggered by an old grandfather clock, which was electrified by my gym teacher, Kovács ur. Gym classes, as in my elementary school, were my favorites. At the Kollégium we had at least two gym classes per week. Kovács ur, our gym teacher, detested all szecskák, whom he considered and treated like babies, stupid little kids he had the misfortune of having to deal with. Like my father, he growled at us and restricted all our moves, including how to get dressed for gym class and how to get undressed after gym class. This was sixty years ago, but I still remember the much-anticipated first gym class as if it happened yesterday. My plan to show off my climbing skills didn't materialize. We weren't even allowed to enter the gym. Instead, we sat on benches in the dressing room as Kovács ur lectured us on how to behave in gym class, how to dress, undress, and so on. During the next gym class we had to color-code our sneakers and were told what we could and could not do once we were permitted to enter the gym. We wore a uniform for gym class, which consisted of black gym shorts with short red and blue ribbons, the school colors sewn on the side, and a white T-shirt. There was only one type of sneakers we were allowed to wear for gym. They were white with white soles. They did not mark the floor, which Mr. Kovács was fanatical about. It was spotless and shiny and no one, under the threat of instant death, was allowed to enter with street shoes on. We could not talk to Mr. Kovács unless we approached him and stood at attention until he recognized us and growled to find out what we wanted. Whatever the request was, as a szecská, the request was, more often than not, denied. His mannerisms and behavior reminded me of my father, which might be why I was not quite as intimidated by him as some others were. I think he liked that. When we were finally permitted to enter the gym weeks later, we were lined up in three rows, taller kids at the head of the lines, the short ones at the end. We were instructed how to line up straight, arm's length from one another, looking straightforward, standing at attention. Well into the first year, I think after the first quarter report cards came out, and once the gymnastic abilities and character traits of the kids were established, a platoon leader, assistant platoon leader, squad leaders, and assistant squad leaders were appointed by Kovács ur. Though a few years later I was appointed assistant squad leader, at that first occasion, much to my disappointment, I was not. A few minutes before gym class ended, we were told to grab large push brooms and sweep the floors like so many snow plows, one broom following another. In later years I became one of Kovács ur's favorites. I looked up to and admired him, and still think of him kindly and with admiration. More about him later.

* * *

A favorite pastime amongst students of this age group (10–13) was Gomb Futball, "Button Soccer." As the name implies, it was played with buttons, which were altered to make them suitable for the game. As in real soccer, each team consisted of eleven players. The teams were named after one's favorite soccer team and sported hand-painted paper tags pasted to the top of the buttons with the real team's colors. My team was named after and wore the colors of a very good Hungarian soccer team, Ferencváros. Likewise, the individual button players were named after real soccer heroes. The objective of the game was to "kick" the "ball," usually a small mother-of-pearl shirt button, into the opponent's goal. The game had to be played on a smooth, slippery surface, such as a highly polished table, but there were very few of these, as most mothers frowned upon button soccer played on their dining room table. I made a highly polished folding playing field, much like the top of a ping-pong table, but smaller. I also made goal gates with netting, which were pretty smart. The boards had all the markings of a real soccer field. The largest button was the goalie, which could not be manipulated, only placed in position once before an opponent's shot at the goal. Opponents alternated shooting, except in the case of a penalty. All other players were of different sizes, all fashioned out of regular buttons. Large buttons, made out of horn for overcoats, were the favorites as they could be easily ground to the shape which was most suitable for the positions the buttons played. The edges of these buttons were ground off all the way around to an angle, which allowed them to be manipulated during the game by one's thumbnail pressing against the ground-off edge, forcing them to slide along the slippery board. The game called for skill, but most importantly for properly ground buttons for players. Nobody's overcoat buttons were safe.

* * *

Over the years, time and again I heard talk about my father hunting game as a young man. The only time and place this could have happened would have been at Bikolypuszta. I vaguely remember some stag horns over a door in the entrance hall of the house. He must have had the skin of one of these animals tanned, and many years later my brother, my cousin Jancsi, and I had lederhosen, short leather pants made from it. Lederhosen were traditionally Tyrolean, very popular in Southern Germany, Austria, and Switzerland. All ages of men, and at times women, wore them. Most were made alike in a traditional design, very short with a fancy flap covering the fly. All had buttons made of stag horns, suspenders made from the same skin, and a small side pocket for a multiblade knife. The older and greasier these lederhosen were, the more fashionable and desirable they became. As they were indestructible, most were handed down from generation to generation.

When I first put mine on it felt like it was made out of wood, stiff as a board. I did everything I could think of trying to soften it. They were purposely made a bit large for us to grow into, and by the third summer their size was just right, and to my delight they were becoming much softer and beginning to show some shiny spots of wear. I wore them proudly for many years and never hesitated to tell anyone who would be willing to listen that they were made from the skin of a stag my father shot.

* * *

Other new and important aspects were entering and shaping my life. During one of our summer visits to my grandmother in Celldömölk, I met a man who was a master cabinetmaker. I no longer remember what his name was or how or why I met him, but for some reason he allowed me to hang around his shop and even taught me how to use woodworking tools. He had a very small shop, no power tools of course—they didn't exist at that time—but even if they did he could not have used them, as I don't believe his shop had electricity. He was a master at his trade, which he achieved after a long apprenticeship without pay, working for years as a journeyman, traveling to other countries to work under other masters, and finally becoming a master himself. He was very talented and very meticulous. The furniture that came out of his shop was beautiful and perfect in every respect. I learned a lot from him, particularly how to finish wood and do inlay work. I worked at his shop as much as my vacation time permitted. He didn't pay me—nor did I want to be paid. Working with him fascinated me and I couldn't get enough of it. It is possible that my love for tools had its start in his small shop. I learned to sharpen chisels, the blades for planes, and generally how to take care of tools. Not too long after working in his shop I discovered a thieves' market in Pápa near the fire station. I really don't think it was a true thieves' market of the Dickens variety, but on certain days all kinds of junk would be spread out on the ground, amongst which were broken or rusty old tools. I could buy a broken chisel for pennies, take it home, clean and shine it up, fit it with a new handle, and when it was sharpened, it was as good as new. I soon built up a collection of tools, which became of major importance in later years—in fact, throughout my entire life.

* * *

The subject matter taught at school was extensive. Starting with grade one, Latin was compulsory, as was German, to which in subsequent classes Ancient Greek or English was added. The problem was that the method of teaching was archaic, obsolete, and not effective. It would have been preposterous to even attempt to mention or try to discuss this with anyone then. At best, I would have been laughed at or scolded for it, but looking back on it now I know I was right, as eight years of Latin or German did not qualify me to order a sandwich at a restaurant. It is possible of course that I didn't make a good enough effort, but later on, having acquired a limited command of the Russian language in a very short time, the same in German, and learning English well enough to get by within a couple of months, seems to prove my point. The school taught all subject matters their way, the way they have done it, I suppose, for centuries. Perhaps because of this, my parents decided that my brother and I should take private English lessons from Frieda néni. She was an old lady, perhaps a retired teacher who somehow acquired knowledge of several languages and sustained herself by giving private lessons. My brother and I went to her house after school probably twice a week for our lessons. We had a textbook, different from the one at school, and a handwritten dictionary in which we put down the English and German words we learned. She was a lovely old lady, but the English lessons would have made an extremely funny comedy routine in a Jerry Lewis movie. The pronunciation of even the simplest English words became a circus. Learning to say the word "the," for example, could at times take up the better part of the hourlong lesson. Practicing putting the tip of our tongue to the edge of our bottom row of teeth, incorporating a *tz* sound into the word, came out sounding like "dzoe," not to mention the saliva flying all over the room. She also gave us German lessons with similar results. Fortunately, my parents did not persist in continuing our language lessons with Frieda néni. On the rare occasions these days when I meet up with old friends from Pápa, I always know who took English lessons from Frieda néni when they spit in my face, trying to pronounce "the" with their tongue pressed against their lower teeth.

* * *

My horizons were getting broader. The studies at school, newspapers, magazines, radio, all helped to expand my knowledge, perspective, and understanding of the world around me. I was beginning to learn and truly understand the real meaning of words, concepts such as friend or foe, allies and enemies. Foes and enemies, I was taught, were despicable, awful people, while allies were all wonderful, faultless, and pure knights in shining armor. Being taught about the great and glorious past of Hungary, victories defending king and country, even the glories in defeats filled me with joy to be a Hungarian. The great and glorious leaders of Hungary's past became my idols, and even thinking of them filled my heart with pride.

Learning the Italian words to "Giovinezza," the fascist national anthem, our entire class singing it loud and with enthusiasm in the second year of junior high school, writing letters to Il Duce on the occasion of his magnificent victories in Ethiopia made me burst with joy over how wonderful it was to have a magnificent ally such as he. But my father and mother didn't share my joy as I told them about what we did in class. They remained mysteriously and very conspicuously silent. For the first time, even my father didn't talk about the glory of service to one's country.

* * *

Math, Hungarian, and world history, geography, Hungarian literature and language, physics, natural sciences, algebra, calculus, trigonometry, music, and so on were all added to our curriculum as we advanced to upper classes. Mechanical drawing was a part of our art class. It was taught by Tóth Sándor ur, Mr. Sándor Tóth, who was an acclaimed artist. I saw some of his pictures, paintings, and sketches and thought they were less than impressive. They were well-enough executed, but recalling them after all these years, I don't think they showed any genuine originality, nor were they much above the artistic level of a penny arcade or street artist. In my opinion, he was not a great or even a better-than-average artist. Nevertheless, he was a good instructor and I learned a lot from him, particularly in the area of mechanical drawing. It was one of the activities I enjoyed, which I find useful even today. We learned to draw an obelisk as an exercise in art class in three views, or elevations: front, side, top, as well as in perspective from a given vantage point. Finishing these exercises first during class was generally considered an achievement, a victory of sorts, and I seldom finished anything but first or second. The first one to finish had to hold up a hand and announce, "Finished," loud and clear. Mr. Tóth then would scrutinize the work for mistakes and execution, and if there were none, one would be considered the winner. At first I didn't understand why he always scrutinized my work more than the work of others. I also didn't understand why on one occasion he seemed to be perturbed by my winning again, and instead of complimenting me he told the class that they should be ashamed of themselves. This came into focus sometime later when I wanted to join the Boy Scouts. He was the scoutmaster of the school's troop, and when I approached him, he simply told me that Jews were not accepted into the troop. This hit like lightning. I never considered myself a Jew, nor could I consciously recall any incident till then of a similar nature. As the next guy, I thought of myself as simply being a Hungarian. By this time I was aware of different religions. The students at my school, which belonged to the Hungarian Reformed Church, were predominantly of the Reformed Church or "Református," as they were called in Hungarian. There were a good number of Catholics, Jews, Presbyterians, Calvinists, and so on, but I never thought of identifying myself in a religious term. To me, religion was something secondary to being Hungarian. All religions—Catholic, Protestant—simply meant being a Hungarian practicing a certain faith. I never mentioned this incident at home, but by then I sensed that certain things were not right in the world. In the following years, indications of this were coming more and more frequently, yet as far as I could tell at that time, it still did not affect my family or me in any significant manner.

* * *

At one time, while we were still living on Jókai Street, my father brought us pigeons—some homing pigeons, tumblers, and some peacock pigeons—as pets. I don't know if these names are correct, I'm translating them from Hungarian. The peacock pigeons were so called, because they spread their tail feathers in a manner of peacocks. We all know what homing pigeons are, but the ones I call tumblers were noted for their ability to fold their wings in flight and just tumble seemingly out of control. I was told they did this as a method of escaping from pursuing predators. I helped Tóni build the cages for these birds and learned from my father how to water young pigeons by taking a mouthful of water and putting the pigeon's beak in between my lips to give them water. As these birds grew and became familiar with their environment, we opened the cages and let them fly. My father explained that they would always find their way home. They did, until one day when we heard a shot, and as we watched we saw feathers fly and one of the birds fall to the ground, dead. One of the neighbors shot it, we didn't know who or why, but the bird was dead. Shortly after, we gave all our pigeons away.

* * *

As winters approached, one of the annual chores was to put our bikes away for the winter. With the heavy snows of Hungary, bikes were useless during the winter. Because they were precious possessions, at the end of every fall we took them apart, cleaned the parts, oiled and greased them, and wrapped them in paper. Even though it was a dirty, greasy, and grimy job, I loved to do it and usually ended up doing my brother's bike as well.

As winter wore on, I would be increasingly looking forward to that first mild day when the bikes could be taken out of mothballs, reassembled, and I could take off.

But winters were also fun. Tóni still made the ice at the PFC, but I now put my skates on myself. My newest treasures were called műkorcsolyák, "art skates" in translation, really meaning figure skates permanently attached to shoes. My skating improved to the point of going into competition. Unlike Liz's training, my skating was almost all self-taught and restricted to the winter seasons only. I started competing first in interclass competition, mostly against my best friends, Sinkó Ottó, or Jocó, as we called him, and Rózsa Miklós, another classmate and good friend. Jocó, pronounced Yoeh-tsoh, was pretty good and usually came in second after me. His older brother, Big Jocó, was a good skater and usually beat both of us in higher-level competition, but in later years I beat him also. There were a number of places to skate in and around Pápa. The PFC was the best and competitions were usually held there. I preferred it for many reasons, one of which was—now that I was a good skater—Mr. Kovács gave me a free season pass, which allowed me to go at any time for free. During one season the sand was flooded at the Strand, but no one really liked to skate there, and after one season it closed. There was another place on the opposite side of town, similar to the PFC, where tennis courts were flooded, but that didn't last either. Aside from competition, the most fun my friends and I had skating was on an artificial pond just a little ways out of town. This pond, a large area of pastureland in reality, was flooded by local butchers for their next summer's supplies of ice. Every time it snowed, the area was flooded again so as not to allow the snow to create air pockets in the ice, which would have made it bad for ice house use. But the resulting ice, always black and so clear that one could see the bottom of the pond through it, was the best ice I ever skated on then or since. Ice hockey was not well known in Hungary at that time. We heard of it and saw pictures in sports magazines, but the only thing we thought we knew about it was that players of opposing teams batted a puck around with sticks to score goals. That was enough for us. We didn't have real hockey sticks but used branches broken off of nearby poplar trees, which had big natural burls at one end substituting for the blade portion of real hockey sticks. They were more like clubs than hockey sticks, but they did just fine as we scooted around the ice, hitting the other guys' ankles more often than the roll of electrical friction tape we used as a puck. There was no warming shed at this pond. By the time we were ready to go home at times after dark, we were well frozen. Our overcoats, which we took off while skating, would be covered with snow at times, or frozen to the ground. The goose liver, which we had plenty of in our pantry, on a generous slice of bread covered with liver fat and dill pickle slices, followed with hot cocoa, did wonders warming us up.

I took preparation for skating competition very seriously. Kovács ur posted the dates, the required compulsory figures, and the length of the freestyle program on the school's bulletin board, which I copied and, from that day on, practiced every chance I got. Kovács ur arranged with the PFC to give us the competitors, practice time during which no one else would be permitted on the ice. The prestige of being on the ice alone is hard to define and explain. There was a single tennis court at the Nátus, our sister school, which occasionally was also flooded. Once again, Mr. Kovács arranged permission for the competitors to use that small rink, but it was hard to practice there. The girls looking at us from the windows were distracting. As I got better, I went to other towns to compete against skaters from different schools. One of my favorite places was a town called Győr. The fire department in this town maintained the ice, which was huge and outstanding. I came in second during my first competition there, and a year later won first. It was fun competing, winning, and getting medals. My medals were not real gold or silver, though they were called gold and silver and were made to look like that, but I know my father was as proud of my medals next to his in the glass cabinet as he was of his own.

The Kollégium was a boys' school, though there were a couple of exceptions. In all, there were probably fewer than ten girls in the entire school while I attended. One of these girls, Horvát Kató, was the daughter of the headmaster of our sister school, the Nátus, an all-girls school. I no longer know what Nátus means, nor is it important to this story. I never could figure out why Kató went to our school, but she did. She was a good skater. She and I skated together a lot and competed against one another. At one of these competitions, Kató, being about two years older than I, was heavily favored to win, but when I beat her she was declared the winner in the girls' category. There was no such thing as a girls' category. The competition was coed. I was first of course in the boys' category, but I knew that something was out of kilter that the rules were changed as the game was played. When the scores were tallied and her marks came in under mine, a girls' category was quickly created, I think, for political reasons. It could have had something to do with her father being the headmaster of the other school, or because the political situation in Hungary was pretty badly deteriorated by then. You will get the picture as I go on. Kovács ur congratulated me, but I sensed that he was troubled or embarrassed by something. I believe he knew that I knew he caved in, and in a strange way I felt embarrassed for him.

* * *

The newspapers and magazines were full of news about the new Germany and her miraculous recovery from the demeaning peace treaty of Versailles after WWI. Most Hungarian publications fell in line, reporting profusely and very favorably on all that was happening in Germany. The 1936 Olympic Games were coming up, and the magazines and sport publications carried long articles with lots of photographs of the new Olympic stadium, arenas, swimming facilities, and the superior athletes of the New Order. There were a number of youth magazines published in German as well as in Hungarian, which had articles about German youngsters training to be pilots. The Versailles Peace Treaty forbade Germany to have an air force, but civilian sport aviation—soaring, flying unpowered craft such as gliders—was not restricted. I wished I could have been amongst those young fellows whose pictures in those articles showed them sitting in open cockpit trainers, or even the ones pulling on the V-shaped bungee-launching slings. All of us knew that these young fellows were in fact training for the future German Air Force as pilots. The magazines made snide innuendos, which clearly indicated that the Treaty of Versailles was openly snubbed and defied. But the wish to fly, my childhood dream, went beyond treaties, the superrace, Aryans, and all things which had kept me out of the Boy Scouts or learning to fly sailplanes. Almost daily more and more activities I loved but wasn't allowed to participate in were added to the list. I did become involved in building model airplanes. Model airplane clubs were cropping up all over, including one at the Kollégium. By that time I had more tools than anyone else in the club, which might have contributed to being allowed a membership. I also knew how to use these tools and was able to teach others. I devoured flying magazines, and before long I designed and built my own model gliders, most of which flew very well.

* * *

My tool collection grew, and before long I was making cases for phonographs. I could buy a portable, hand cranked–type phonograph—gramofón, we called them—for a reasonable amount of money, and I would then transplant the mechanism into a handsome wooden case I made and sell the phonograph for a good profit. Photography also became an important new element in my life. I was about twelve years old when my brother loaned me his new camera so I could take pictures of, you might have guessed, Vera Neumann. I loved the camera. I loved looking through the viewfinder, which on that camera strangely twisted the images as the camera moved from side to side. Sándor had no interest in photography and didn't mind me holding onto the camera as my own. I read some articles about film processing and decided to try it. My tools and ability to use them allowed me to make primitive photographic equipment for a basic darkroom. At that time one could not buy readymade photo chemicals. I had to order the chemical components to make the developer, stop bath, bleach, and fixer. I also had to order a sensitive little scale to measure the chemicals, a variety of beakers, and some brown bottles to store the mixed chemicals. One of the local photographers, a browbeaten husband of an immense, overpowering wife, allowed me to work in their dark room, printing my own photographs in exchange for doing work for them. Before long, I built my own enlarger, a curious contraption made out of wood and an old bellows camera, but it worked great. In fact, it worked so well that in no time I had a couple of orders from other kids, amateur photographers like me, in the school. My next enlarger was a much-improved version over the first one. It was made out of an aluminum milk can, which made it look almost store-bought.

As my collection of tools grew, more and more hobbies were added to my already extensive list, which kept me from devoting proper attention to my schoolwork. Most of the time I slipped by, but I failed the fourth class (age fourteen) and had to repeat it. During that year I was out a lot due to illness and missed a lot of classroom time. I also believe that I didn't get on well enough with my teachers. One teacher stands out in my memory. His name was Nagy Jenő, never mind the English pronunciation—a huge, bent-over old man who either liked you or hated you.

He hated me, and frankly the feeling was mutual. He taught Latin in my first grade, thundering at us if our pronunciation of "terra, terrae" was not to his liking. I don't know why he disliked me, but he did. When I got him back in fourth grade as my literature teacher, I knew I was in trouble. One of his assignments had to do with a historical subject matter I was familiar with and liked. Here was my chance, I thought, to get into his good graces by writing a paper he was going to have to like. I worked hard on it, and when it was finished it was almost twenty pages, much longer than a normal paper would have been, but I knew it was good and hoped he would reward the extra effort. Our papers were graded on three levels: contents, grammar, and appearance. Each of these areas was marked. The best mark was 1, and with an asterisk it denoted superior work; and the worst mark was 4, or failing. In between were marks such as 1/2, which was between 1 and 2; or 2/3, between 2 and 3. I was devastated when my paper came back with just about failing marks in all three areas. As my handwriting wasn't too good, I didn't expect a good mark for appearance, but I didn't think that the bad mark I received for appearance was deserved. The equally bad mark he gave me for contents I knew was based on his intense dislike of me. I failed his course, and I believe I also failed math. Having failed two major subjects, I had to repeat fourth grade. It was a demeaning experience. What helped a bit was that a classmate and good friend of mine, the local Presbyterian minister's son, was also left back, so I didn't feel totally alone in a class of younger kids. The silver lining in this cloud was the appearance of a new teacher that year at the Kollégium, Csipő Lajos. Unlike all other teachers in school, he was young with a cheerful, pleasant smile, constantly in good humor. Best of all, he was our literature teacher. In spite of Nagy Jenő, I loved to write. When my first papers came back with good marks from Professor Csipő, I asked him to read my long history paper that Professor Nagy marked down. Mr. Csipő didn't comment on the bad marks; instead, he suggested I recopy my paper and send it to a student publication that was running a literary contest along the lines of my paper's subject matter. I did as he suggested. My paper won and was published in the magazine.

Several other teachers were antisemites. I already mentioned Tóth Sándor, my art teacher, Varga László, a natural history teacher, my math teacher, and a few others whose names I no longer remember. But there was one who stands out. Molnar Benjamin, an English teacher at the Kollégium, became the head and commander of the district's Nyilaskeresztes (Arrow Cross Party) organization. This was the Hungarian equivalent of the Nazi Party in Germany. Though, until these events, it never occurred to me to think about antisemitism, or if indeed it affected me, I mention it here to tell you that unlike other kids in my class, for me school was becoming an uphill battle. Yet teachers like Csipő Lajos and Mr. Kovács somehow made up for the rotten apples. I know now that I was able to rise above this very bad situation and make the best of it. I never acknowledged nor dwelled on my difficulties. Nor would I let anyone, certainly at the student level, express or exercise any antisemitic behavior towards me. I think this was accepted by most who knew me, and in a strange way I suspect I was respected by even the most committed antisemites in school. Indeed, my best friends were almost all Christian. Whenever I was with them, there was never even the slightest hint of any difference between us. Nor should there have been any. They came up with a nickname for me, Horkay ur, Mr. Horkay. If I ever knew how this name came about or what it meant, I no longer remember, but it was a very Hungarian-sounding name and I didn't mind it. Some of my classmates I still correspond with and saw, when Mom and I visited Pápa three years ago, remembered it also. It is strange, particularly in retrospect, to try to put this aspect of my life in perspective and to pass this perspective on to you, who, I'm sure, had a very different idea of my background.

In my earlier years there was no mention of religion or religious differences within, or outside of, my family. I recall no awareness of it. Whatever there might have been, as I alluded to it in connection with the differences between my father and my mother's family, was never discussed with us children. When the concept of religion entered my life around the time of grammar school, it was something that was there without any influence on what I considered normal life. When it first became obvious, it was hard to understand on any reasonable level. As far as I could tell, I didn't look, act, think, or do anything differently from anyone I knew, including some who were bent on proving that I was somehow different. I knew I wasn't. I certainly didn't feel different when I was with my friends, which in later years was most of the time. Yet the newspapers, radio, newsreels kept hammering away at a "difference," until even I was beginning to question if, indeed, there might be something to it. One of my heroes, Dr. Kabos, winner of the 1936 Olympic Gold Medal in saber fencing, was snubbed by Hitler who wouldn't shake hands with him, as he did with all other gold medal winners, because he was Jewish. By 1936 I was a beginner fencer. It was a sport I loved—a sport of skill and intellect for gentlemen. My fencing instructor was Mr. Kovács, who was regarded by all of us, his students, as well as my father and other adults who knew him, as a perfect gentleman. It was a thrill every time it was my turn to take instruction from him. Each individual lesson lasted about fifteen minutes. He would start with the basics, cursing and slashing at his students if they didn't do the moves right. At the end of each session he would allow a few seconds of free fencing, when the student could execute an attack against him. On one of these occasions I attacked him with such ferocity that he was forced to back up, and as good as he was, the unexpected attack surprised him. Instead of reprimanding and dismissing me at the end of this lesson, he called one of the upperclassman, a champion fencer, over, and put me up against him. By this time the adrenaline was pumping hard, and when I attacked, the results were even fiercer than before. He put me up against other good fencers after this incident, though this was not the norm for my age group. I knew that this was his way of encouraging me. It's called pushing the right buttons, and he certainly knew how to do that. He was one of my idols. He and Mr. Csipő will probably keep cropping up as I go along.

There were other reminders to tell me that, indeed, I belonged to another club. Before the end of the decade Germany's intentions became obvious. While Mr. Chamberlain waved the now famous piece of paper declaring, "Peace in our time," the newspapers, radio, motion pictures in Germany and Hungary left no doubt as to the direction we were really heading in. As far back as the publication of *Mein Kampf* in the late twenties, Hitler's intentions were clearly stated and it did not bode well for the world, particularly not for people of the Jewish faith living in Europe. At first, in the early thirties before I first heard Hitler speak on the radio at my grandmother's house in Celldömölk, most people did not believe he would ever be allowed to rise to power. This was, of course, wishful thinking in most cases, and not caring in others. But he did rise to power. Men like my father, who liked and trusted the military, believed that the combined French and English forces would easily defeat Hitler. When Hitler walked into Alsace-Lorraine and the French caved in, my father was shaken by the news. The newspapers declared in bold headlines the overwhelming desire of the Austrian people to join the Reich. This was born out by newsreels showing hundreds of thousands of Austrians waving small swastika flags, jamming the streets of Vienna, and welcoming the German army with the outstretched-arm Nazi salute. Danzig, the Sudetenland in Czechoslovakia, switched hands equally easily, and there was no doubt in anyone's mind that this was only the beginning. A new set of laws took effect in Germany called the Nuremberg Laws. They were designed exclusively to curtail the civil rights of Jews, communists, labor unionists, and other "undesirables," restricting them from conducting certain businesses and regulating private activities and private ownership. News of these laws and their reported extremes reached us on a daily basis. The Aryan race exerted itself, declaring its purity. Many Christians, even some Nazi Party members, suddenly discovered a Jewish ancestor, which relegated them to non-Aryan status, stripping them also of their civil rights. In order to gain racial purity in Germany as the Nazi Party grew bolder and more powerful, one had to prove Christian ancestry going back to 1775 or some arbitrary, ludicrous date. A political joke—oppressed people at times find the occasion for self-effacing humor—quoted that the letters INRI on the cross above the crucified Christ meant "Irataimért Nazarétbe Repültem, Jézus." Meaning, "I flew to Nazareth for my papers,

Jesus." The underlying message was that even Jesus, a Jew, had to get some papers to prove his Christian faith.

As these events negated some of the intended purposes of converting to Christianity, or as an expression of disagreement with the older brothers, or, perhaps defying the times, possibly to appease my mother, or for reasons not known to me, my father decided that both my brother and I should be confirmed in the Jewish faith. At this stage I prefer to believe that he no longer believed in the validity or the righteousness of converting to Christianity. More than likely, he never did. My confirmation bar mitzvah was going to happen on the prescribed day, decided by those who knew the dictates of the Jewish religion. To say the least, this was bewildering for me. Until this time I was reminded more than a few times that I was born a Catholic. By this time I suspected that my father and his brothers converted to Catholicism, but I had no concept of what a Catholic or a Jew really meant. I received no real religious instruction in either of these faiths and knew less than little of each. The Jewish grade school I had attended had some religious instruction, but they didn't amount to more than bible classes and stories. There was a religious Jewish school in town and those who desired an Orthodox religious education went there. Religion, particularly this event, was thoroughly confusing to me. I understood that it signified achieving manhood and becoming a member of the adult Jewish community, but what about the other side, the Catholic community? It was strange that throughout all those years, I had more contact and affinity with Christian than with Jewish children of my age. At this point I didn't understand where I belonged, a determination which in a few more years was clearly decided for me. I couldn't read Hebrew, nor did I understand the ritual. No one in my family understood Hebrew. It was a strange ritual for me to say the least, yet in a strange way I enjoyed being the focus of it. This was one of the few occasions I was in the large, and I might add, very beautiful and historic synagogue in Pápa. I remember that my mother couldn't sit with us. Men and women were separated, not even visible to one another. A party followed this ceremony at our house. There were an awful lot of people there. Relatives, friends—some from distant towns—kept coming and going. One family, which was conspicuously absent, was Uncle Matthew, his wife, Aunt Margaret, and their son, my cousin Gyuri. I do remember collecting an awful lot of presents and money.

\* \* \*

From about the mid-thirties on, some lucky ones with foresight and money managed to leave Germany, Hungary, and other parts of Europe. Towards the end of the decade when it became painfully obvious that the situation would only worsen, I overheard my parents discussing the possibility of sending my brother and me to America to Uncle George. Whenever this or similar subject matters were discussed, my parents always talked in German and usually only if they thought we were not within earshot. In spite of daily reports of terrible things happening in Germany, nobody, certainly no parent, could have easily made a decision of parting with their children. Besides, everybody was hoping for the best, a miraculous reversal of the situation. In our case, by the time my parents came to terms with the possibility of my brother's and my leaving them, it was too late. All exits were closed; Hungary was cut off from the rest of the world, except of course its neighbors and allies. Yet, miraculously, Hungary remained an island of relative peace as war raged all around us. German and Italian troop trains were going through Pápa with regularity, but Hungary, a tiny little nation, somehow stayed out of the war and life went on as before. In fact, my father's business picked up. He started a small pork-processing business some years before the war, selling a certain type of bacon and ham to England. This business continued even after the war broke out, but the product was sold locally. I know there were large business transactions with Baron Eszterházy's estate in my father's large animal business. After some of these transactions my father would travel, a week, two weeks at a time. On one occasion, I happened to walk into my parents' bedroom as a money belt my mother made on her sewing machine was stuffed with a lot of strange-looking money, possibly the day before my father left on one of these trips. I often wonder if there is a bank account somewhere, perhaps in Switzerland, with quite a bit of his money in it.

While I know that everyone, including my parents, feared the worst, my father never openly considered the possibility of any harm coming to us. The Hungarian people and the government, he proclaimed, would never permit it. But the most important thing was that no one, even those with the most fertile imagination, could have foreseen or guessed the disaster that was to come.

Shortly after the takeover of the Sudetenland, some people moved into one of our neighbors' houses. Most of the time they stayed indoors. I got to know one of the younger ones who, though older than my brother or I, was interested in photography. One day, as I was taking pictures in our garden, we struck up a conversation across the fence in my limited German. He seemed scared and would not tell me who he was other than being a relative of our neighbors visiting from Prague. These neighbors were somehow related to Vera Neumann's parents. She told me that the young man I met over the fence escaped from Prague. The Germans took his parents away. But life in Hungary went on, as I said, almost as before. I continued in school, continued competing in fencing, skating, and gymnastics. I did my photography and spent as much, if not more, time with my friends, particularly with Jocó, who by then was my best friend.

* * *

Some unusual, interesting events took place around this time. Shortly after Germany and Russia signed the unexpected and now well-known non-aggression treaty, Russia returned some flags they captured during World War I to Hungary. The ceremony of receiving these flags took place in a northeast town called Kassa and was broadcast on the radio. In the course of the ceremony, "The Internationale," the Soviet anthem, was played by a Hungarian military band. My father was beside himself. Looking back on this incident, knowing he fought the Russians in World War I, I can understand his behavior. In spite of everything, my father, your grandfather, was an unbending patriot and an outspoken anticommunist—a nationalist even then—who just couldn't comprehend how the Russian Communist anthem could have been played on Hungarian soil. Returning the flags was an expression of Russia's "peaceful" intentions towards Germany and her Hungarian ally. I must mention again that the chronology of these events is not very clear. I could have looked it up, but the time frame isn't terribly important. There was another event that I think should be mentioned here. With Germany's vast political power by this time, they were able to put enough pressure on Hungary's neighbors to return some of the territories that the Versailles treaty stripped away from Hungary after WWI. The radio was playing Hungarian martial music for days; the nation was celebrating and there was an outpouring of gratitude towards Germany and Hitler for this wonderful deed. It sealed an alliance, which even then didn't end in actively joining Germany's military activities. Of course the German presence was felt. The political jokes, for which Hungary is known under whatever occupation, were quoting the wonderful relationship between the two countries, "Hungary supplying Germany with food in return for the world's best harmonicas." But Hungary got more than just harmonicas from Germany, namely tanks, airplanes, all sorts of state-of-the-art military hardware and instructors, drawing Hungary closer into World War II.

* * *

Then disaster struck. My father was called to active service in the military. His behívó, as the document which called him up was called, had the large, black block letters SAS stamped on it, which we were told meant that he had to report immediately. He left the following day for Hajmáskér, an artillery camp not too far from Pápa. We did have some money to fall back on, and my father's military pay, which wasn't much, helped, but his business stopped completely. My Aunt Manci and her husband, Dr. Zala János, came to stay with us for a while and encouraged me to come with them to Budapest. They knew an old man who made some very fine and unique lampshades, and Manci néni thought she could arrange to have the old man teach me. She knew I was very good with my hands and tools, and she probably figured that I could make some money, which we needed, making lampshades. I went with them when they returned to Budapest. There was one less mouth to feed at home and I was learning a trade and a potentially profitable business. The stay in Budapest was wonderful. I had my own room at my aunt's apartment, and every morning I went to work at the old lampshade maker's shop, learning his craft. One of his main specialties was lampshades made of old maps. These maps, some of them printed over a hundred years ago on heavy paper which we treated to look like old parchment, were sold only at a few select shops. I learned how to make the frame from heavy wire, solder it, cut the paper, and cover the frame. Some of these lampshades were custom orders. At times a porcelain vase was brought in with a flower design. The old fellow taught me how to trace and paint the matching design onto the paper the shade was going to be made out of.

At lunchtime I walked down to the Danube, just a few blocks from where I worked, and went swimming in one of the uszoda, swimming places. There were a number of these along both banks of the Danube. They were wooden structures with a perimeter of a boardwalk and connecting changing booths. The river flowed through and under this structure and it was great to swim against the current, trying to make it to the upstream end of the swimming area. On weekends my aunt and uncle took me swimming at a truly unique and incredible swimming complex, the Palatinus on Margit Sziget, "Saint Margaret Island," in the Danube River. There were several very large pools. One of them, like the one in the Gellért Hotel, had artificial waves. There were also thermal pools with hot water, some with sulfur, which incidentally smelled like rotten eggs, and one half-circle–shaped pool surrounded by white marble columns. This pool had armchairs under the water, sculpted also from white marble, arranged in a way so that one could sit in them while playing chess with an opponent, the marble chessboards being just above water level. We went to open-air concerts in the Angol Park, "English Park," which was a very beautiful amusement park. But my absolutely most favorite place they introduced me to was the transportation museum in the Városliget, "City Park." This museum had the most beautiful working models of locomotives, all of them handmade and true to scale, as well as a very large collection of miniature railroad cars, automobiles, and planes. I just could not get enough of this place and went whenever I had the time.

It didn't take very long to acquire the skills needed to make lampshades. By the time I returned from Budapest with two large crates full of lampshades, summer was almost over. My father was home. As we corresponded by letters only, my mother didn't have a chance to let me know before I left Budapest that my father was coming home for the weekend. My lampshades were much admired and I was ready and anxious to start taking orders.

It wasn't hard to tell how happy my father was to be home. Yet he was very quiet, almost withdrawn, and spoke very little of his daily activities in the military. My brother and I walked with him to the railroad station as he was going back to his post. On the way to the station, a soldier, a local boy who might have known who my father was, perhaps thinking that under the New World Order he did not have to salute a Jew, walked right by us. My father's face turned as red as I have ever seen it. He was a quiet man, but did have a very short fuse and an explosive temper. His face then conjured up images of a volcano about to erupt, and it did. What follows, obviously, played out in the Hungarian language. My father turned, eyes sparking, his voice booming, "Private!" The soldier stopped in his tracks, turned on his heels, both palms pressed against his sides, standing in rigid attention. "Do you know what these are?" My father pointed to the stars on his tunic collar. "Yes, sir," the private responded. "Don't you know how to salute?" My father's voice was still booming. "Yes, sir," the soldier replied. "Salute," my father commanded. The soldier snapped a salute. "Do you know that you are supposed to salute me three steps in front of me?" My father ordered the soldier to walk back and forth and salute him every time he got three steps from him. Finally he let him go and we went on to the railroad station. I was so proud of my father my chest almost burst. Until that time I never saw him in uniform, except in photographs. He looked wonderful, powerful, and exuded authority. I know my brother felt the way I did at that moment, but my father was strangely subdued. He hardly spoke to us during the rest of our walk to the station and as he got on the train.

Some weeks later, by which time I sold a number of lampshades, my brother, Sándor, and I bicycled to Hajmáskér to see him. Just as we got to his quarters, a soldier brought and served him his lunch. We had our usual picnic lunch in our backpacks, and my mother even packed some goodies for my father, but his food looked very good, including a large portion of apple cake, which we all shared. As he finished lunch, there was knock on the door and my father called out, "Enter." A soldier came in, saluted, and told him something to the effect that they were ready. My father got up, put his cap and a pistol belt on, and told us that we could come with him. The soldiers under his command were formed up in front of the building and he took the report, after which the troops were dismissed. This reminded me of my gym classes, which always started with a similar drill. We all would form up, just as the troops were now in front of my father, and Kovács ur would take the report from one of the students who was the class commander. Shortly after this visit, my father was released from service and came home. There was endless speculation as to why he was called up. Hungary was not at war, though it was obvious that everyone expected Hungary to enter the war on the German side. But he was a civilian again, trying to put his business together. This time it didn't seem very difficult. The Eszterházy account started right up, bigger than ever, and the hog business moved to a new area in town, somewhere behind the Calvary Cemetery. He no longer processed the hogs. It was a feeding operation only, where I spent most of one of my more memorable summers. My brother and some of his friends, and a couple of my other friends, and I worked for my father, feeding hogs. It was without a doubt the dirtiest, most disgusting job I ever had. But Jocó and I had the best time. We started in the morning hauling dried corn on the cob in dusty burlap sacks on our shoulders from silos to a hand-cranked machine in a shed, which removed the kernels from the cob. I can still smell the dust, which stuck to our sweat-covered skin. The kernels were ground in another hand-cranked machine, and mixed with some other feeds. Before we could feed the hogs, their pens had to be cleaned out. This was the worst part of the job. First, the hogs had to be herded into an adjoining pen, then the pen was hosed out and the pigs were let back in. There were about four or five pens with as many as fifty pigs in each. After all the pens were clean, the feed was poured into a long trough running the full length of the pens. All of us wore old clothes and shoes, which by the end of the day were covered with muck, dust, sweat, and smelled like the pigs. So did we. The fun was to get out of these clothes at one of the sheds and hose each other off. Then we went swimming at a mill on the far end of town.

On occasion I also helped out herding cattle. Unlike this country, in Hungary this was done by herders on foot. Most of the cattle my father bought and sold were driven or brought to Pápa by rail. A bunch of herders, me included at times, met the shipment at the station and unloaded the animals. They were tied to one another by their horns, four abreast, and driven through town to our stables near the huszar kaszarnya, cavalry barracks. In the course of this I learned to use a bullwhip. With a proper "snapper" at its end, the whip would make a noise as loud as a rifle shot. I loved to crack it. Life went on.

# Chapter 7

# 1939 – 1943
# THE WAR YEARS

My father was recalled to active duty again. At the same time, a lot of other people in Pápa mostly his age were also called up. They were all Jews, and all of them, including my father, were to report to a military camp other than Hajmáskér, which was the home of my father's artillery unit. If my parents knew what this meant or even what the implications were, they didn't say. There was a lot of speculation about the significance of calling up Jewish people only, all reporting to the same camp. The year of this event escapes me, but it had to be in the early forties. The tone of the first letter from my father was disturbing. He talked about having to remove the red backing from his tunic collar under the stars denoting his rank. The red color indicated artillery. One statement in the letter intended to put a silver lining in what obviously was a dark cloud in his life said, "Nincs puskánk!" meaning "We have no guns!" Perhaps he wanted to assure my mother that there was no immediate indication of dangerous service. Instead, he wrote about doing construction work projects around the military base. While it was a relief to know he was not in a dangerous situation, his disillusionment was obvious. He was always proud to be in the artillery. When he was ordered to remove the red color from his collar, to him it must have meant that he no longer belonged to the unit he was so proud of. Every arm of the Hungarian Army was identified by a color. Cavalry, the most exclusive, aristocratic arm of the service, was signified by the blue color. Infantry, considered the most common service, was green. The loss of this identification with the arm of the service he loved must have been as great a disappointment to him as the empty pistol holster, which was still part of his uniform, but instead of a pistol it was stuffed with old newspapers.

Even this call-up didn't last for long. He was released after a few months, but for the first time I thought I detected a change in him. He never mentioned anything about this latest service and no longer talked in his usual glowing terms about service in the military.

* * *

Sometime during the late thirties, my mother had gallbladder surgery. Comparing it to present-day surgical procedures requiring a two- or three-day hospital stay, this sort of surgery was a lengthy, complicated, difficult, and, more often than not, a very dangerous procedure. She had to prepare, as I recall, for months in advance. She had to reduce her weight, which for her was always a problem. She also had to reduce her blood sugar level. She was diabetic, though not to any great, advanced extent. After months of dieting, she and my father went to Budapest to check her into what at that time was probably the best hospital for this kind of an operation. With the help of all the doctors in the family, she received the best possible treatment and care, but I know she was horrified. Some years earlier, her father had had a kidney ailment. He had been operated on in Vienna in probably the finest hospital in Europe, where the best surgeons in the Austro-Hungarian Empire removed the good kidney. He died shortly after the operation. It wasn't hard to understand why she was horrified of hospitals and frightened by the surgery. It was an emotional experience as my mother left for a projected six weeks' absence. I don't know if she didn't expect to come back, but once again she fell back on her God's Big Book philosophy, bordering on almost blind fatalism. Even though Fáni was there to take care of our day-to-day needs, the house seemed empty without her. My father called once or twice a week, always giving positive reports, though there was nothing really to report other than she was in the hospital, making whatever preparation was called for.

I recall my father talking years before about the Hungarian peasant mentality as it regarded hospital treatment. According to this philosophy, when a sick person didn't go to the hospital and died, the family saved the hospital expenses. If he did not die, the hospital expenses would not have been necessary. He always laughed relating this. Of course, none of us subscribed to this philosophy, and we knew that in my mother's case the operation was an absolute necessity. I witnessed her having severe gallbladder attacks more and more frequently by this time, causing much pain and necessitating almost continuous use of morphine. The operation was done some weeks after my father took her to Budapest. We didn't know in advance when this was going to happen. If my father knew I'm sure he would have told us, but when he called to say that mother was operated on and was doing as well as could be expected, it was at the same time a tremendous shock and relief. I somehow wanted to give thanks to God but didn't know how. Throughout these weeks I prayed for her in my own way silently, whenever I was alone. I hoped that in God's Big Book, the description of her life was going to allow her to live. It was to be so. My father, who came home time and again after the operation to attend to his business, took my brother and me to Budapest to visit her in the hospital. He prepared us for what to expect, what to do, and what not to do. He told us that she was much thinner than before and, therefore, very weak. She needed a lot of rest and we were not to exhaust her with too much conversation. I will never forget her smile as we came into her room at the hospital. She was propped up on her own embroidered pillows, her hair was done, and she had lipstick on. It seemed though that her lipstick, one of the few cosmetics she ever used, was heavier than usual.

When she came home after many weeks of recuperation in the hospital, she had to continue with bed rest for months. Eventually she returned to her former activities, cooking, knitting, and spending quiet afternoons with friends.

* * *

Hungary continued on what by then seemed to be an irrevocable commitment to the German cause. Almost all aspects of our daily life were affected. The classical music of opera, symphony, the light and vibrant tunes of Strauss and Lehár, slowly gave way to more and more patriotic martial music. In school we were taught to goose step, as we occasionally marched in formation through the streets of Pápa. Looking back over a half century ago, I find these aspects of my life strange, but then goose stepping, for instance, was an accepted, expected way of life in a military country, and, as in my case, in school too. I liked it. It was a sort of a military-type activity I did with my friends and it fitted in with my love for my country, which I was taught to respect all my life in school and at home. The glory of Hungary's thousand-year-old history was coming at me from all directions. Monuments of the heroic past were all around me on just about every square and street corner. There were war memorials in most towns of Hungary commemorating and honoring heroes of the past. My schoolbooks were full of accounts and reminders of a millennium of glory. But none of those monuments and accounts made as much an impression on me as listening to my father talk about our country. I knew about some of his exploits, one in particular which I mentioned already, but when he talked about one of his brothers who had been killed on the Russian front, when he talked about my Uncle Miklós, the whole concept of the glorious battles of the past, the individual heroism and sacrifices warmed my heart, became personal, and made me proud to be a Hungarian. So as I was slamming my feet down hard on the pavement, commanded to do so by our platoon leader, saluting an army officer standing on the sidewalk, it made me feel glad to be part of it.

\* \* \*

We still went to Celldömölk to visit my grandmother during the summers. The trip no longer had the childhood magic. My brother and I hardly ever took the train anymore. Instead, we would hop on our bikes and beat the train to Celldömölk. I was a good bike rider, which in Hungary then represented a mode of transportation. Even prominent adults such as doctors and lawyers used bicycles for their local transportation. For us kids, bikes were primarily fun, and extensive outings to distant places were commonplace. After we'd done it a couple of times, going to our grandmother was easy. The bikes also came in handy while we were in Celldömölk. My brother and I could go to the vineyard on Sághegy, even go see friends in nearby towns. Certain aspects of these visits to my grandmother never changed. We still had to wash up on arrival, and when we stopped in to see my Aunt Ilonka, her husband the dentist still insisted on checking our teeth. A free service extended to the family, followed by his lecturing us on the importance of proper dental hygiene. After those few initial minutes, I didn't have much contact with him for the rest of our stay in Celldömölk. His wife, Ilonka néni, the oldest of my mother's sisters, was married for the second time. She had a son, Zoli, and a daughter, Sari, from her first marriage. Zoli, perhaps ten years older than I, lived at my grandmother's, who had taken him in before my aunt's second marriage. He was a nasty sort and I didn't have much to do with him. Sari, on the other hand, was a very beautiful young woman whose wedding I vaguely recall. She married one of two brothers who jointly owned a wholesale grocery, oil, and gasoline business. They had a younger brother, Hertzfeld Sanyi, exactly my brother's age, who attended the Kollégium in my brother's class. At one time he lived with us during the school year. Ilonka néni also had two younger daughters with her second husband, Kató the older and Marta. Kató was one year older than I. She was very good-looking and she was a flirt. I'm not sure if she was a student at the Nátus or at the Kollégium, but she had boys running after her from every direction and I knew she loved every minute of it. She had lots of girlfriends in Celldömölk, which helped as about this time most of the days were spent playing various games, all of which somehow ended up in necking.

I no longer remember which vacation it was—I think it had to be the one before I fully discovered girls and the "birds and the bees" aspect—when some of my friends (all boys at that time) in Celldömölk and I decided to create an explosion. I was "into," as we would say today, chemistry at the time. I learned about how gunpowder was made a long time ago in the many forts of Hungary during a siege. The flowered-up, glorious accounts of scraping saltpeter, a key ingredient of gunpowder, from the dungeon walls of the fort and the subsequent making of gunpowder intrigued me. Hertzfeld Sanyi showed us large amounts of saltpeter growing naturally on the stone walls in one of their old warehouses. The other two ingredients of gunpowder were going to be easy to get. Sulfur came from my grandmother's storeroom in the form of sulfur candles my grandmother's winemaker used to disinfect wine barrels. We bought a small bag of charcoal for a couple of cents. The charcoal and sulfur were mashed to a fine powder and sifted. Saltpeter was scraped off the wall, dried in the sun, and also sifted. The three ingredients were mixed in the proper proportions, which I no longer remember. We dug a relatively small hole in the ground to test it, behind Sanyi's brothers' warehouses, and put a small amount of the powder in a tin can. I fashioned a primer from some steel wool tied to two nails on a small wooden board to detonate it. Two electric wires were twisted onto the nails, the idea being that when electricity was applied the steel wool would ignite and detonate the gunpowder. A very simple practical device, except that it didn't work. When we plugged the wire into a long extension cord, it promptly blew the fuse in the house, which I was able to fix; but we knew we had to find another power source. They had automobile batteries for sale at Sanyi's brothers' store, so we borrowed one without asking anybody of course, and dug up the tin can with the gunpowder only to notice that a portion of the steel wool did burn in spite of the blown fuse. We reasoned that there wasn't enough gunpowder in the tin and perhaps it wasn't quite dry to ignite. Sanyi brought out some old shotgun shells they had in the house. We carefully opened these up, threw away the shot, and emptied the powder from the shells into the tin. For good measure we also dumped all our own powder into the tin, reasoning that after the explosion we wouldn't be allowed to use whatever we had left anyhow. This was sound thinking. So as not to have pieces of the tin can fly around as it exploded, we decided to dig a much deeper hole. We placed an old doghouse filled with old bricks and rocks over the filled in hole to muffle the explosion. This time the battery and my detonator worked. As we made the connection to the battery, an ear-shattering explosion threw up a mountain of dirt, fragments of the old doghouse, and bricks and rocks. It blew half the leaves off a big old horse chestnut tree branching over the explosion, broke more than a few windows in Sanyi's brothers' warehouse, and probably rattled hundreds in the area. My ears were ringing and I was stunned, not wanting to believe what happened. We had a lot of explaining to do and I didn't play with explosives after this incident.

* * *

My grandmother was getting very old. She seemed smaller somehow, and both she and Mári talked less and moved slower. My Uncle Márton and my cousin Zoli were still living at her house, still out of work, and nastier than ever. They mistreated my grandmother awfully while taking advantage of living at her house, eating her food, and still expecting her to pay for their clothing and expenses. Márton slept late every morning. His room reeked with the smell of rancid urine, as he used a chamber pot kept under his bed. The problem was that by this time my grandmother had no live-in help besides Mári, who at her age would empty and clean the chamber pots every morning. I found Uncle Márton's attitude appalling. I heard my father saying at one time that he would have loved to have Uncle Márton serve under him in the army. I might have been fourteen, fifteen, when I asked Uncle Márton why he still used chamber pots. His answer was that it was too chilly to get out of a warm, cozy bed to go to the outhouse. He said this with a condescending smile on his face, which I thought was kind of wicked. I don't really remember what I told him, but whatever it was made him angry and he yelled at me, telling me to mind my own business. I was much younger than he. The respect for my elders I was taught all my life made me back off, but after this incident I liked him even less than before. My grandmother's lifestyle changed little. She and Mári still stayed up at night, arguing or just sitting around in the kitchen with one kerosene light. My brother and I bicycled to the vineyards and on more than a few occasions got sick on freshly pressed grape juice. We no longer stayed with my grandmother over the entire summer. Sometimes we would go for a couple of days if and when we felt like it.

Looking back on my life, I can't help but compare some aspects of it to your young years. Maybe because we lived in a small town, there were far fewer restrictions imposed on us as children than on you and other children of your generation here in this country. Even as a youngster around the age of ten and younger, I would wander away from my house, explore the fields around town, or just stand on the bridge over the railroad tracks without getting permission from or telling anyone where I was going. The rigid guidelines my school imposed did not apply during the summer. For instance, when school was out, I was free to go on distant outings with my friends on our bikes. Sometimes we rode up to the Bakony Mountains, divided into two teams, and played war games. All of us would wear numbers on our forehead and on our backs, trying to infiltrate the other team's area. One was considered dead when one's number was called. Sometimes boys and girls would go together, but at those times there were no numbers and the games were of a different variety. Usually one of the older girls would be designated as a chaperone, which was like asking a pigeon to guard a bunch of cats.

* * *

It had to be in the very early forties when my brother and I went to spend our Christmas vacation with my cousin Jancsi and his sister, Magda, at their parents' home in Magyaróvár. Their mother, Jolán néni, was my mother's sister. She was married to Dr. Weisz Gyula, who as I mentioned earlier was a very highly regarded doctor. By this time he no longer practiced medicine, as he suffered from some rare disease which affected the bone structure of his skull. The bone thickened, and as his head grew to grotesque dimensions, his brain was squeezed, and the disease eventually caused him to lose all mental and bodily functions. By the time of this visit he could hardly walk, his speech was slurred and most of the time unintelligible.

He must have been in constant excruciating pain, for which there was no remedy. Yet he was a kind man, happy to see my brother and me, and spent quite a bit of time with me showing me how to use his microscope and how to color slides. He had a very large medical office, an entire wing built onto his house, which by this time was not used. They lived in an immense house in a western Hungarian town, Magyaróvár ("old Hungarian fort"), and were extremely wealthy. On top of his medical practice, he received a large retainer as one of the household physicians to a Hapsburg duke. The house was one of the first ones in Hungary that had central heating. But it had a wood-burning furnace, which by the time of this visit was seldom fired up as the onetime large household staff was reduced to I believe two maids, who either didn't know how or simply refused to work the furnace. Jancsi fired it up and it was amazing to feel the heat coming out of the radiators just a few minutes later. Their large and beautifully furnished home showed signs of neglect. I don't know what the reason was, but the dirty bathrooms, an equally dirty kitchen, and neglected bedrooms made me uneasy. Both Magda and Jancsi were older than I. She was a quiet and shy pretty little girl, the complete opposite of her brother, who was big, loud, boisterous, and mischievous, but carefree and most of the time was fun to be with. He could be charming, very likable, except he was constantly looking for and getting into fights. One evening, after I observed lots of hushed conversations with his friends and my brother, he announced that he was taking us over to the house of one of his friends. It was bitter cold and already dark as we left his house. He wouldn't tell me where we were going other than that we were not going to any friend's house, and he had me swear that I wouldn't tell anyone where we went. It turned out that he decided to treat his friends and my brother to an evening at the local house of ill repute. I was not allowed to go in; instead, I was told to wait for them in the street. By the time they came out laughing hysterically, slapping each other on the back, I was frozen, but as I was sworn to secrecy, I couldn't go back to my aunt's house by myself. Jancsi, the oldest and most experienced in this sort of thing, told my brother that it was a good idea to urinate after such an encounter to clear one's urinary tract. I watched as he, his friends, and my brother had a pissing contest at the sidewall of the whorehouse. Whorehouses, incidentally, were not unusual at that time in Hungary. Every sizable town had at least one under medical and police supervision, which claimed to keep the working girls off the streets and ensure at least a minimal measure of success against the spread of disease. I thought this was a disgusting thing and wondered how my brother could have gone along with it.

Jancsi and Magda visited us a few times in Pápa. It didn't take long before the local boys discovered Magda, and before Jancsi discovered the local boys to pick fights with.

* * *

I learned to play tennis. It was fun to put on white shorts or even long white trousers with a cotton sweater over a light knit shirt. Tennis rackets and balls were another thing. They were expensive, but I managed to buy a used racket and learned to restring it. My friend Jocó showed me how to restring a racket. He learned it from his brother, who must have learned it from who knows whom. I made a sort of a clamp to hold the racket while it was being restrung. We needed several ice pick–like tools and a short, round hardwood dowel to wrap the string on as it was being stretched. We did a good job and picked up some pocket cash doing it for some of our friends.

By this time the two of us were partners in a number of enterprises. We did our photography together, and Jocó even helped me with my lampshade business. As I had the tools, we offered Mr. Kovács to fix broken fencing swords. At times, during a bout or lesson, the tip of a sword would break off, leaving a jagged point which made the blade unsafe to use. The broken tip had to be heated and folded back onto itself. When a blade became too short or totally unusable, it had to be replaced with a new one. This involved threading the handle portion of the new blade, which I could do. Mr. Kovács was delighted, as until then he had to send the blades out and pay for the repairs.

Jocó and I also learned to play a game much like tennis, a game I haven't seen played anywhere before or since. Mr. Kovács gave us tambourine-like rackets, about a foot in diameter, having a round hardwood frame with rawhide stretched over it. Grasping the hardwood ring by its edge, one would strike a rubber ball about the size of a regular tennis ball without the felt covering. The game was played on a regular tennis court with regular tennis rules. Jocó and I played this game for hours at the Nátus on its single tennis court.

I took up skiing, which was then very different from what skiing is today. Just about then it was coming into its own as an increasingly popular sport. I couldn't tell you where my first skis came from. I know they were real, and I suspect I must have bought them secondhand from someone. Jocó's older brother had skis and Jocó usually borrowed them, but I remember the two of us working on the skis, shaping, painting, and waxing them, doing what we learned from reading sports magazines. He and I would get up at the crack of dawn, sometimes even before, and take a train to a nearby town, Zirc, on top of one of the Bakony Mountains. The train would chug up this mountain, arriving at Zirc around seven in the morning. Just as light was coming up, Jocó and I would walk out of town towards the ski area with skis on our shoulder. Actually, there really was no ski area, as we know it today. There were no lifts, lodges, and runs, just a hillside, which was naturally clear enough to ski down on after we climbed to the top. The climb was exhausting. We usually had a cup of hot chocolate or tea from a thermos in our backpack before we strapped on the skis and went schussing down the mountain. Neither one of us knew how to ski. But we learned fast, falling, crashing into trees and rocks, and laughing all the way to the bottom of the hill. We would ski back up towards the top of the mountain, cross-country style, which incidentally was the only style then. We'd then climb to the top again, have another cup of tea, and come crashing down the slope again. After a few runs we would've had it for the day and walk back to the railroad station and take the only train back to Pápa in the late afternoon.

On one occasion, by which time we thought we were pretty good, we decided to ski all the way home to Pápa. I don't know how far it was but it couldn't have been very far, and we talked ourselves into believing that it would be an easy downhill cross-country trip all the way. It was logical to think so. After all, the train going to Zirc was going uphill all the way. But it didn't turn out that way. It seemed that at the bottom of every down slope was a ravine with deep snow–covered shrubs and rocks, making skiing very difficult. And the unexpected up slopes, most of which we had to climb with our skis on our shoulders, seemed as steep as the down slopes were. Long before lunch, we were lost. It was an overcast day, snowing lightly now and then, and we had no idea which way was which. We roasted a slab of bacon over a fire for lunch and went on following the downhill slopes whenever possible. Shortly after lunch the snow got heavier, but we found a road going downhill and continued to cross-country on it. It wasn't hard going. The snow was fresh and the gentle slope of the road had us going without obstacles of trees, rocks, and shrubs. But it was getting dark fast, even though it was only around three o'clock. The snow was coming down harder, swirling and making it difficult to see. By the time it was almost totally dark, we were still on the road, trying to feel our way, getting nowhere. We knew we were in pickle. Neither one of us said anything, as we didn't know what to do other than to go on. Sometime later, we heard a truck behind us. We waved it down and it stopped. There were three men in the cab. The driver told us they were going through Pápa and that we could climb in the back. We were saved. The truck ride seemed to take forever in the heavy snow. Once in Pápa we banged on the cab and the truck let us off at a corner on Main Street and the street leading down to Tókert, towards our homes. It had to be around seven or eight o'clock as we walked the rest of the way home. Jocó and I thought it was a great experience, but my mother didn't think so. Not knowing what had happened, fearing the worst, she was very upset as I walked into the house. She reprimanded me near tears, while at the same time I felt she wanted to hug me. My father was in the room also. He asked me what happened. I told him. He didn't comment, just left the room puffing on his pipe. I thought he was, in his own way, pleased with the way we handled the situation. He seldom voiced approval, but by then I knew that at times his approval was indicated by the lack of his disapproval. One of his favorite expressions was, in translation of course, "You can't eat hot soup too fast." He used this expression often, usually meaning that at times when the situation seems worse, one still has time, or hope, as one has to wait for the soup to cool down before one can eat it. He didn't say this then, but I thought he might have thought about it. I did.

* * *

In addition to making lampshades, I started making complete lamps. I was able to buy very attractive baked clay vases at the open-air market for relatively little money. I learned to electrify these vases and sell them with one of my lampshades as a complete unit. They sold well and my lampshade business was booming, until one of the dealers in town told me that he was no longer going to pay the prices I asked for my shades. He was one of my better customers, the owner of a large store in Pápa that sold radios, phonographs, lamps, and electrical appliances. Dealing with him was very convenient, as I didn't have to carefully pack and ship my lampshades and I could just deliver them in a large box. This was a big loss as he not only bought my shades for his lamps in his store, but also recommended me to people who wanted custom shades made. He told me that one of his clerks had learned to make lampshades and he was going to make his own shades from then on and sell them in competition with me. This took a lot of wind out of my sails. It didn't take my father too long to sense that something was wrong, but he never asked me any questions. He simply told me one day that he was going to Győr, a nearby town larger than Pápa, and suggested that I come with him and bring my samples to show in the stores in Győr while he was attending to his business. I didn't much feel like it, but he encouraged me and I went. We got into Győr a couple of hours before noon and the hired car stopped right in front of the biggest store, which my father told me would be a good prospect. He told me where the other shops were and that he would meet me around four o'clock. Then he helped me get my two large sample cases out of the car and left. There I was, standing on a sidewalk in a strange town with two large cases of lampshades. After a while I worked up enough courage to walk into the store and ask for the owner. The upshot of the situation was that the owner genuinely liked my shades. He asked a lot of questions then ordered a few of my standard shades, and I walked out of the store feeling a couple of feet taller. The same thing happened at the next store. I knew my lampshades were very nice, much nicer than the commercially made variety, and I sold them for just about the same price. I did very well that day. At exactly four o'clock, the car with my father pulled up to the curb. I wrestled my two cases into the backseat and got in next to my father. We were on our way back to Pápa. I didn't think my father had a very good day as he didn't say much, but as we were quietly riding along he finally asked how I did. He seemed pleased, but offered no comments for a while. "One thing I learned in the army," he said quietly sometime later as we were coming into Pápa, "is that one is not defeated till one gives up." It was a statement almost out of thin air, seemingly apropos of nothing. He made no reference to my shying away from my business because of the threat of competition. In fact, I don't remember him saying anything else for the rest of the trip home. It came to mind some time after this trip—and I'm as convinced today as I was then—that he didn't have any business in Győr that day. He concocted the entire trip to get my business and me back on track.

I went to work on the Győr order, starting early the following morning. On my father's advice, I photographed every shade I made and put the pictures in an album with a short description of the shade. Who it was made for, when, for how much, and so on. He gave me a small portable typewriter and showed me how to keep books for the business. This became very helpful as about a year later I hired a salesman. Well, I didn't actually hire him. Looking back on this, I think he hired me. He was, I was told, a distant relative who just happened to show up at our house one day for a short visit. During lunch he told me that he had heard about my lampshades and asked if he could see them. When I showed him my samples he wanted to know if anyone was selling them for me. He told me that he traveled constantly selling various merchandise, and if it was all right with me he would show samples of my shades. He turned out to be a big help. I made two photo albums full of pictures of my shades and lamps. All the pictures were black-and-white, but I hand colored some, which made them interesting. The biggest surprise was when he gave me a bigger order than I had ever gotten from the dealer in Pápa who had threatened to compete against me.

For years after that trip with my father to Győr, I wondered if I "gave up," let's say, when I lost an athletic competition. Inwardly, I never thought I gave up when I lost to someone who was bigger, older, more experienced, and better than I. Slowly I came to understand that one can be beaten, but "one is never defeated till one gives up."

* * *

The political situation worsened steadily. Germany had been at war for a couple of years by then, conquering country after country at will, and in most cases with very little or no resistance at all. The German army seemed unstoppable and invincible. Its obvious successes were flowered up in the sympathetic and slanted Hungarian press. Every day more and more troop trains were going through Pápa, and the field-gray color of the German Wehrmacht and black SS uniforms became commonplace. So did the increasing number of refugees, mostly Jews from Austria, Poland, Romania, and Czechoslovakia. The tales they brought with them were horrifying. They talked in hushed tones and with stricken faces about unbelievable atrocities. An occasional beating, or murder, or the burning and looting of one's home paled in comparison with the mass deportations to unknown places where, according to these stories, thousands would be slaughtered. From our perspective, judging on the basis of our own lives, these stories seemed far-fetched and exaggerated, if not totally unbelievable. But if they were untrue, why did all those people flee their home, in most cases with nothing more than the clothes on their backs? We saw pictures of the main gate of a camp called Dachau in Germany. The inscription on this gate read, "Arbeit Macht Frei," loosely translated, "Work Will Liberate You." It was a labor camp. The article accompanying these photographs told the story of the camp, built to hold the enemies of the Reich: communists, homosexuals, Gypsies, and all undesirables, such as Jews. All those who were committed to this camp lost their German citizenship, civil rights, and personal property. All official news reaching us was closely controlled. The domestic press was a translated carbon copy of German propaganda. Everybody became an interpreter of the news, trying to read between the lines and hoping to find even the slightest offering of hope. I recall listening to the radio to one of Hitler's speeches in the Reichstag in response to President Roosevelt's letter requesting guarantees of a list of countries and nations. Hitler read the long list. As he read, an obviously well-orchestrated snicker started in the background. It grew in intensity as the list continued, and broke out into thunderous laughter as Hitler mockingly read off "Palestina." Hungary was also included on this list. The "experts," those optimists who read between the lines and interpreted the news, immediately declared that President Roosevelt and America would not allow any harm coming to us. America was our only hope. But as big and as rich and powerful as we thought America was, it was on the other side of the world, far and safe from German aggression with little interest or reason for fighting Germany. This was confirmed by hearing that America was intent on staying out of a war so far from their own shores. It made sense. Why, we asked, should they worry about other people's problems? France, Belgium, Holland, Denmark, and Norway were defeated, and from the way the situation looked, it was only a matter of time before England would fall also. The newspapers showed photographs daily of London burning, and the radio blared news of England being defeated from the air by Hitler's powerful Luftwaffe. We listened to the BBC, the British Broadcasting Company, hoping to get if not good news, at least some denial of the German propaganda. But the BBC at that time couldn't offer much encouragement. We knew they made an effort to soften the bad news by reporting that their fighter planes, the Spitfires and the Hurricanes, shot down large numbers of German planes. Yet every day the Hungarian press and radio brought new accounts of more victories by Germany in the air. We knew that the news was slanted on both sides and it was hard to say who was closer to the truth, but the Germans seemed to have an inexhaustible supply of airpower, contradicting British claims. The losses the Germans admitted to were far below the BBC's. Even the most optimistic interpreters of the news had to admit that day in and day out, German planes were raiding England, while the largest portion of the BBC broadcast was devoted to silly theatricals, such as two Welsh coal miners, obviously actors, discussing world events in Hungarian. The real news took no more than a few minutes at the beginning of every broadcast. In other words, they really didn't have anything good to report. The BBC broadcasted twice a day. Listening to these broadcasts was strictly forbidden, which made it interesting, almost comical, to see windows closing all over town a few minutes before 2:15 in the afternoon and at 10:15 in the evening. We would huddle around our radio, tuning it to the BBC frequency, searching for the familiar Morse code signal - - - —, - - - —, - - - —, or VVV, and to hear the first bars of Beethoven's Fifth Symphony, followed by the imposing voice of the announcer: "This is BBC, London." A monotonous, almost disinterested voice would come on in Hungarian: "Sok német repülőgépek megint bombázták Londont tegnap este." ("Large number of German planes attacked London again last night.") They usually listed some hospitals, churches, and schools hit, disclaiming damage to military targets, and they always claimed many more German planes shot down than the Hungarian radio admitted. Then the "Welsh coal miners" would take over for the rest of the newscast.

Though our lives still showed very little change, the general mood in the country changed visibly. Hungary was still not officially at war, but the "Volunteer Hungarian Army and Air Force units of solidarity" fought along

Germans in Russia. A military airport was built just outside of Pápa. Young Hungarian cadets were training to fly German aircraft and a parachute regiment was stationed there.

One afternoon Jocó and I were playing tennis at the PFC when three German planes flew over us very low, bearing Hungarian Air Force markings. They were Junkers Ju 86 medium bombers. I recognized them instantly, though until then I never saw any real monoplanes, let alone twin engine ones. But I devoured aviation magazines, German and Hungarian, and knew all about every plane flying at that time. On one occasion, most of the upperclassmen marched out to the airport to witness a flying demonstration. It was amazing. We saw little bi-wing trainers doing aerobatics and a large bomber dropping a sack of white powder on a target as a bombing demonstration. Some of the students who declared their intention of joining the air force didn't have to march back to school. As future airmen, their privileged status became obvious as they passed and waved to us from the back of an army truck being driven back to school. Jocó's brother was one of them. Military service was compulsory in Hungary. At the age of eighteen, all males were conscripted for a minimum of three years of service. Those who graduated from a school such as the Kollégium in peacetime conditions were released after one year as cadet sergeants. For the next three years they would report to summer maneuvers for a commission as officers, and remain in the reserves for the rest of their lives. Many Kollégium students were in uniform by this time. They usually came back to the school to visit and show off their snappy uniforms. They would come to the gym first to salute Mr. Kovács, who would acknowledge their salutes and shake hands with them. As much as I envied them, by this time it was clear to me that I would not be allowed the same privilege.

# Chapter 8

# 1942 – 1944
# BAD TIMES START

My brother and I went to Celldömölk for our summer vacation. One of my mother's sisters, Jolán, was visiting us in Pápa. She and my mother took the train while my brother and I bicycled. We made it in almost the same time the train took. By this time, I went everywhere on my bike. It became a part of me. I could do tricks on it, even ride it backwards, and on one occasion was in a group of kids from the school who performed on bicycles at our traditional year-end celebration, the Tornavizsga. The Tornavizsga—there really is no accurate translation of the word—loosely describes the event, meaning "Gymnastic Test." It took place towards the end of every school year, when my school and the Nátus, our sister school, put on a show of gymnastics and other athletic exhibitions. This was a big, much-anticipated event that all of us looked forward to. We would practice the mass exercises throughout the school year and prepare for the individual presentations as well. On the day of the event, all students would congregate at school in uniforms of black pants, a white T-shirt, a blue sash tightly wrapped around our waists, and, of course, our school cap with a feather. We were encouraged to wear medals won in athletic competition. The classes would form up in platoons and march to the soccer stadium in the town park, the Liget. We would march to the cadence of drums, right onto the field to prearranged positions. The whole thing was always well rehearsed and ran like clockwork under the direction of Mr. Kovács. When all the platoons were in place, the national anthem would be played from a phonograph record as a grandstand full of people, parents, townspeople, and those who traveled from long distances just to see this event would stand and sing It was a wonderful, proud moment. Over the years since Kovács ur started this event, it became well known and very popular. Right after the national anthem, after some commands from Mr. Kovács, the platoons would spread out, filling the entire field evenly. Then music would start, usually Lehár or Strauss, and the students from both schools would do the well-rehearsed calisthenics routine. The exercises were all designed by Mr. Kovács. On a sunny day it was a spectacular sight to see the hundreds of girls and boys perform in almost faultless unison. When the group exercises were finished, on the command from Mr. Kovács the platoons would form up again and march off the field. Even as this happened, a team of students would be erecting gymnastics equipment, such as parallel bars, pommel horses, high bars, and rings, which would be finished just as the gymnastics team in tight-fitting white uniforms reached the spot. They would go into their routine, performing on the equipment. When their number was over, other groups, fencers, javelin and discus throwers, and shot putters would take to the field one after the other, followed by other exhibitions. In later years I was a member of the gymnastics team, the fencing team, and the shot putters. On at least one occasion I was also part of the bicycle team, performing a routine on bikes decorated with colored paper.

* * *

Then there was dancing class. I don't remember exactly, but I had to be fourteen, fifteen, perhaps even sixteen years old. Dancing then didn't resemble the type of dancing one sees in movies or in discos today. It was the foxtrot, the tango, and of course the waltz. But just learning the steps wasn't the whole thing. It was learning how a gentleman should behave with ladies on and off the dance floor. The lessons took place at the Nátus in a large, empty room on the second floor. Kovács ur, the perfect gentleman, attended some of these classes, but the main teacher was a lady whose name I've forgotten long ago. She was tall, always in a long, black dress, her hair put up in a bun, and in her hand she always had a clapper, which she slammed into the palm of her other hand to the rhythm of the piano music as she counted cadence: "One, two, three—one, two, three…" Boys were seated in a row of chairs along the window side of the room facing the girls, who were similarly seated across from us on the opposite side. We were told how to sit and how to stand and how to walk across the room to ask the lady of our choice for a dance. Then came learning the steps, learning how to hold the lady's hand, how to have our other arm around her waist, with an appropriate separation between bodies. Needless to say, there was much discussion of these classes afterwards, amidst giggles and laughs as we imitated our teacher and some of the girls, mostly the less popular ones. Of course, there were some very popular girls also. Some were beautiful and so popular that they were intimidating. One of these was a gal a year younger than I, Horvát Hajnalka, the younger sister of Horvát Kató, my skating partner/opponent. Hajnal, meaning "Dawn," Hajnalka a term of endearment, was my idea of the most beautiful girl in the world. At this time, this estimation was based on seeing her from a distance only, or saying hello or exchanging a few words at the skating rink, and now in dancing class. Unlike Vera Neumann, who was also very beautiful but shy, Hajnal was vivacious, always smiling, and never lost for words. I was kind of tongue-tied dancing with her for the first time. We met lots of other girls at dancing class, which after a while became something to look forward to, though I'd never admit it.

With the new acquaintances made at dancing school came another bit of activity, which I still remember fondly. The girls circulated large notebooks amongst the boys in my school, in which everyone was invited to write remarks. Every page had a question at the top of the page, put there by the owner of the book for the boys to answer. Such questions as, "How tall do you think I am?" were simple teasers to see if the boys could figure out who the book belonged to, which was supposed to be a secret. But the girls all hoped to get some nice comments from the boys they cared about. Whoever answered these questions correctly indicated he knew who the book belonged to. There were questions, which gave an opening to the boys to identify themselves. For example, "Do you have a nickname?" was an open invitation to someone to identify himself if he wanted to. But even if one did not identify himself with a nickname, there were other ways to let the girl of your dreams know who you were and to let her know that you knew who the book belonged to without revealing it to anyone else. That was the most fun, as it usually centered on a secret shared by two people only. When the books were full, they were returned to the Nátus and to the owners, identified by a number.

* * *

I can't recall when this event took place—I think it was in the winter when the dancing classes concluded, and we had a formal dance, much like a prom in this country. I remember a certain anxiety over being able to invite your choice amongst the girls, hoping she would accept your invitation.

Even this was accomplished in a traditional, formal manner. All girls had to have a dance card. It was a nicely printed little card dangling from the wrist with a tiny pencil attached. By the rules of the event, the girls had to accept invitations to a dance by whoever approached them first, until midnight or ten o'clock or whatever the time limit was, after which they could write in the names of their choice for all dances to follow. I guess I don't have to tell you that my date was Horvát Hajnalka. But this didn't come about without anxiety. By this time the mood of the country was definitely antisemitic, and since I was considered a Jew, both my parents were certain that Hajnalka and her parents would turn me down. I didn't think this would happen, yet understanding my parents' reasoning and concern, understanding all the increasing signs of antisemitic feelings around me, even I was hesitant. But blind love won out and I asked Hajnal to be my date at the dance. All of us were surprised when she accepted. It was a bit intimidating to sit with her parents at dinner, but it turned out to be a very lovely, memorable evening.

* * *

As the subject came up, let me say a few words about the wave of antisemitism that swept the country. There was always a certain amount of antisemitism in Europe, more in some countries than in others. Hungary was no exception. I don't have to tell you there still is. In fact, I doubt that there is a country in the world where antisemitism never did, nor does not, exist today. But by the early forties, this situation had become drastic in Hungary. Most of those who until this time had antisemitic tendencies but suppressed them became outspoken advocates of antisemitism and racial superiority. Even those who did not endorse antisemitism paid service to it by remaining silent. By this time, it was quite clear to me that I and my family, regardless of my father's and his brothers' conversion, were now considered Jews. Even without antisemitism, this wasn't entirely unreasonable. None of us participated in any activity of the Catholic faith. We did participate in some activities of the Jewish faith. My mother and her entire family were well known in the Jewish community. So were my paternal grandparents. My brother and I went to a Jewish elementary school. My father's and his brothers' conversion to Catholicism, if it indeed took place, was never publicized, and was talked about rarely even within the family. Even without the new laws, it was reasonable to understand that the world looked at me and my family as Jews. Until the early forties this was not a problem for me, but the situation was noticeably changing. The incident of being refused by my art teacher Tóth Sándor for the Boy Scouts had to have happened around this time.

* * *

America entered the war against the Japanese, and, as you know, Germany declared war against the US a day later. Needless to say, my family was delighted. This was a huge reversal by my father, but it was more and more obvious by every passing day that the country he loved so much and served so well was selling him, his family, and his entire race down the river. He still refused to believe that Hungary or the people of Hungary would allow anything to happen to those sons who fought on her behalf. He thought that all the problems could be traced to Hitler's Germany, and that Hungary only followed under duress. To some extent, this was true. Hungary was still not at war, having not declared war on Russia or on any of Germany's enemies. With Hungary out of the war and with the United States now in it, there was cause for optimism.

All of that abruptly changed one day in 1942. The radio stopped broadcasting in the early afternoon. A few hours later martial music started, followed by an announcement that Admiral Horty was going to address the nation. He was Hungary's regent—a nice word substituting for dictator—who, as our history books depicted, liberated Hungary from the yoke of Béla Kun's Bolshevik regime, which had immediately followed World War I. He ruled Hungary continuously since then. He was an admiral, though Hungary had no seaports nor navy by this time. His new title was Kormanyzó, literal translation "Steerer," meaning "Helmsman," one who holds the reins, or "Leader." In his radio address that day, he told the nation that one of Hungary's principal northeast cities was bombed that day by two Russian bombers. There was quite a lot of damage and loss of life. He declared war on Russia and from that day on Hungary was at war, committed to and fighting alongside her German allies. The quality of our lives deteriorated rather rapidly from this moment on.

The country mobilized, committing itself one hundred percent to the German cause. Rumors were flying that one of the two Russian planes that bombed our city in the northeast was shot down or crashed, and turned out to be a German plane with a German crew, with phony Russian markings. The likelihood of this being true was very good, but true or not, Hungary was now on a road of no return. The reserves were called up immediately, but my father was not. Not until some time later, at which time his call-up papers did not refer to his rank but prefaced his name with "Munkaszolgálatos," "One in Labor Service." He was stripped of his rank, effectively demoted to serve in what became known as labor battalions. He was instructed to report immediately and to bring with him eating utensils, a blanket, and clothes suitable for heavy labor. Being the defiant man he was, he packed his old uniforms denuded of rank and unit designation. Many others—all Jews—were called up at about the same time to report to labor units. It didn't take long for the confirmed optimists to come up with a silver lining. This was the only effective way they explained that the Hungarian Government could counter the German practice of deporting a conquered country's Jewish population. It was tough, they said, but as long as our men were in the Hungarian Labor Service, they would not be deported. This explanation made a certain amount of sense. By then we knew that Jews had been deported from German-occupied countries such as France, Holland, Belgium, and Poland, and that none of these countries was in a position to oppose the Germans. The one country which stood alone was tiny Denmark. France, Holland, Norway, even some of the occupied British Channel Islands had their collaborators and quislings. But the King of Denmark declared that if his Jewish citizens were forced to wear a yellow Star of David, he would be the first to put one on. The entire Danish nation united behind their king in an effort to save Danish Jews. Ordinary Danish people risked their lives and the well-being of their families, smuggling their Jewish citizens night after night to Sweden during the German occupation. In spite of incredibly cruel retaliation, the Germans were unable to stop it. As I understand it, relatively few Danish Jews were deported.

Though Hungary was not occupied, German authority was no longer questioned. Yet no Hungarians were deported. In fact, with some minor and a few major variations, my life went on almost as before. I continued going to school, compete in fencing, skating, and gymnastics. My lampshade business was actually booming, helping with our living expenses. Jocó and I still played tennis, did our photography, and built model airplanes together. It was an insane, illogical, upside-down sort of a situation.

The first real blow came when my brother finished school. On completing Class Eight, the finishing class at the Kollégium, one could voluntarily take an examination called érettségi. "Maturity," I guess, would be the closest in translation—a test comparable to the French le bachot. This exam usually lasted about a week and took in all subjects studied during the past eight years at the school. Accomplishing this test successfully meant an automatic entrance to Hungary's best universities, cadet or officer status in the armed forces, and in general a privileged status in Hungarian society. But there was to be no university or any of the traditional privileges in my brother's future. As of 1942 or so, Jews were excluded from Hungarian universities. Having completed his érettségi with better-than-average marks, he went to work for a local machine shop, which, being blue-collar labor, just a few years before would have been unheard of and unacceptable for our social position. But he always wanted to be an engineer, and under the circumstances the machine shop was a sorry second. Understanding the situation, he went off to work in the machine shop without a word of complaint. All of us were devastated, but we couldn't have been prouder of him. I had another year of school and was wondering what I was going to do after my érettségi. In some ways I thought I was in a better position. I was already in business for myself with my lampshades, so I could have worked for a carpenter or cabinetmaker, could have done photography or whatever came up. I wasn't worried.

\* \* \*

My brother and I decided to visit my father. Oddly enough, he ended up at Hajmáskér, his old artillery post. We bicycled from Pápa leaving in the early morning, our backpacks stuffed with food and goodies my mother prepared for my father. It being Sunday, people dressed in their all-black Sunday bests were going to or coming from church. As expected, small Hungarian sheepdogs—Pulis—chased us on the main streets as we rode through these little towns, but I always had a baton attached to the handlebar of my bike fashioned out of an old broom handle to fight the dogs off with. We arrived at my father's camp around ten o'clock and were made to wait till visitors were assembled in a group. We were told that certain items such as weapons including knives were not allowed in the camp, and that all our packs would be examined. They did look through our backpacks and cut open a rolled cake, I suppose to see if I had maybe a hand grenade in it. Obviously I did not. But this was a far cry from our last visit to Hajmáskér and the installation we visited him in previously. The labor unit he was in was housed in what might have been an old abandoned warehouse. Everybody slept on wooden platforms just inches above the dirt floor, covered with some straw and blankets for minimal comfort. The compound was surrounded by barbed wire and there were armed soldiers outside the fence. There were a few soldiers loitering around in the camp, posturing, trying to look important, and obviously enjoying their superior status. My father ignored them. Some of the younger people came by, the ones who had no visitors that day, and told us a story that made me burst with pride.

To fully appreciate it, you must understand and believe me that under the best of conditions a person in the Hungarian military, just one grade above a private, for example, had almost absolute authority over persons of lower rank. All orders given by a higher-ranked person, however tough or difficult, had to be obeyed and carried out at once without question or hesitation. In this camp, we were told that all the Munkaszolgálatosok, those in labor service such as my father, having no rank at all, were considered to be below the rank of the lowest private. In other words, their cadre, soldiers in charge of the Labor Service System, mostly privates, were all superior and their orders were to be instantly obeyed. Some, as it often happens with lowerclass people who suddenly find themselves in a position of authority, reveled in and took advantage of their newly found power. Unreasonable, stupid, and most of the time impossible orders were given, which could not have been carried out, and many were severely punished for disobedience for not being able to carry out these orders.

As it was related to us by some of the younger men, the entire unit was digging some kind of a ditch with picks and shovels when a very young, and probably very stupid, cadre started issuing stupid orders. The more those orders were complied with, the more he was encouraged and the more orders he issued. He was particularly hard on some of the meek and older people. Finally, my father, who was witnessing this, had enough. He jumped out of the ditch with shovel in hand, towering over this cadre, and bellowed at him.

"Én harcoltam az Oroszokat amikor te még mindig a pöcsöddel játszottál a homokba. Lelápni." I don't think that my limited Hungarian language skills will do justice to this statement, particularly without your ability to fully appreciate the circumstances and the desperation of the situation. As best as I can do, my father's outburst meant, "I fought the Russians when you were still playing with your pecker in the dirt. Dismissed." This statement stayed with me, ringing in my ears over all these years, with all the subtleties of Hungarian Army language. As my brother and I were told, the young soldier backed off and my father became the hero of the camp. All the younger people sought him out to congratulate him and let him know how much they respected him for his courage and what he did. All called him Laci bácsi, "Uncle Laci," and when they spoke of him, they referred to him as Laci batyam, or "my big brother Laci," a very endearing and respectful mannerism.

We stayed with him for most of the day. Had lunch together, joined by some of the younger people sharing the food my mother prepared. Then it was time to go. Thinking that my father might need money, I stuffed an envelope with money before we left Pápa. I handed him the envelope as we were preparing to leave. He didn't know what it was, but as he looked into it he immediately understood. For the first time in my life I saw tears come to my father's eyes. He hugged me but said nothing. It took some time for him to gain control of himself, clearing his throat, trying to cover his emotions.

It was getting late. He told us to take care of our mother and look in on the others in the family. A few minutes later my brother and I were on our way back to Pápa.

The ride seemed long. My brother and I weren't talking. I had a lot of time to think, as we pushed ourselves trying to beat the oncoming nightfall. The visit with my father was a demeaning, disturbing experience. Why was he in that camp? Why was he made to do work he never had done before? Why was he kept behind barbed wire, guarded like a criminal by gun-toting soldiers? Was he a prisoner, and if so, why? I found the whole thing very unsettling. To see him—a proud man he was all his life—under those circumstances was, to say the least, a very troubling experience. Though my brother tried not to show it, I knew he was also very upset. I was furious and frustrated at my lack of ability to do something about the situation and wished it wasn't so. I didn't want to talk about it and sensed that my brother felt the same way. It raised questions that I couldn't answer, and even I started to hide behind the reasoning of the optimists that by conscripting my father into labor service, the Hungarian Government was saving him from things far worse at the hands of the Germans. If that was so, why was that no-account, probably illiterate, despicable little shit of a private permitted to make impossible demands on people and order them around as his personal slaves for no other purpose than his own amusement? I had no answers. It was very upsetting.

* * *

As our situation deteriorated, others in town visibly benefited from Hungary's joining the Axis. Our food, which until then was always plentiful, items such as sugar, salt, vinegar, meat, flour—almost everything—became rationed. Everyone was allotted certain portions which had to be claimed with food ration stamps. Even yard goods were rationed. A black market flourished, as did black marketeers. Though black marketeering was against the law, somehow these people openly flaunted their newly found wealth and position. Some tore around town on new motorcycles, even in new cars. All of them wore long leather coats and a pair of lace-up high boots that I believe were called Bürgerli, or something like that. These boots were very popular. Parachute troops had them, and they somehow denoted a nationalistic position of the wearer. Perhaps it was a sign of solidarity with the times and philosophies of the era, and almost all who could afford them wore them. Much to my regret, Jocó wore them. I didn't like to see him in those boots, but he was my best friend who gave no indication, other than wearing those stupid-looking boots, of endorsing Nazi ideologies. We still spent as much time as possible in each other's company. Did what we always did, and managed to get into trouble together.

One evening, with permission to stay out after curfew, Jocó and I were on our way home on the sparsely lit streets after an evening of night photography. Our cameras were slung over our shoulders, folded tripods swinging from our hands, and as we rounded one of the corners we bumped into our German language teacher. I don't remember his name, but he was a caricature of a little man. He was small, skinny, and bald with an enormous bushy mustache trying to diminish a very large hooked nose with a wart on the tip. He walked with a funny gait, bent over like a hunchback. He looked at us and before we had a chance to say good evening or explain that we had permission from our homeroom teacher to be out after curfew, he turned and ran. Jocó and I didn't know what to make of this, but that quarter I flunked German.

* * *

My class went to Budapest on an excursion. We stayed in a big dormitory with double-decker beds arranged in rows. One single bed where our chaperone, Varga László, our natural history teacher, slept had a night table next to it. The whole room was buzzing with the discovery that Mr. Varga had a pistol on this night table. I have no idea why he carried it and why he displayed it so openly. One of the activities was a concert at one of the best concert halls, the Vigadó. It was a great evening of classical music. We also visited some of the better-known landmarks, the Fisherman's Bastion, and some museums, and one night we were allowed to strike out on our own. Some graduate students from the Kollégium who by this time were attending universities in Budapest were showing us around. One of these fellows took Jocó and me to a little tavern on the Buda hillside, overlooking Pest and the Danube River. It was a beautiful sight in spite of the blackout. The bridges were no longer lit up, nor were the side-wheeler boats running between Budapest and Vienna. The blackout was the only reminder that Hungary was at war. We sat outdoors in a garden on the hillside in a booth covered with rose bushes, eating pörkölt (meat stew), and drinking beer, as we listened to quiet Gypsy music. It was a beautiful evening.

* * *

The BBC no longer broadcasted long sessions of the philosophizing Welsh coal miners. Instead, news took up more and more of each fifteen-minute-long broadcast. The Hungarian newspapers still headlined great victories in Russia, but the articles now also talked about "strategic withdrawals," "consolidation of units," and "the realigning of front lines." By comparing the local news to the BBC, one could reach conclusions which we believed were closer to the truth than what was reported in the Hungarian newspapers or radio. For instance, when the United States entered the war in 1941, the German and Hungarian newspapers carried items about the American fleet having been destroyed and that America had no armies. They carried photographs of ill-equipped American troops training with wooden rifles. The papers also reported profusely and in glowing colors of the German American Bund, claiming an overwhelming pro-German sentiment in America. We saw the photographs of Bund rallies—Americans in Nazi-type uniforms—arms outstretched in the Nazi salute, carrying swastika flags.

But in spite of German and Hungarian propaganda, we knew that the tide was changing. We knew that the Americans had landed in North Africa and heard about the air raid over the Ploiești oil fields in Romania. We saw more and more large formations of American planes flying high over Pápa, filling the skies with white contrails, hearing the hundreds of engines reverberate long before the formations appeared and long after they were out of sight. We also heard the rumble, like low, distant thunder, as the American planes dropped their deadly cargo on Wiener Neustadt. Shortly afterwards, the formations returned heading home in the opposite direction. The war was definitely changing, but the signs still indicated that the end was not yet in sight. One after the other, German troop trains were going through Pápa, laden with gigantic tanks, guns, trucks, and troops.

More and more people were called up into the army, and more and more Jews were sent to labor service camps. But my father was released and was exempted from further labor service because of his past military record and decorations. Though he never talked about it, the reports we got from some of the labor service camps were devastating. Young and old were harassed and severely brutalized for even the most minor infractions. Torture, mostly for the amusement of the cadre, was common. Having one's hands tied behind one's back, at times with thin wire, then hoisted up high with a rope attached to the wire around one's wrists was a standard form of torture. Most of the time the thin wire cut the person's wrist to the bone. A person hoisted up in that manner was left hanging for hours, overnight at times, until his shoulders gave out and both arms were twisted out of their sockets. Not all fared this badly. Depending on the individual commanding officers of these units, the treatment in some of the units was relatively humane, though in others it was brutal in the extreme.

Csipő Lajos, my favorite teacher, was called up. Less than four weeks later he was killed on the Russian front. News of his death came like a blow. I truly loved and admired him. He was a genuine friend. With all the terrible things that surrounded us by this time, his death somehow signaled worse tragedies to come.

All students at school were going through a sort of a paramilitary training. All students were assigned to levente units (the marching band I described in the first chapter of this account was part of such a unit) and drilled at least once a week. Mr. Kovács called all Jewish students into his office one day, as the rest of the students were about to march off to their levente training. He explained that under the laws of the country, people of the Jewish religion were not permitted to participate in military-type activities, and henceforth we could not be part of levente training. Instead, also keeping with the current practices in the country, we would be assigned physical labor while the others did military drills. We were to dust some old gymnastics equipment in a small, dark, murky storage room. He put me in charge, though I wasn't the oldest in the group. As he was about to leave, I followed him and asked to be relieved of being in charge. He said something to the effect that somebody had to be in charge, and turned away from me muttering something I couldn't understand, but I thought he said that it didn't matter. He left the room. To this day I believe he was very embarrassed having to do this. I went back to the others and dusted some old equipment.

* * *

These events, as other events elsewhere in this account, are not in a proper, chronological order. I'm relating them as they come to mind, but all the events which I talk about here happened during the period of 1940–1944. These events as they affected me and my family intensified towards the end of that period. It was odd how some very bad and very good things could, and did, exist alongside one another. For instance, every new day brought further information which seemed to be getting us closer to disaster. On the other hand, the news from every source indicated a definite turn in the way the war was going. There seemed to be no new spectacular German military conquests or successes. Hungarian military personnel at home on leave from the front brought news of devastating losses inflicted by the Russian Army and the incredibly severe Russian winter. We heard stories of the battles in and around Stalingrad with entire German divisions capitulating or being annihilated. At the same time, large formations of German transport planes, each towing two gliders, were flying over Pápa on their way south to some Balkan destination, and the troop trains kept going eastward every day. The formations of four-engine American Liberators seemed to grow larger as they flew over us with increasing frequency. For me, they were a beautiful sight to behold. While all German and Hungarian planes were painted either dark or camouflage colors, the bare, sparkling aluminum of unpainted American planes almost daringly declared their overpowering presence. They seemed invincible and offered us a glimmer of hope that the end of the war and the prospect of peace was getting closer.

\* \* \*

By this time I'd been taking violin lessons for years. I loved the violin and was reasonably good at it. I always liked music, had an ear for it, and could remember and play most songs or a melody after hearing it only once. I even composed a couple of songs which Jocó and I sang in Mr. Csipő's class. He was one of the few teachers who came to our house or allowed us to visit him at his home unannounced. On one of these visits he mentioned that he needed some bookshelves. I was going to surprise him and Jocó and I set out to get some suitable lumber from some abandoned fences around town, which were the major source of lumber for my model airplane and woodworking hobbies. I built the shelves quickly and we decided to sneak into his small apartment, install the shelves as a surprise, and leave before he came home. Because all walls in Hungary or perhaps just around Pápa were built of brick, in order to hang anything one had to chisel into the wall, cutting a small cavity into which a small piece of wood would be cemented to hold a nail. We came properly prepared with my tools, cold chisels, sledge hammers, little wood blocks, mortar, nails, and so on. What we didn't know was that Mr. Csipő's small room was partitioned off from a larger room belonging to the owner of the house. Wanting to do the job quickly, we hammered away at the wall thinking it was one of the usually massive brick walls these houses were built with, but this was a thin partition wall, which gave under the pounding and broke through into the owner's living room. I was terrified. Fortunately Mr. Csipő came home unexpectedly, helped us replaster the bricks into the wall, and promised to set the situation straight with his landlord. He liked the bookshelves.

\* \* \*

More and more young men were called up for labor service. I knew that my time was getting closer as young men only four or five years older than I were already in the service. It was time to prepare. I started making a backpack. It was going to be strong, designed to expand with compartments for everything. Even the straps were made from a type of a hose, hollow on the inside, where I planned to hide some money. The material I chose was waterproof and strong, but lightweight. It was green in color and had a rubberized backing. I even put rubber cement on the seams to make it as waterproof as possible. I also made a shoulder bag, which could be attached to the backpack or to rings on the straps in the front. I knew that if and when I was going to be called, I had to take with me summer and winter gear and a blanket. I also had a small pouch, which fitted in a special place containing medicines, first aid supplies, and a sewing kit. Some of my tools had to come with me also. Obviously I couldn't take all the tools I owned by then, but I put together a basic toolkit as well as some supplies such as nails, a few spikes, and a small coil of tying wire. The back portion of the pack was lined with a slab of thick leather, in case my shoes needed to be resoled. I made all the straps, latches, snaps, rings, and buckles myself. When the backpack was finished, I set out collecting the supplies to put in it. I bought a very tough pair of work boots at Vera Neumann's father's store, also a very good waterproof outer jacket like a parka, a strong, wide leather belt, and some other supplies, all with money made in my lampshade business. Then I put the whole thing in a closet for when it was going to be needed. But I wasn't called. It was almost disappointing to see some of the young fellows I knew going, but I was still in school and wasn't called. Neither was my brother, and in spite of the rapidly worsening situation all around us, our life went on almost as usual.

* * *

The Germans were retreating along the entire front in Russia. The Allied forces were driving the Germans out of Africa and coming up the Italian peninsula towards Austria and Hungary. Ditto for Greece and the Balkans, but in Hungary nationalistic fervor was getting stronger. It seemed that anything that went wrong or was bad was said to be caused by and blamed on the Jews. At least that is what the headlines blared, and that is what most people paid lip service to, whether they believed it or not. Jewish business was more and more restricted, as was every facet of life in a very antisemitic environment. The noose of the Nuremberg Laws tightened, curtailing Jewish life.

But life still went on. My father's business was better than ever. It was booming. Maybe it was the war; the need for meat and for animals of burden was great. He was now working almost exclusively for Baron Eszterházy, his biggest and best client, with Eszterházy's majordomo, the general manager whose name I wish I could remember but I can't. Every now and then the circuits in my brain try to click and a name, something like Lustig, keeps coming up, but I can't be sure if it is correct. This man was also a big man and, like my father, also had a mustache, and also walked with a cane—which was fashionable in Hungary at that time. Money was pouring in, but I have no idea what happened to it. As I mentioned earlier, very large sums had to be deposited somewhere. There was never any talk about it.

The BBC increased the number of daily broadcasts to, I believe, four. The Welsh coal miners were gone and hard news came in larger doses. A new item was instituted, leaving much speculation about its real purpose. At the end of some of the broadcasts, strange messages and announcements were read. I can't quote any of these verbatim after so many years, but in essence they were something like: "My brother-in-law will pick apples this winter," followed by "Joska, go see your aunt." None of them made sense, but it wasn't long before some claimed to be able to decipher and assign meanings to these mysterious messages. But even without understanding them, somehow they offered hope of the war going more favorably for the Western Allies and getting closer to its end. People started to talk about an underground, and we believed it as the BBC openly reported on the activities of the French Underground and Russian partisans sabotaging the Germans. There was more and more open opposition to German occupation in countries around us. In Yugoslavia the Germans were now continuously fighting an unseen guerilla force, the Chetniks. In Czechoslovakia entire villages such as Lidice were erased from the surface of the earth in retaliation for such anti-German acts as the assassination of Reinhard Heydrich, the Nazi gauliter of Czechoslovakia. The Jews incarcerated in the Warsaw Ghetto rose up, fought the SS, and after a surprisingly long period were defeated and brutally annihilated. The German reprisals were brutal beyond description. For every German soldier killed, ten, fifty, a hundred people, entire villages—young, old, men, women—were brutally murdered at the whim of the SS. Whenever such reprisals took place, the news and the papers gave graphic accounts, at times even photographs of retaliation to deter further repetitions. Ten people hanging from common gallows, hung by thin wire or from butcher's hooks, were printed in some of the papers. News of extermination camps was beginning to circulate, but these rumors were so incredible that they were hard to believe.

German propaganda magazines such as *Signal* or *Der Stürmer*, the official magazine of the SS, were translated and published in Hungarian. Lots of people read them. Some younger people thought it was kind of smart to be seen with one of these, folded and tucked under one's arm, leaving no guess as to where the person's sentiments lay. New Hungarian propaganda magazines also appeared. In them, articles and serials, most likely orchestrated by the German propaganda machine, hammered away at the Jews. One serial I remember was called "Tarnopólból Indult El," meaning, "He Started in Tarnopól." A town in Odessa, Tarnopól was heavily populated by wealthy Orthodox Jews. Over many weeks this serial gave a detailed and obviously fictional and ludicrous account of how one of these Jews came to Budapest and infiltrated and tried to corrupt Hungarian society. Some of the movies I loved so much, *The Virginian* with Gary Cooper, *Broadway Melodies*, Disney cartoons, were replaced by German propaganda films. Not just masterfully crafted newsreels or documentaries such as *Triumph of the Will*, but feature films produced exclusively to generate and stir up sentiment and trouble against Jews. One of these films was *Jude Süss*, or *Süss the Jew*. I went to see this movie just to see firsthand what everyone was talking about. It was a demeaning, horrible, sick bunch of lies and fabrications portraying Jews as vermin. German propaganda films slanted towards Nazi ideology were more and more frequent. I hated these films, but I loved movies. My hobby, photography, slowly led to an interest in movies. Though there was no way I could make movies then—small movie cameras and film were beyond my financial reach—I read everything about movies and filmmaking I could lay my hands on and knew even then that some day, movies would be my life's calling.

\* \* \*

The year was 1944. I built an air raid shelter in our garden. It was about ten feet deep and four feet wide. I lined and roofed it with heavy timber, and covered it with about three feet of dirt. The steps at both ends joined the shelter at right angles so bullets of strafing aircraft would be blocked. In all, as I recall, there were about three air raids in Pápa, but no planes ever came and dropped bombs or did any strafing while I was still there. Aside from those who came to admire the shelter, no one ever spent a second in it under raid conditions. For what I know, it might still be there and the present occupants of 12 Pozsonyi ut might be keeping potatoes in it.

While we lived at Pozsonyi Street in the Tókert, I learned to bind books. Jocó knew something about it and showed me how he did it with the help of very crude, makeshift equipment. I picked it up quickly and easily. Within a short time the two of us joined our efforts. I made good equipment to do the work with and established contact with a professional bookbinder in town who had large equipment and, for a few cents, trimmed the edges of our bound books for us before we added the hard covers. We picked up a bit of pocket money with our bookbinding.

I also did a lot of skating, though by this time I was barred from competition. The long winter of 1943–44 broke suddenly, giving way to unusually mild March weather. On the fifteenth of March, Hungary's independence day, as every year before the entire school, all students and faculty, marched to the square in front of the school to listen to patriotic speeches in front of the statues of Petőfi Sándor and Kossuth Lajos, the heroes of Hungary's independence. For the first time other Jewish students and I were excluded from this traditional celebration. I watched from the sidewalk as my classmates sang, "Isten áld meg a magyart…" "God bless the Hungarians…" Hungary's national anthem, with glowing faces and goose feathers stuck in their caps. I resented being excluded. The following day, we were back in school in our regular classes. News of Russian troops grouping at the Hungarian borders and the imminent invasion of Hungary were openly discussed. On the eighteenth of March, the Hungarian radio stopped broadcasting. I can no longer remember if it was on this day or a day later, but when the radio came on again it played soft folk music. It was repeatedly announced that Admiral Horty was going to make an important speech. When it came, it was not to be believed. He announced that under the circumstances and in the face of an overwhelming force, the shedding of Hungarian blood was no longer justified. He announced a cease-fire and the stopping of hostilities between Hungary and the Soviet Union, calling on all Hungarian Army units to lay down their arms. I ran home but instead of jubilation found my mother and father ashen-faced, speechless. Nobody knew what to make of the situation or figure out what it actually meant.

The following day, I was back in my classroom. Some of the students, including me, were wearing the Hungarian tricolor rosettes called kokárda on our lapels. Around eleven o'clock we heard a loud rumble coming from the square in front of the school, but from our windows on the far side of the building we couldn't see anything. When the break came, all of us ran out to the square. Two enormous German tanks sat in front of the Nátus, their guns pointing upward and to the side in opposing directions. German military vehicles, trucks, personnel carriers, small jeep-like cars, and motorcycles were racing through town, coming and going in every direction. It looked like there were thousands of them. In the middle of the square a German military policeman with the quarter-moon metal shield hanging from small chains around his neck was directing traffic with a round dish at the end of a baton. The bell rang, calling us back, but there was no class. After a while a teacher came in and sent us home.

From this moment on our lives rapidly turned for the worse.

\* \* \*

I will never forget that day: March 19, 1944. It was, perhaps, the most important turning point in my life. There was a tremendous, nationalistic, anti-German sentiment that swept Pápa. I don't know if this was so all over the country, but it was definitely the case in Pápa. It was as though overnight or from one minute to the next, Hungary's German allies became the enemy. Everyone knew we were being occupied. Sometime before when Italy tried to jump out of the Axis, a number of trains with Italian soldiers, held prisoners by the Germans, came through Pápa. It wasn't hard to see how quickly an alliance could break apart, and former allies become enemies. Jocó and I walked around town at times nearly run down by German motorcycles driving at breakneck speeds on the sidewalks. We hated them. By this time the Gypsy music on the radio was replaced by martial music again, which, as on so many other occasions in the past, stirred up nationalistic feelings and signaled changes for the worse. Jocó and I decided to get even with the Germans. We went home and folded some newspapers, which we were going to soak in benzin (benzine) and use them to burn German cars with that evening. At nightfall, the two of us walked into the center of town looking for German vehicles to burn. Surprisingly, there were a lot fewer than we thought. Two of them were sitting half on the sidewalk on Main Street, not far from my aunt's store. They were the small jeep-type vehicles, top down, with backpacks hanging from their sides. There were some German soldiers around, as well as a few local people. We kept looking. There were a few more cars, trucks, and motorcycles in front of the big church on the Main Square, but they were guarded. We walked through the archway across from the big church into Kossuth Street, which was relatively empty of people as well as cars. At this point I think Jocó got cold feet. He said it was getting late and he wanted to go home. He did. There I was, alone with a small bottle of benzin, a homemade cigarette lighter, and some folded newspaper strips in my pocket. I turned into Saint László Street, the first side street on the right off Kossuth Street. The street was deserted, but there was a lone German car with backpacks hanging from it and not a person in sight. All of us I believe do some extremely stupid things at least once in our lives—things we regret throughout our lifetime. My turn came at that moment in Saint László Street. As I recall, I walked towards the lonely German car trying to appear very nonchalant. There was no one in sight. I took some of the folded newspaper from my pocket, stuffed it into the backseat, poured some benzin (benzine) on it, and threw the lit cigarette lighter into the car. Until this moment I was relatively calm, but when I saw the flames flare I panicked, possibly thinking that someone else may also have seen the flames in the dark. My heart skipped a beat and I started to run down the street and into an alley. To this day I don't know if the car did catch fire and burn.

It took the better part of my life—occasionally I still agonize over this—to realize that if I were caught, I would have been hanging from piano wire from some lamppost perhaps along with my family. Fortunately I didn't get caught, and even if the car did burn, in the long run it would have accomplished very little. I kept running, coming out of the alley at its far end, when the air raid sirens came on. It had a calming effect on me—a lesser calamity negating a bigger one.

In spite of everything that was affecting my life at this time, my brother, as most young men of that age group, and I were junior air raid wardens. We had to serve several nights a month, sleeping away from home, patrolling the streets for four hours at a time, checking and warning people if there was light showing from any of their windows. I had an armband denoting my junior air raid warden status. As the sirens were blaring, I remember putting my armband on and walking quickly towards the air raid shelter beneath Eszterházy Castle. Funny, how one remembers insignificant details under grave circumstances, but I recall that it was a breezy, cold March night with thin clouds racing over a half moon in a steel-blue sky. The air raid shelter was almost full of people when I got there. Shortly after I got to the shelter, German soldiers, a military band, came in carrying instruments. Within minutes they put on an impromptu concert, playing Strauss waltzes, some spirited polkas, and Hungarian folk songs. As a musician I found it hard to believe that the concert was as impromptu as it seemed, unless this band rehearsed and played Hungarian folk songs regularly. Little by little, the hostile atmosphere in the shelter changed. No more than a half an hour later, a festive atmosphere replaced the animosity towards the Germans in the shelter, as the local people sang along with the tunes the band played. More and more German soldiers came in, and festive people slapped them on the back in friendly gestures. So much for the nationalistic fervor and anti-German sentiment on the heels of Hungary getting out of the war and being occupied by the German army.

The following day, rumors claimed that there was no danger of an air raid the night before. The rumors claimed that the Germans concocted the air raid to bring people to the shelter and the concert. It worked in Pápa. Nationwide, the following morning the radio announced that a new Hungarian Government was formed, and rumors claimed that Admiral Horty was arrested and taken to Germany, and one of his sons was killed.

# Chapter 9

# 1944 – MARCH | APRIL | MAY | JUNE
# "SHAVE EVERY DAY..."

N ow is the time to put this book down, perhaps even burn it. As I warned you in the prologue, lots of my past life's aspects are difficult to talk about, very probably hard for you to understand, and reading it might cause discomfort. Yes, from here on this account is going to get rough.

* * *

Under the new Hungarian Nazi regime, things happened fast. Within days a national edict forced Jews to wear a yellow star, twelve centimeters in size in public. Few were exempt from these laws. My father believed that on the basis of his military service and decorations, we were exempt. The problem was that somehow he lost or misplaced the documentation to one of his medals. He wrote away for a duplicate, but the missing paper was not replaced. My mother sewed the yellow Star of David onto all our garments so even by mistake we wouldn't go out without it, which carried a severe penalty. The local police took it on themselves to vigorously enforce these laws. The worse were the gendarmerie, csendőrség, "guardians of quiet" in literal translation. What a joke. The gendarmerie was a nationwide police organization in military uniforms except for their hats, which were similar to black bowlers with a large rooster tail stuck into the band. They patrolled the countryside in pairs, sometimes on bicycles but most of the time on foot. They were a feared and deservedly hated sadistic and vicious bunch.

As everywhere else in all German-occupied countries, Jews had to register at a so-called Jew office. The leaders of the Jewish community administered this office under the new laws. They were responsible to the local police, the gendarmerie, and the Gestapo. When everybody was registered, an order was issued that all Jews, with the exception of those who were exempt from these laws, were to move into an area of town designated as a ghetto. There wasn't much notice given. In a matter of days we had to vacate our home. Each person was allowed to take—I no longer remember exactly—a certain amount of personal effects. It was some ridiculously low amount, perhaps twenty kilograms. No other items, jewelry, gold, works of art, bankbooks, securities, furs, fine porcelain, rugs, radios, phonographs, cars, motorcycles or bicycles, anything of value were allowed to be taken. All holdings in one's home were to be taken out of cupboards, wardrobes, closets, trunks, and other storage, laid out on tables and floors, inventoried, and left behind. We went about complying with the order. When the inspectors came to our house, my father showed them his medals and explained that the missing document had been requested and should be received any time. But it never came. Somebody sat on it no doubt, suppressing it. I totally disregarded the orders. First, I gave all my photographic equipment and lots of my tools to Jocó, then I methodically made numerous runs on my bicycle between our house and my grandmother's house on Bástya Street. As her house was located in the designated ghetto area, that is where the whole family was going to stay, crowded but in relative comfort, as opposed to some of the other houses where two, three families were crowded into single rooms. On some of these runs I had a five-, perhaps a six-foot-long stovepipe under my arm. The stovepipe was stuffed with winter and summer clothes, as well as anything else I thought of having practical value that would fit inside it. There were right-angle elbows at each end so one could not see into the pipe and whatever I had inside it couldn't fall out. Though by this time I had a large yellow Star of David on my clothes, nobody ever stopped me as I whizzed through the streets of Pápa on my bike. My Uncle Miklós, who was a war hero and whose papers were in order, his wife, and his young son were exempt from wearing the star, as well as from moving to the ghetto. The designated ghetto area was to be sealed off by a twelve-foot-high wooden fence, which was to be erected at designated points, separating the ghetto from the rest of the city. A labor force was put together to build these fences and gates. I was one of this group. A recent history book of Pápa paid lip service to this event in the short paragraph reprinted here.

Translation: "Beginning with the end of the 1930s, the new Jewish laws significantly restricted the rights of the Jewish population of Pápa. In April of 1944, Endre László, Minister of Interior, in his directive to the mayors and regional leaders, ordered the registration of Jews per street address. On the eleventh of April 1944, a new directive by Endre László, amongst other things, forbade the lard and sugar rations to Jews. Their telephones were to be disconnected, radios confiscated, stores closed, and personal possessions put under lock. The wearing of the yellow star was mandatory. Freibert Lajos [possibly a onetime partner of my father], Director of the Bacon & Meat Company, Steiner József, owner of the brickworks, Gutz Emil and Patkay Lajos, lawyers, were interned. In May of 1944, Rókócy, Eötvös, Petőfi, Saint László Streets, self-including portion of the city, including Bástya Street, were designated as the ghetto. Thirteen and a half hectares of the self-enclosed ghetto were surrounded by a two-meter-high wooden wall. Dr. Körös Endre and his wife, the retired head of the Reformed Church Women Students' Institute, Korein György, and, further, Dr. Glück Sándor, gynecologist, and his wife committed suicide before they would have been taken to the ghetto. In all, 3,600 people were locked in, amongst them nine hundred from the Devecser and Zirc districts."

Once the fences and gates were up and everybody moved into the ghetto, the gates were guarded by the gendarmerie and the police. People had to ask for permission to go outside these fences, indicating the reason and designating the time needed outside the fence. My father totally defied this order and every day regularly went through the gate, walked around town, went to the post office, and came back with as many newspapers as he could buy. Radios and telephones were forbidden, and these newspapers were our only contact with the outside world. The news, we knew, was slanted, inaccurate and untrue, and usually weeks behind, by which time they could no longer be denied. We could estimate where the front lines really were, having learned how long it took the Hungarian papers to admit bad news. In other words, if the newspapers claimed that in a certain section of the front lines "a strategic withdrawal" or "a consolidation of the forces" has taken place, we surmised that, in fact, that event has taken place at least two to three weeks before it was reported, without the German Army being able to reverse the situation. Consequently, any defeat which was reported was final and we could assume that further defeats were in progress to be reported weeks later.

While at Bástya Street, I built a secret compartment into the attic of one of the outbuildings. It had a trapdoor installed amongst the beams of the ceiling, which could not be seen but could be triggered to open from the opposite end of the building by pulling on one of a number of hooks in a beam. Unfortunately, I couldn't completely finish the final touches to the triggering mechanism. The tragedy was that we had precious little to put into this hiding place. Most of our beautiful things were left at our house, though I managed to give some linens and tablecloths to Joco's parents. My mother also gave some hardly ever used damask tablecloths to one of our neighbors, an elderly retired judge and his wife. Without my parents knowing about it, these neighbors permitted me to bury a few items in their garden, which was a criminal offense under the new laws. I still have some of these items. One is a silver cigarette case with my father's initials *LL* engraved on it, and a small, gold Schauffhausen wristwatch, which belonged to my mother. I sealed these items in an empty cookie tin that I soldered shut. Unfortunately, the can rusted through. The silver cigarette case could be cleaned up, but the delicate workings of the gold watch I think are beyond repair. Somehow, I have no desire to have it repaired or reconditioned. In its present shape it reminds me of my mother and those terrible times.

Our situation infuriated me. I was still stupid enough to think that I could do something about it, which is what led to my second incredibly stupid act only weeks after the car-burning incident. Sometime after we had to vacate our home, I went back into our house without telling anybody and, defying the directives, destroyed most of our Meissen, Dresden, and Herend china, lead crystal bowls and vases, all sorts of other items of value and beauty. Some of these items were laid out on the floor. I walked over them, kicking and trampling and smashing them. I used a silver candelabra as a club, destroying it as well as I smashed the china and glassware on the floor and on the large dining room table with it. I destroyed some silver bowls and a silver fruit plate on a pedestal of a female figure. In a matter of minutes I destroyed a small fortune in beautiful art, accumulated over several lifetimes. I knew or suspected that our things would probably be picked over by some no-account son of a bitch, higher- and lower-level party functionaries and their friends. We had a large, white marble statue of Venus on a pedestal. The last thing I did before leaving our home for the last time was to push this statue and its pedestal over, smashing it into the glass and carved wood display cabinet, vitrine, as we called it, which used to hold delicate Meissen figurines, silver, and my father's and my medals. The case, glass, and wood were smashed and splintered, totally destroyed. As long as we weren't going to have it, I saw to it that no one else would. I never stopped to consider what would have happened if this was discovered. Somehow, I thought that if I told my father, he probably would have scolded me for breaking the law while silently approving of what I'd done. Actually, by this time I was sure that his past patriotic sentiments were no more. In fact, I was certain that his former devotion to our country was completely gone. In view of all that happened to and around us, this was only understandable.

* * *

Living at Bástya Street was no fun. Even though the house was occupied by only our family, it was a large group. Besides us four, it was my elderly grandmother, my crippled Aunt Józsa, her son Imre, daughter Klári, her husband József, and their little daughter Ágnes. Ten people crowded into an old house, parts of which might have been a couple of hundred years old. We had one outhouse-type toilet built into the house at the end of a long, covered walkway alongside the house. We also had one flush toilet, one bathroom, and one kitchen. What made living under these conditions very difficult was that all of us spent all our time in the house or in the yard. Everybody was very conscious of our situation and overly careful to be considerate, not to disturb or aggravate anybody else in the house. We could no longer buy firewood and therefore heating water for bathing had to be carefully rationed. Wood was to be preserved for cooking and next winter, which never came.

Sometime before we were to move out of our home, Fáni was forced to leave us, as Jews were no longer permitted to have domestic servants. After some twenty years of being with us, becoming one of the family, she went back to her village and her family amidst tears and disappeared without a trace during the following year. Mári's case in Celldömölk was even more heartbreaking. Having spent her life with my grandmother, she didn't want to leave. She had no other home, no family, not even friends. As I put it together on the basis of information received from some local people in Celldömölk after the war, some idiot told Mári, perhaps as a demeaning

141

joke, that she could stay with my grandmother if she sewed a Star of David on her clothes. Being the simple trusting person she was, she did sew a Star of David on and was hauled away for mocking the law. She must have died shortly after, perhaps of a broken heart. Beyond the Star of David story, I haven't been able to find out anything else about what happened to her.

Otherwise, the old house at Bástya Street was relatively comfortable. Because it had thick stone and brick walls, it was cool during the usually hot and humid early summer months. But day by day, without adequate sanitation the stench created by all the people crammed into the relatively small area of the ghetto grew worse. There was no garbage collection or street cleaning. Overstressed cesspools flooded, and on hot days the stench was sickening. Yet every day, when my father came in with the newspapers, we talked ourselves into believing that this was to be a short-lived situation as Germany was just about defeated and the war was almost over. In fact, for Hungary the war was over. The Russians were advancing slowly but steadily towards and into Hungary. Horty's declaration of cease-fire didn't work. The Germans occupied the country and the Hungarian Nazi government, which took control, continued on an overzealous, reckless, irrevocable alliance with Germany. Hungarian troops were still fighting alongside the Germans in spite of the fact that some areas of the country these soldiers were from were already under Russian occupation.

Almost all the young Jewish men were conscripted into labor service. The morning my brother's age group was formed up on the main street of the ghetto, my father and I went with him. It was early morning as his group was marched out of the ghetto through one of the gates I helped build. Without asking anybody's permission, my father walked out of the ghetto to go along with my brother's group to the railroad station. I don't remember the exact date—the days had a way of flowing together in the ghetto— but it had to be in May or April. One of the most demoralizing aspects of living in that house through this period was the silence. Nobody talked. Everybody walked around the house or in the garden without words like zombies. Every now and then somebody would ask a question or make a statement, more to break the silence than really wanting to get a response. In fact, I knew that when I would answer any of these questions, in some cases my answer wouldn't be heard. After my father would return with the papers, there would be a very short, at times overly optimistic discussion about the way the war was going, what the Americans were doing, and guessing about how long it would be before the Germans were defeated. It was life, more accurately an existence expecting the worse but hoping against hope for a miracle. Every now and then my mother hugged and kissed me, quietly without words, and smiled or forced a smile in quiet resignation. My parents knew or suspected a lot more than they let on.

On the afternoon of June 6, my father burst through the massive wooden gates of the house with an armful of papers that headlined the invasion in Normandy. He was very excited and sounded optimistic as he read us the account of the invasion. Of course the Germans claimed that the invasion forces were contained on the beach and the papers predicted that the American and British would be thrown back into the channel before nightfall. The headlines about Hitler's miracle weapons and how they were going to turn the war into Germany's favor again were larger than ever. My father read us the articles of the invasion over and over again and explained the significance of this momentous event, which in his opinion signaled the rapid defeat of Germany and the end of the war. It was the light at the end of the tunnel, which, to use a cliche, did turn out to be an oncoming freight train.

After that day the ghetto was sealed off and the only papers we could get were usually days old, brought in by the police who extorted large amounts of money for them.

* * *

Then it was my turn. The ghetto office announced that men of my age group were to report for labor service. As in the case of my brother leaving, it was painful to see the anguish this caused to my family and I wanted to get it over with quickly. I packed my backpack and strapped on a blanket my father gave me. It was a rough, hand-loomed Romanian virgin wool blanket, but he told me that, being virgin wool, it was water-repellent and very warm. He bought this blanket during World War I and in a way I felt badly about taking it from him. I strapped my hunting knife, an antler-handled Bowie-type knife, which I wore on my belt during our outings in better days, into its compartment in my backpack. Nobody slept that night in our room. I could hear my parents talk in hushed tones but couldn't make out what they were saying. I finally fell asleep to be awakened by my father telling me it was time to get up. I dressed and one by one said goodbye to everybody in the house. It was dark and quiet in the rooms. My grandmother in her bathrobe with her long, gray hair down said goodbye to me. Józsa néni was half sitting up in her bed—she couldn't lie flat—as she said goodbye. When my mother hugged me and I felt the warmth of her bosom, I felt like saying something comforting, but I couldn't. She didn't talk either. Her face was twisted in agony, her lips clenched together in what seemed a grotesque smile of love, saying goodbye forever.

My father and I walked to the main street of the ghetto, which by then had a large group of young men. I knew most of them though not very well, as in previous years we didn't have extensive contact. The gendarmes, bayonets fixed to their rifles, were everywhere. In a short time the group was formed up. My father put on a brave face and told me that if all other avenues failed, Uncle Miklós was to be our center of communication. He told me to keep in touch as much as I could and to write my brother regularly. The group was marched out of the ghetto towards the railroad station at the far end of Eszterházy Street. Passing the house of my early childhood brought back fleeting memories of good times. My father walked alongside our group, the only person on the streets in the early morning. His military footsteps and his cane beat a tattoo on the pavement expressing his futile defiance. As erect as he was, his forced brave face was ashen, stricken, and unable to hide his grief. A young man's sensitivities and perception combined with a lack of thorough understanding of the situation didn't permit me to fully evaluate and appreciate the situation. Or perhaps it was a built-in defense mechanism, which falsified the true situation and shrouded it into acceptable levels. My deceptive brain might have been saying, "Tell him not to grieve, I'll be all right. These terrible times will soon be over and everything will be fine." Of course I couldn't talk to him, in fact couldn't understand how my father could have just walked out of the ghetto, defying strict orders and a whole detachment of the gendarmerie. I wondered if later on he might have been punished for his defiance.

There was an empty train of boxcars waiting for us on one of the sidings not too far from the bridge where as a child I used to stand in the steam and smoke as the trains rolled under me. The cars were very familiar to me. They were the same boxcars in which our cattle used to arrive in better days, a far cry from the plush, velvet upholstered first-class compartments we used to travel in, which now seemed ages ago. My father came over to me and patted me on my shoulder. "Shave every day," he said. Though I didn't understand why he wanted me to shave every day—I hardly ever shaved until then—I nodded as I was pushed aboard the train. The doors of the boxcars were slid shut and shortly after the train pulled out of the station. Through the high window I could see him standing erect, his homburg on straight, his walking stick held like a sword. He stood there as I lost sight of him and the train chugged on to an unknown destination.

# Chapter 10

# 1944 – JUNE | JULY | AUGUST "THINK OF US OFTEN..."

There was hardly enough room in the small boxcar to stand, let alone sit or lie down. One young fellow I knew from school, Kardos Dénes, was in the car with me. He was one, perhaps two years older than I, so until this time we weren't close friends, though we knew each other. His father was a prominent lawyer in town, also a decorated officer of WWI, and a wounded veteran. He also was to be exempt from the Jewish laws because of his military service, but as Dénes told me then, about a week before the Jewish population was to go into the ghetto his father was arrested, taken away, and they weren't able to find out what had happened to him. It was suspected, as in so many other cases, that some party functionary or police official arrested people on trumped-up charges in hopes of extorting large amounts of money or valuables. As mentioned in the excerpt from the history book, most of the wealthiest members of the Jewish community of Pápa were taken away and disappeared at about the same time.

The train sat on sidings for long time periods at just about every station en route. We spent the night in the boxcars, Dénes and I huddled in a corner of the car, trying to catch a few snatches of sleep, which was impossible. A few seconds after my eyes would close, someone would lean, step, or fall on me in the dark. The boxcar lurched, squealed, making all kinds of noises, and some—asleep on their feet—would lose their balance and fall. The worse thing was that I couldn't stretch my legs. They were pulled up to my chin all night long, totally numb by the time I tried to stand up. During the night, as the train was standing in a station, we heard one of the neighboring car's door being slid open. One of the young fellows was taken out of the car and brutally beaten by the gendarmes. We heard his agonized screams for some time, then it abruptly stopped. He must have passed out or passed away, and I never found out exactly why he was beaten. Some said he was hiding a knife, which turned out to be untrue. I think he was beaten and

tortured for the sheer pleasure of the gendarmes. By the time morning came we were in pretty bad shape, but at that age—I was seventeen and a half—one recovers fast. The train stopped in the early morning and sat for some time on a siding before the locked doors of the boxcars were pushed open by the gendarmes and we were told to get out. We were at the railroad station of the town Kőszeg, meaning "Stone Nail," which I knew had a large military installation. The gendarmerie turned us over to the military and we marched to the barracks, a short distance from the railroad station. We stood for hours in a parade ground–sized square surrounded by large buildings.
It was a hot and humid June day, and some in our group fainted. It almost seemed like nobody knew what to do with us. Finally, around noon we were lined up in front of a row of tables where soldiers recorded our names. From there we went to get our hair cut bald, which reminded me of my summer haircut long ago. There was no end to the snide, derogatory remarks by young soldiers, who were obviously trying to outdo one another being nasty, enjoying our humiliation and discomfort and their own superiority. We were issued the only items of uniform: a standard military cap, a wide yellow armband, and two pairs of kapca. My cap was a bit too big, but I thought that would be all right, as I expected my hair to grow back and make it fit right. Unlike some of the caps given to others, mine was brand new and had flaps that could be pulled down over one's ears in cold weather. Ironically, I thought it was handsome. The yellow armband was to be worn at all times on the left sleeve of the outer garment, replacing the star. Let me explain the two pairs of kapca. In the Hungarian military service, the lower ranks would not be issued socks. The Hungarian military could not afford them, nor would they have been appreciated by the recruits, most of whom never wore or had socks in their entire life. Kapca were two more or less identical-sized square pieces of cloth, which was to be folded over one's foot and worn instead of socks. One pair I was given was cotton, the other flannel for cold weather. I almost laughed when I took mine. I had enough fine woolen socks, hand knit by my mother, for a whole squad.

Then it was lunchtime. We lined up before a couple of large vats brought out from one of the buildings as soldiers dispensed noodles, with some greenish-yellowish goo poured over it. I didn't know what it was but was hungry, and I always liked noodles. It was a pleasant experience to taste it. The noodles were good and the green sauce had a wonderful, sweet new taste. When I went back for seconds I was told it was soybean sauce and surprisingly was given an equal portion to the first one. But the day dragged on, as we stood around with nothing to do. I couldn't get my father's image out of my mind and wondered why he told me to shave every day at a time when we might have been saying goodbye to each other for the last time. I thought there was a message in there somewhere, but the more I thought about it the more difficult it became for me to try to figure it out. Some time later I did figure it out, but more about that later.

My mother's contorted, grief-stricken face in the subdued early morning light kept coming back to me. At that moment, as I was walking around aimlessly under a large, old acacia tree, her whole sweet being came to bear on me. There was a buzzing in my ear, which grew louder to an almost unbearable pitch and intensity. I knew I was on the verge of a breakdown. I finally realized that if I allowed this to take over, I would surely lose my mind. My father's image, marching erect alongside our group the day before, was almost like a slap in the face, which brought me back to reality. It made me snap out of my state. The high-pitched whistle in my ear stopped and I knew that I had hurdled my first test. It gave me tremendous strength, though I suspected that I would never see my parents again.

* * *

That night we slept under the arched corridors, open on one side to the square. The Romanian blanket was surprisingly comfortable. I shared it with Kardos Dénes, who only had a thin, lightweight blanket. The next morning we were formed up and stood again for hours as more and more groups of young people were arriving. Then we were organized into smaller units, and one by one these small groups were marched out of the barracks. My group marched through town through some fields to what looked like an abandoned farm. There were some stables and barns in very bad repair. It was to be, we were told, our home during our training. The first task was to clean out one of the old barns, our new quarters, and make it livable. There was a stack of hay outside the buildings, which we used as our bedding. Over the next period of time, I don't remember how long, we were taught all sorts of "useful" things such as how to form up, march, carry a shovel, salute, and so on. Obviously I'm being sarcastic. Military formations, marching in step, left turns, right turns, about-face were not new to me. The training I received in Mr. Kovács's class qualified me more than the training I was receiving from a young private whom we had to address as Oktató ur, or "Instructor sir." One of these fellows wasn't a bad sort. He had some education, and after a while we became pretty friendly. But others were the scum of the earth. I won't describe the misery, anguish, and hardships they caused, which turned out to be relatively insignificant in view of what was to come and therefore not very important. What was important was that I was young, in superb physical shape, with an iron determination that nobody was going to get the better of me no matter what. To some extent, I enjoyed the physical aspect of the training. It was like an athletic contest and gave me an almost perverse satisfaction to outrun, outdo the "instructors." It was, I suppose, a way of saying to them and to myself, "I'm the better one."

Digging and filling in trenches we just dug was the full extent of our training. I wrote and sent postcards home to my parents, to my brother and my Uncle Miklós. I assured everybody that I was all right, which was true, and that under the circumstances I was enjoying myself, which was not. But I thought this would help relieve some of their anxieties. I also thought that my father would be pleased with me. I brought with me a small stack of penny postcards with the stamps printed on them. Our so-called training didn't last long. It was obvious that the military didn't know what to train us for or what to do with us. Perhaps there was something to the rumors that the government was trying to save us from the Germans.

* * *

I received my first news from home. Over the next two months I received several letters from my parents, from my brother, and from Uncle Miklós and his wife. I don't know how, but I held onto these letters throughout the war, and I still have them today after more than fifty years. Rereading them now while working on this account made me choke up and filled my heart with sadness as the voices, which have been silent for so long, reverberated again, recalling the events and situations, making me relive that terrible part of my past so long ago. I translated these letters and postcards, trying hard to stay as close to the original Hungarian language and meaning as I am able to with my remaining, limited command of the Hungarian language. Due to the intricacies of the Hungarian language, the translations are at times verbatim while at other times only a loose meaning is achieved. To facilitate the continuity of the story, I won't present all the cards and letters here. They are grouped by date at the end of this book, originals and their translations, and I hope you'll read them. For now, I will quote some of the significant portions from them.

The first correspondence I received from home was a postcard from my mother (Postcard #1). It was her usual sweet, uncomplaining, loving account, but her underlying fear of the future was obvious. In the first sentence she said, "We still don't know anything..." meaning that they were expecting bad news. The reference to the work I couldn't finish, which she thought Klári, my cousin, couldn't finish was the secret compartment I built into the attic but didn't have time to complete. She finished the card, "Think of us often." When I read that it tore at my heart, and I thought I might not hear from her ever again.

But the second postcard (Postcard #2) just two days later was also from her. In it she tells me about a suit which was to be made for me, but the tailor couldn't finish it. This was a bit of a loss for me, as I loved the wool fabric. I picked it out myself months before, purchased it with my own money, but didn't rush having it made as winter was far away. Under my situation then, I would have liked to have the warm suit.

The third card (Postcard #3) dated the same day, June 23, 1944, was from my father. I don't know what the position was that he refers to, but I suspect it had something to do with a leadership position within the ghetto community. His handwriting is difficult to read, particularly now after more than fifty years, as the Hungarian words and their meanings have faded, as did the cards. True to his form, he admonished me to be careful with my clothes, food, and money. He explained that he knew this would be so by my own volition, but he said, "It comforts me to be able to give you advice." On the basis of all the rumors, the bad news we have been hearing, I interpreted this as saying that he didn't know how much longer he might be able to give me advice. He finished his card, "Continue behaving in a manly manner, as until now." Another long letter came within days (Letter #1) from my mother, in a package with some meager foodstuff. I remember wishing she hadn't sent the food as I was actually well fed and I thought that they might have done without some of the things they sent me. Her letter was upsetting. It was less cryptic than the previous cards, talking about but not describing the bad things that were happening as their situation was steadily deteriorating. Such statements as "A lot has happened since you went away," or "Do not upset yourself over us, the good God will help us," or "I know that you are our true good children and even if we won't be with you, you will behave as if we could see you, and this knowledge will give us strength for all eventualities!" Her last sentence—"The good God be with you, my little son, and think of us always"—in fact, the entire letter sounded like she expected it to be the last.

As it turned out, it was her last letter, but I received one more postcard (Postcard #4) from my mother. Her first sentence came like a bolt of lightning. "I write quickly as we are packing and getting ready for a trip, I don't know where." The next short sentence confirmed the worse possible news. "We are at peace with our fate, my son." She told me to communicate with Uncle Miklós, who, being exempt from the Jewish laws, remained in Pápa. She told me to maintain contact with my brother, Sándor, to keep my things in good order, not allowing them to become disorganized. The last sentence devastated me. "God be with you, my little son, our blessings will follow both of you. With our love forever, your parents." I knew this was the last I would hear from her. I felt devastated and guilty for not being able to do anything about it. But there wasn't anything I could have done. All of us expected this to happen, but none of us really wanted to believe that it ever would.

The hastily scribbled postscript baffled me. "Since Thursday, we are at the fertilizer factory." I didn't know they were not in my grandmother's house in the ghetto. I didn't even know where the fertilizer factory was or how they got there, and why.

A postcard from Uncle Miklós (Postcard #5) dated the same day, July 2, 1944, confirmed the worst. In it he says, "The parents of Horkay András left on a trip today without future address with the entire family. Horkay's letter did not get to them." Horkay András, you might recall, was the nickname my friends gave me in school. Knowing that my letters were censored by the military, this was his way of telling me that my parents and my entire family were taken away amongst some 3,600-some-odd other people from Pápa.

Just last year I got hold of a recently published history book of Pápa, from which I had quoted in chapter nine. It gave the following brief account of this event:

> On June 29, 1944, the people were herded from the ghetto to the Fertilizer Factory. At dawn, on July 4,* they were jammed into boxcars and taken to Budapest, then Kassa. They arrived in Auschwitz on July 13. Only three hundred returned.

How did my elderly grandmother walk to the fertilizer factory miles away? How did my Aunt Józsa, who was crippled most of her life, get to the fertilizer factory? How did my mother, an overweight person, walk to the factory? Why and how did they live in a fertilizer factory? The questions were tearing me apart, but there were no answers until about a year later.

Even if the date of July 4, 1944, as quoted in the history book, is correct, being jammed into the boxcars for nine (but most likely eleven) days in the scorching heat of the summer, without food, water, or sanitation, would have most certainly killed a very large number of the people in the cars, whose decomposing bodies would not have been removed until arrival in Auschwitz.

\* \* \*

I don't have to tell you about my mental state at that time. Fortunately, my company was moving to a new billet. Preparing for and taking the trip mercifully took some of the pressure off my heart and mind. Once again I found myself traveling in a boxcar, which at this time was not as jammed as it was during my trip to Kőszeg. There were forty of us in the car, the designated number of troops per car by the Hungarian Army. Of course even forty is a large number in a relatively small car, and we were very uncomfortable. But we had our doors open most of the time.

---

* The date in this history book, I believe, is wrong. The postcards received from my mother and Uncle Miklós both put the departure date at July 2. They were both postmarked July 2, 1944. Of course, it is possible that they were locked into the boxcars on the second, but the train didn't leave until the fourth.

We had food and water, and most importantly most of us were young and strong. For some reason, I haven't been able to figure out why, the car doors were closed and locked at certain stations. Perhaps it was more convenient for the cadre than having to watch us, so we couldn't get off and wander away from the train. At almost every station where the train stopped, somebody in the train from that part of the country would throw out or give someone a message, asking them to deliver it to a relative or friend in town. I sent such a message at one of these stations to a classmate of mine, who I knew lived in that town. He came to the station shortly with a brown bag full of hastily assembled foodstuff and a couple of bottles of half-finished wine. His name is Csonka József. He still lives in Hungary—and as an interesting footnote, years later, under the Communist regime, he also found himself in a boxcar amongst others on their way to Siberia. Fortunately for him, his train was turned around and he was allowed to return home.

Some days later our train arrived in a small town, Zsibó, in what is Western Romania today. Zsibó was to be my home for the next couple of months. We were billeted some distance from town in another abandoned barn. Once again the first order of the day was to clean out the barn and under the circumstances make it as livable as was possible. There were some more permanent buildings around—the remainder of a onetime farm— which were cleaned out and turned into quarters for our commanding officer, a first lieutenant, his second, a second lieutenant, a sergeant, and assorted other cadre of about six soldiers. Our commanding officer was a very decent man. He was an elderly schoolteacher who didn't much enjoy his assignment.

The barn obviously had no hygienic facilities. There was a small stream nearby with enough clean water for washing up and doing laundry, but the water had to be boiled for cooking. It was I who came up with the idea to put a narrow footbridge some distance away and downstream from the barn over the stream with a heavy log alongside and a little above this footbridge. The log served as a latrine seat over the stream, big enough for ten, even more of us to use at the same time as a community facility. The stream continually carried away most of the excrement and was completely flushed out on rainy days. It was a much better arrangement than the usual stinking slit trenches would have been.

I also found myself in a most envied position. Our unit was issued a number of bicycles commandeered by the military from somewhere, all of them in very bad repair. At one of the early formations shortly after getting to Zsibó, we were asked if any of us could repair bicycles. I said I could. When I was asked what kinds of tools I would need, I said that I had the tools, which I believe clinched the job for me. I then said that I would need someone to help me and recommended my friend Kardos Dénes.

The first day, as my unit marched off with picks and shovels on shoulders to some work site, Dénes and I reported to one of the old buildings where we were to set up my bike repair operation. For the next couple of weeks I was fixing bicycles. True, some of them didn't really need much fixing, but we fixed them anyhow. The ones that did need work were fixed well, much to the amazement of our CO as well as my own. Unfortunately this good duty didn't last very long. The CO went home on furlough and his second-in-command took over command of the company. He turned out to be a first-class son of a bitch. One of his first official acts was to discontinue the bike repair. By this time all the bikes were in as good a shape as I could make them, and truly there was no need for day in, day out bike maintenance.

The following morning Dénes and I, shovels and picks on shoulders, marched out with the rest of our unit. In a way, this was a good thing. We were building railroad tracks, extremely hard work in the summer heat, but over the next few weeks I became very strong. I approached the work as athletic training. If there was something heavy to lift, I would lift it. If there were rocks to shovel, rails to carry, heavily loaded carts to push, I wanted to outdo all others. Our food was good and plentiful, and I ate like a horse and put on weight, all muscle. I actually liked the work, which incidentally I also found interesting. Laying out the course for the rails, building and preparing the beds, laying the ties, spiking the rails, and underpacking the ties were to me all interesting work. I particularly liked underpacking the ties. It was done by a four-man team, two guys at each end of the tie. All of us had special pickaxes, the broad ends of which had heads like hammers. That was the business end. One of the guys would start a chant and a rhythm going. The verse I liked most started with the words "Kutya fasza, kutya fasza," meaning "A dog's pecker, a dog's pecker." He would tap the beat with his pick on the rail, and at a certain time in the rhythm he would strike the rocks under the tie. The guy diagonal to him at the other end of the tie would strike next, then his partner, then the other fellow at the other end, bringing the sequence back to the starter. As long as the rhythm was maintained, the picks would hammer away at the rocks like a machine to the cadence of the chant. As we became good at maintaining the rhythm, we learned to jump to the next tie to be packed without losing the rhythm and stopping. It was fun. It was almost like skating to music, but it was nevertheless hard, backbreaking work.

I was in a good frame of mind in spite of the terrible news or the lack of any good news. My mother's Big Book in Heaven philosophy was the greatest help. Things were the way they were ordained, and there was nothing I or anyone could do but try to make the best of it. I did hope for the best, as all of us did. No one did—nor would accept—the worst. None of us had any idea about what actually happened to our families and to all the other people, but all of us hoped that one day this terrible situation would be over and we would be reunited as life returned to normal. There were lots of horrible rumors about camps, but even the worst of these didn't come close to the truth as I later found out. At that time all of us lived on hope from one day to the next, believing that our parents, our families, were alive somewhere. Though we did manage to keep somewhat abreast of the news, we'd not heard of Auschwitz. Most of us corresponded with someone and even though no one could write hard news, as all our mail was censored, at times it was possible to get some sort of message by reading between the lines. Some weeks later one of the fellows got hold of a radio which someone in the unit fixed with my tools, and most nights we were able to listen to the BBC. This was a very dangerous enterprise. Very elaborate security was designed to tip us off if someone from the cadre was approaching. In such a case, though it never happened, we had a procedure to quickly dismantle the antenna, a long copper wire, and hide the radio in the back beams of the old barn. Only two could listen at any one time. We had a pair of headphones which were separated for two people who, after the newscast, passed on the news. At times some of us could buy an old paper from one of the cadre or from some local people. But listening to the BBC offered the most hope. We knew that the Russians were getting very close, though not fast enough for us. Dénes, a few others in our group, and I had a plan according to which we would escape the moment we spotted Russian troops and join up with them. We were convinced that the Russians were fully aware of our situation and were all prepared and anxious to help us. Under our circumstances, it never occurred to us to think otherwise.

\* \* \*

Throughout this time I was in communication with my brother, Sándor, some of my other relatives in Budapest, Jocó, and most importantly with Aunt Alice, Uncle Miklós's wife. In a postcard (Postcard #6) Aunt Alice informed me, "Unfortunately there is no news of the others [my parents, family, all from the ghetto] since they left." She also wrote that Uncle Miklós was operated on again but was all right. Uncle Miklós, as I mentioned earlier, was a wounded veteran of WWI. The injury to his right leg never healed right and he underwent one operation after another continuously since World War I. He was constantly in pain, as his leg was literally cut off piece by piece. Aunt Alice also mentioned in her letter that my friend Jocó was going to take a trip to the area I was in. I was also in touch with Jocó, who communicated with me through Aunt Alice. That was the way we designed it to keep in touch with one another in order not to possibly involve him in something that could have been bad for him. Needless to say, I was delighted over the prospect of Jocó's visit.

A postcard from my brother (Postcard #7) also dated July 24 came at the same time. At times cards and letters were delivered promptly, at other times weeks would go by for a card to arrive. This was due to the military or the postal service mishandling the mail or delaying it on purpose. The rapidly deteriorating situation in Hungary such as the bad rail service didn't help. These two pieces of correspondence, both received at Zsibó, indicate that I must have arrived at Zsibó some time before the date on these cards but after the first week in July, when I received my father's last card at Kőszeg.

My brother had no news of our parents either. He also heard the rumors that they were somewhere near Kassa, which may have stemmed from the fact that their train did go through Kassa and someone might have seen the train there. He also confirmed the possibility of Jocó's visit; in fact, he mentioned that he was sending a photograph to Jocó. I never found out anything further about this photograph.

\* \* \*

I'm reasonably certain now, though I didn't think of it then, that my mother, grandmother, and Aunt Józsa must have all been dead by this time. If they did not perish in the train during that cruel, terrible trip, they were surely murdered on arrival at Auschwitz.

\* \* \*

Receiving letters was a most wonderful experience. It really didn't matter so much what the letter said, as long as one knew that the sender was alive and in a position to write and send letters. By this time I was only receiving letters from Sándor and Aunt Alice. The relatives in Budapest fell silent. I was never able to figure out why, particularly as I found Uncle Matthew, his wife, Margit, and their son, Gyuri, alive and well in Budapest after the war. My mother's sister Manci and her husband also stopped writing.

\* \* \*

I would recognize my brother's writing from a distance even before his letter was handed to me. Reading it almost became secondary. Just knowing that he was alive to write was a tremendous relief. It was now August and by this time I, as most in my unit, had just about given up hope of any good news of our families. Aunt Alice's next card (Postcard #8) confirmed my fears. It said, "Unfortunately there is no news of Laci [my father] and the others, as they are definitely not at the previously indicated place." Another sentence told me about her relatives, the Darvases in Budapest, who, in Aunt Alice's words, "suffered the same fate as those in Pápa." In about a week I got a card from Sándor (Postcard #9). He must have suffered tremendous anxiety. "If you have any true news, write immediately." Unfortunately I had no news at all. He indicated that I would be receiving a letter from Horkay Sanyi. He adopted the Horkay name with his given name attached and used it as a third person to circumvent the censors. That is to say, as there was no such person as Horkay Sanyi, he could tell me more than he could have over his own name. The good news was that he was able to get away from his billet to mail the letter. He was in a so-called air raid unit. I suppose they stood by to help clean up after an air raid, which until this time fortunately didn't happen in Szombathely, the town where he was.

\* \* \*

The day-to-day existence in my unit became routine. Reveille was at five, and by seven we were hard at work building railroad tracks. We had

Sundays off. It was a day to write letters—if there was anybody to write to—do laundry, get a haircut, repair our clothes and equipment. Some Sunday evenings a few of us would walk to a little nearby village and buy bread from some local people. There was also a sunflower seed mill at the edge of town, which at this time of the year was going seven days a week pressing sunflower seed for oil. We would buy a couple of bottles of hot, freshly pressed sunflower oil and eat it on the fresh-baked bread. It was delicious.

It was also interesting that our daily lives, our routines, gave very little indication of one's grief. I don't know exactly what to attribute this to. Perhaps the human brain has some sort of defense mechanism built in which kicks in as it is needed to dull one's senses and pain. It is also possible that under certain circumstances, one accepts things which, under normal conditions, would be very hard to deal with. Further, I believe that a young person is not as emotional as older people can be. Besides, though we all suspected, there was no proof, no indication, that our parents were not alive. We had hope and we clung to it desperately. Those who buckled, though very few in my unit did, suffered awfully. In most cases they lost their mind and never recovered.

I did not buckle. I was naturally very strongly affected, but the worse the situation became, the more of an effort I made to fight it. Strangely, I was beginning to understand why my father wanted me to shave every day. I followed his instruction and it made me feel good. It made me feel that in spite of all, I was in control of myself, and every time I shaved I thought of him. I kept my clothes, my equipment, all my belongings in as good a shape as was possible under the circumstances. Dénes and I still shared my Romanian blanket while we slept next to each other, his blanket covering some straw underneath us. The friendship with Dénes became very strong. Other friendships formed also; mostly groups of people from similar backgrounds or common places of origin grouped together. I wrote a poem about this sometime during this period. Along with my postcards and letters, I held onto it till today. It is written in Hungarian of course, but just last week I translated it. I made two translations. The first attempted to translate the poem into English verbatim, staying as close to its original meaning as possible. But the Hungarian language is almost impossible to translate verbatim with its idioms, flowery phrases, and innuendos. The process becomes more complicated as one attempts to translate a poem, which is not great to start with, after a half a century without full command of the Hungarian language. Consequently, what came out of my effort is neither a poem nor a good account of our lives or circumstances at Zsibó.

The second attempt, trying to resurrect it as an English poem, fared a little better. It describes some of the people in my unit while attempting to maintain their character traits as closely as possible to the intents of the original poem.

*Zsibó, late summer, 1944*

MY FRIENDS

It came to my mind, once during hard labor,
to list my comrades in verse, neighbor to neighbor.
And now, it being Sunday with free time on my hand,
I start this foolish thing, hoping to reach the end.

The things I'll write about them, if they'll ever find out,
some of them, rightfully might punch me in my mouth.
Describing who sleeps where, slowly will I start,
let them think my poem is nothing, but pure art.

Kohn Gyula, mountain man, known also as "the peasant"
sleeping next to him is said to be unpleasant.
Meat cutter and butcher, he is by profession,
he emerged as leader of his friends from Bakony.

Here sleeps Klein Pista, also from Bakony,
his voice can be heard, in the evening mostly.
Fighting with his neighbors he keeps everyone up,
till a voice from the dark pleads, "Won't you shut the xxxx up."

Followed by Walthauser, midget by his physique,
I've heard bad tongues say though I do not believe,
at one time as a babe, he was thought to be dead
when his nurse carelessly dropped him on his head.

Weltener trudges in line, like the tong of a bell,
when it comes to food though, his fate does go quite well.
His uncle is chief cook in our unit's kitchen
he gets double rations as portions are given.

Révész Laci comes next, also known as "Brain Plus"
he knows more by himself than any twenty of us.
Speaks languages, six or maybe even seven,
doubles up on dinner, once head count is given.

Meyer Nándor sleeps here, at this end of the place,
when locating food stuff, he's the leading ace.
Who knows where he gets it I ask, please do not dread,
when he asks, on return, "You want dark, or white bread?"

I have to skip a space here, do not think me as terse,
but it would be me who'd follow in verse.
What can I do therefore, but wisely keep my mouth shut
think of me what you will, all of you in our hut.

Next to me, my dear friend, the Dinye, he's so fancy,
complains always about his lack of small currency.
Otherwise he is called Kardos, first name, Dénes,
grew a bushy mustache in the labor service.

Now comes the women's dream, please believe my poem,
he laments "hey" sighing, if I could only go home.
Dressmaker's shop I'd go, not to buy their dresses,
but to see, once again, my Rosie's lovely tresses.

Hoffman Miska is next, he moans in his sleep, as in pain,
till Uncle Richard strikes him with his crooked, old cane.
Never gets up in time to answer reveille,
arrives to the latrine, later than any.

And now, friendly listener, pay attention to me,
as I don't know how long my form will stay with me.
The one I write about now, in this God forsaken place,
Left his heart in Dunaszerdahely with a sour face.
His mouth is always moving, like a duck's ass, it twitches
Goes frequently to sick call in funny, old black britches.

And the two Róts sleep at the edge of the group
Always are together, working in the same troop.
They joined finances and live on their shared money
Together with each other, the best of anybody.

Now I'll stop twiddling with this account of the bunch,
as the cooks are yelling, calling us to lunch.
Alongside with others, I rush to line up for chow,
…the verse is finished, …
        So long my friends, …
                …for now.

* * *

By this time I had learned a lot about building railroad tracks. I was
always good at trigonometry and engineering design at school, and now
I was able to put those skills to work in actual practice. I knew how to
lay out a curve, or how to bank a turn, or how to measure a grade, and so
on. Obviously I wasn't allowed to do most of these things, but I did get a
tremendous kick out of telling some of the engineers or foreman how we
could do certain tasks easier, faster, or better. I also learned a great deal about
trains and engines. I knew how to get hot water from an engine to shave or
to do laundry. I loved the smell of the steam and the engine's smoke, as it
reminded me of the days on the bridge over the railroad tracks in Pápa. I also
learned that most Hungarian rolling stock, all of the lower-grade cars such as
boxcars, or flat freight cars had friction, sleeve bearings. All the wheels, each
pair on a common axle, turned in sleeves having no ball or roller bearings.
The sleeves were heavily lubricated with oil in a container over every bearing.
These containers were covered with a lift-up cover so the oil could be easily
refilled. At times long troop or equipment trains went through our section

on the newly built tracks. Whenever any of these trains stopped near us, at times waiting for a train to pass from the opposite direction, I would walk alongside the waiting train and dump a handful of sand into the bearing housings here and there. I never knew what happened to these trains, but I am pretty sure that some of the bearings I put sand into heated up, melted, or fused, and, I hope, stopped the trains on the open track, blocking and halting traffic in both directions. I felt very good about this, and in retrospect, I wish I had done more of it.

\* \* \*

It had to be late August or early September when my company, which, incidentally was called KMSZ 103/304 m. század, or 103/304 Labor Service Company, was ordered to move. We were building a section of track when one of the orderlies came to the site on a bike and told us to return to barracks at once. We stopped our work, formed up, and marched back to the old barn. We were told to pack and be ready to move out early next morning. Dénes and I were ready. According to our escape plan, we were always near completely packed. All we had to do the following morning was roll up our blankets, and we were ready.

Very early the following morning we had our usual breakfast, some black liquid called kávé, coffee. There wasn't a drop of coffee in our kávé but it was warm, and with a slice of brown bread it got us started. The bread, incidentally, was given out every three or four days, one brick-shaped and -sized loaf per person. It was up to us individually to ration it so it would last till the next distribution. It was called Kommissbrot, a German word left over from the Austro-Hungarian Army, meaning a coarse, vile sort of bread. It was dark, hard as a rock, and it was rolled in sawdust for some reason, but it wasn't vile or bad. In fact, I loved it. With butter and salt on it, it had a very special taste and it was extremely filling.

A train of boxcars was waiting for us some distance from our camp. After everything was loaded aboard, kitchen, orderly room, officers' and cadres' quarters, and tools, we boarded the train, twenty-four of us to a car. This was considerably less than the usual forty the Hungarian Army put in one of these boxcars. In fact, there was a sign on every boxcar, some still in German dating back to WWI: "40 menschen, oder sechs pferden," meaning "forty men, or six horses." But those numbers were for temporary,

163

quick transportation, not for living in the cars, as was going to be our case. Even twenty-four was very uncomfortable, particularly at night when we all wanted to spread out, and there just wasn't enough floor space in the small car for all of us to sleep in any kind of comfort.

Rumors had it that we were on our way to a large marshaling yard which was bombed the day before. I no longer remember where this place was, it might have been Kolozsvár, but when we got there the effect of the bombing was not to be believed. The yard was completely destroyed. Most of the buildings were in rubble. Broken, twisted-up railway cars of all descriptions were in heaps, one on top of the other in stacks three and four high. Some of the tracks that were hit were bent straight up by the blast, pointing at the sky at each end of the crater, standing like giant ladders, ties still attached to the rails. It was a devastating, though, for me, an encouraging sight. It was a powerful indication, the first concrete evidence I saw that my enemies, the Germans and the Hungarians, were finally getting their comeuppance. But fixing or even cleaning up the mess seemed impossible. We didn't have the equipment or the technicians to deal with huge engines smashed into one another. So instead, we were ordered to build twin tracks around the destroyed railway yard. Labor service units were arriving from other places to work beside professional railroad people. The work was accomplished in less than three days. The first train to use these tracks was a German hospital train loaded with wounded, heading west. Another beautiful sight!

In the subsequent days, once two-way traffic was reopened, we worked with the railroad people cleaning up the yard. The engines, tracks, and railroad cars were cut apart with torches, and the ones which could be fixed were either towed or carted away. When the yard was more or less clear of debris, we started rebuilding the destroyed tracks. It was hard work.

* * *

During this period I commandeered some heavy lumber, which wasn't hard as it was strewn all over the place, and built two platform bunks in our car. This allowed six of us per platform to sleep in relative comfort. Some of the guys "liberated" some mattresses I don't know from where, and we also got some seats from wrecked cars, which I installed in our car facing the doors. All the comforts of home! The best things I put up were the luggage racks for our packs, which I also "liberated" from a wrecked third-class passenger car. So outfitted, our car was much admired, envied, and imitated, but none was as good as mine. We lived in this train for some time. During our free time, which we didn't have much of, we went looking up other units, hoping to get news and information about our families. No one knew anything. It seemed that the events of Pápa in June and July were played out all over Hungary. Thousands of people were rounded up in ghettos, jammed into boxcars, and taken away to unknown destinations. Beyond that, no one heard from any of their relatives. The Hungarian railroad crews of these transports were taken off at the Polish border and claimed to know nothing.

* * *

At about this time and during the following weeks, I received one more postcard from my brother and also a letter which he signed Horkay Sándor, a friend. In the card (Postcard #10) he says, "There is still no definite news of our dear parents. There is a lot of bad news we hear, which is not at all certain. For instance, I have heard that they are in the vicinity of Kassa, or that the exempted ones will be brought back." He also mentioned that his unit was moving to "another [district] in the same place," but gave no address.

Because of our move, not knowing where I was going either, I couldn't let him know, but receiving his postcard and letter confirmed that the mail was being forwarded and I wrote to his old address. I don't know if he ever received my letter, as I did not hear from him after that.

Some time later, two letters came from Aunt Alice. In the first one (Letter #3) she told me, "The news that they [my parents] are around Kassa is in error, as they are not there." Then, "Sándor didn't write for some days, I don't know if he is still where he was, the last he wrote they were moving…" In her second letter she once again said, "Sorry that we know nothing of Horkay's parents…" Their own situation in Pápa might also have deteriorated somehow, as she mentions in this letter that "this uncertainty is terrible."

These were the last letters I received. Afterwards, there was no news of, or from, anyone.

* * *

We were still getting some general and, in most cases, unimportant news as reported by the local papers we got hold of on occasion. We still had our radio, but listening to it in the train was very difficult. We knew that the war, if ever so slowly, was getting closer to its end. From our train, sitting on a spur as we worked in the marshaling yard, we couldn't help but see and notice the increased frequency of hospital trains going west, while fewer and fewer troop and equipment trains were going east. As we were going into September, rumors had it that the Russians were only a short distance from us. Yet we were still building new tracks, which my friends and I privately hoped were going to be used by the Russians.

* * *

Then the yard was bombed again. We were working in the middle of it when I heard the characteristic undulating hum of a large formation of planes. We couldn't see them, but the engines' roar got louder and I knew it was time to get out of there. I, as well as another couple of hundred people, ran in every direction. The planes were coming from one direction; I was running in the other. There was a cemetery next to the railroad yard. I ran through it. I now saw the planes coming directly at us and kept running. When the first bomb hit, I dove into a ditch. There wasn't anybody else around. I held my ears and watched the bombs do their work. As the railroad yard was swallowed up in a cloud of dust, the explosions kept coming towards me across the cemetery. I bounced like a ball as the ground heaved. Headstones, wooden crosses, pieces of coffins were tossed high in the air. At one point I felt a pain, as though a bee stung me in my right leg just below the knee. When my hand went to feel it, there was a hot piece of metal sticking out of my leg and a little blood was oozing out of the wound. I pulled the small, jagged piece of hot metal out and tied my handkerchief around my leg. I recalled hearing a loud buzzing noise just before I felt the sting. The next couple of days I dug more pieces of shrapnel out of my leg with a razor blade. I washed the cuts with iodine for a couple of days, and they healed rapidly. Most of the shrapnel, which remained in my leg and showed up on X-rays for years, came to the surface or dissolved long ago.

After the explosions stopped, it took some time for the planes to disappear. I got to my feet and started back towards the yard. The dust was thinning out, but now smoke and flames were everywhere. The work we had done over the past couple of weeks was totally destroyed and it couldn't have made me happier.

There were lots of casualties, dead and wounded, but miraculously no one was killed or seriously hurt in my company. We had very little medical help. Superficial wounds like mine were self-doctored most of the time. Our train was moved further away from the yard, which meant that we had to walk a good distance to and from work, but I was happy to be away from the yard, an obviously important target. Our futile efforts—at least I hoped they were futile—went on. First we rebuilt the double loop around the yard, and then once again started cleaning up the immense yard.

* * *

There was a chill in the air as we were drinking our morning kávé in almost total darkness. We knew the summer was over. A few weeks before it would have been already daylight at this time in the morning. As the eastern sky was getting brighter I noticed some symmetrical, rectangular-shaped objects, almost like large crates, on a crest some distance away. As I watched there was a flash of yellow light in front of one of them Moments later I heard a thump, and about the same time one of the boxcars exploded behind me. Somebody yelled, "The Russians!" Dénes and I got to our boxcar about the same time. We grabbed our packs and jumped out of the car on the other side. As we were running away, a thought struck me. What about food? The kitchen car was just abreast of us and I jumped up into it. Everybody was running all over the place as I grabbed two little wooden boxes of marmalade. Then I rejoined Dénes and some others, and we ran deep into the woods, as far from the train as we could. By evening, I was sure we would join up with the Russians.

# Chapter 11

# 1944 – SEPTEMBER | OCTOBER
# DESERTING

The explosions continued behind us. We saw the flashes and heard the sounds of our train being blown apart. In a way it was almost sad to know that the car I outfitted and lived in was probably no more. On the other hand, a new chapter was about to start and the anticipation of joining up with the Russians filled us with excitement and anxiety. We even fantasized about joining the Russian Army, fully expecting the Russians to be aware of our situation and our sentiments and being anxious to have us fight on their side. I've had no communist tendencies; in fact, until my parents were taken away I considered myself an anticommunist. But now the situation changed. It was no longer difficult to decide who was friend and who was foe. The Russians didn't haul away my family; they fought those who did, and I wanted to help.

Hours must have passed and the shelling had stopped, but there was no sign of Russians. We waited. We could see a road from our position in a depression near the edge of the woods. It had quite a bit of traffic on it. Hungarian military vehicles were going in both directions, and there was surprisingly large civilian activity on the road also. Some overloaded horse- and ox-drawn farm wagons with old people and young children sitting on the top of some of them formed an endless convoy. There were lots of people on bicycles, on foot, and some pushing carts and wheelbarrows. They were all going in one direction, west. Time was dragging ever so slowly, yet we could do nothing but wait. It started to rain slightly. At first the trees offered some shelter, but as the rain picked up we had no cover. By the time night came we were soaked; still, no sign of the Russians. Some of us were better off than others. There were about ten, maybe twelve of us—I don't remember exactly, but that is the figure that seems to surface from my memory. Those who ran from the train were without as much as an overcoat. Dénes and I had all our belongings. Our escape planning paid off, but some of the others did not fare that well. In the sudden panic of the shelling most of their belongings were left on the train, which we thought no longer existed. It was getting dark, but we didn't want to light a fire. We reasoned that if the Russians advanced, we would see them on the road and would join them. If they did not, we didn't want to give our position away, running the risk of being arrested for desertion. We opened one of the small cases of marmalade in the semidark of the evening. Dénes and I had some bread and we distributed it amongst all of us. My knife came in handy slicing it and spreading the marmalade. Then we tried to sleep. The noise of the endless procession of people on the highway could still be heard, telling us that the Russians still had not arrived. It was scary being in the woods. By now it was completely dark; one couldn't see the tip of one's nose, and all we could do was huddle and wait for morning. But morning was taking its time coming. When it finally did come, some decided to go back to the train to see what had happened to it and if there were anybody around from our company. They also hoped to collect some of their belongings. Dénes and I didn't go. We told the others we would wait for them. Hours went by before the others returned. They told us that the train was totally destroyed, most of it burnt. The guys did manage to collect some clothes, not necessarily their own but just about anything that was left more or less intact. By this time Dénes and I figured that we were in a pickle. If the Russians didn't come and we were discovered by Hungarian troops, we could and most probably would be considered deserters. The prospect of that was not good. As an alternative to staying put and waiting for the Russians, we decided to join the people on the road and head west. If on the way we found another labor service unit, we would join them. Our excuse of our unit having been destroyed was the truth, and we thought it would be accepted by whoever might question us. The rain let up a bit by noon. It made little difference as by then we were completely soaked. We decided to gather our stuff and walk onto the road. By this time there were considerably fewer people on the road than the day before. Military vehicles were still going in both directions. I have no idea where we were or how far we walked that afternoon; all I remember is that I was very tired, being drenched all this time, carrying a heavy backpack. We came into a small, rural, typical Hungarian country station of one small, yellow-painted building. There were a few people around spending the night, which is what we decided to do. The following morning most of them were gone as we were about to start out. The ever-present small luggage cart, which every station in Hungary had, was next to the station. We thought it would make our lives a lot easier if we appropriated the cart and pulled our packs instead of carrying them. There was no one around to stop us as we loaded up the cart and took off.

All I can tell you about the following couple of days is that we walked, got soaked again, and walked some more. We crossed the Tisza, one of Hungary's principal rivers, and passed lots of military activity, but no labor service units. The remaining portion of our bread and the marmalade were long gone and we were hungry. At one point we dug up some sugar beets from a field along the road and ate them raw, mud and all. Night came again and we spent it just off the road, half asleep waiting for the Russians and the morning to come. Morning came, but the Russians did not. We were wondering where they were. Just a few days ago their tanks were within eyesight and shooting at us, but now they were nowhere. We kept walking west. Budapest was ahead of us, perhaps a few more days of walking, and we thought going there was our best bet. Our objective was to make it to Budapest and join a labor unit there. Budapest, we thought, had to have lots of them. The cold rain started again. This time it was coming down in buckets as we trudged along alone on the road. All of a sudden, an army truck passed us at breakneck speed from the opposite direction. We heard its breaks and tires squeal as it stopped and backed up to us. A young sergeant jumped out of the cab, pointing at Dénes, me, and one of the other guys. "You, you, and you," he shouted at us, "into the truck." We were in no position to argue. The three of us jumped up into the open bed of the truck, yelling at the others to go to Budapest; we would find them there. There I was, in an open army truck without my belongings, driving rain penetrating my skin, going back in the direction I just came from. At that moment I didn't think things could get much worse. The truck kept going. In less than an hour we were stopped by a German military policeman on the west side of the Tisza River at the very bridge we crossed the day, perhaps two days before. There were two 88 mm antiaircraft guns leveled horizontally pointing across the bridge, obviously expecting Russian tanks. The officer in our truck showed some papers to a Hungarian officer, explaining that he was acting on direct orders to go across the river to some factory that had a safe he was ordered to pick up. The Hungarian officer passed him. We crossed over the bridge onto a dirt road and arrived at our destination, some sort of a factory, about a half hour later. The wire link gates were chained and locked, and there wasn't a soul around. Dénes, the other guy who was with us, the sergeant, and I climbed over the fence into the factory grounds. The sergeant had no idea where the safe was. We went from one building to another breaking down doors, looking for the safe. We finally found a safe in an office building. It was about the size of the truck we came in, and it was built into the wall. Obviously it was locked. One would have had to dynamite it to open it, and we had no dynamite.

I still wonder about what might have been in that safe. I don't think it was military material. Later on, when Dénes and I speculated about this incident, we figured that the "Safe Rescue" operation was not an official one. We speculated that the sergeant and the young officer in the truck probably heard about a safe in this factory which they must also have heard contained money, perhaps other valuables, and decided to go after it as a personal venture. When it became obvious that the safe could not be removed or opened, we went back to the truck and climbed over the gates again. The officer in the truck, the driver, and the sergeant were anxious to get going, not wanting to be cut off from the bridge and captured by the Russians. The truck hightailed it back to the bridge. The German guns were still there leveled at us as we crossed the bridge, while overhead a small Russian plane, a Rata, was circling. Occasionally it swooped down to fire a burst at the guns on the west side of the river. Our truck didn't even stop. We were going west again and I was hoping that we would pass our friends with our packs. We were waved off the road by a Hungarian military policeman as it was getting dark, and the truck was directed into a busy military compound. Hungarian troops were digging in, obviously expecting a Russian attack. The young officer in the truck was questioned by a captain. He showed his orders and told the captain that he had direct orders to report back to his unit. The captain cursed and said something to the effect that the papers were shit, not direct orders, and the young officer, the sergeant, and the driver were to remain with his unit to fight the Russians. The three had no choice. The captain wanted to know who we were. I told him who we were and that our train was shot up by Russian tanks, and we were trying to find our unit. He wanted to know if we could fire rifles. I told him that we had no training with guns. He told us to get out of there, which was music to my ears. As much as I would have liked making contact with the Russians, the one thing I didn't want was to be captured amongst Hungarian troops. We were on our own again, wet, sleepy, and incredibly hungry. I don't remember where we slept that night. What I do remember was the most beautiful sight I could have wished for the following morning as we started out on the highway. Way in the distance coming towards us were some guys pulling a small cart. I knew then that God was looking out for me. They were our friends, pulling the little railroad cart with our backpacks on it. Somehow they had gotten hold of some bread, which was totally soaked but tasted very good. We walked on towards Budapest.

* * *

I don't know how many days we spent on the road, but the rain finally stopped and our clothes, which we hadn't changed since we left our train, dried completely. Food was another story. We hadn't had any for almost three days by then. Strangely, the roads were empty. No civilians and only an occasional military vehicle. We arrived at a military airport near Budapest called Ferihegy, which incidentally is the international airport of Hungary today. We saw some Hungarian Air Force troops on the outskirts of Ferihegy. We talked with them, explaining our situation and asking if they would feed us. We were all weak from hunger. The fellow we talked with told us to follow him. It was evening as he took us to their kitchen where soldiers were cleaning up. Fortunately they had some leftover soup and some bread. We ate and ate. They couldn't believe how hungry we were and laughed as we put portion after portion away. They told us to find a place to sleep and be at formation the following morning.

We found a room on the second floor in a bombed-out building. Dénes and I unrolled my Romanian blanket and fell asleep. The following morning we did form up with the air force unit. We were still weak and exhausted but were told to group at the low end of the unit by ourselves. The commanding officer took the morning report, gave his orders, and the unit was dismissed to do their assigned jobs. I thought it was odd when I found out that the commanding officer's name was Háry János. The reason I thought this was strange was because his name was the same as that of a legendary Baron Munchausen–type tall tale storytelling, a Hungarian folklore character. But he turned out to be a very decent man. Through his subordinates he let us know that we could stay with them. Each of us was assigned to work with the soldiers in the unit. I ended up helping hoist bombs up into Messerschmitt 111 light bombers. I also helped load ammunition for the machine guns on the planes. To the amazement of the soldiers I knew a lot about the planes. These were a decent bunch of people who treated us well. We ate well, and in the next couple of days had a chance to clean up our clothes. During our walk west I had missed a couple of days of shaving. When I finally did shave at Ferihegy, it felt wonderful. It reminded me of my father and I wondered where my parents might be.

During the next couple of days, a Russian plane the soldiers called "the Singer" appeared several times a day and bombed us. But it was almost funny as the plane was an old WWI-type bi-wing plane with an open cockpit. It usually came down very low. We could clearly see two people in it wearing goggles, one of whom tossed out three bombs by hand. The plane would appear two or three times a day, and the fellow in the rear would toss out three bombs without any regard of a target. After a while, unless the plane was directly overhead, no one even took cover. Instead, we watched the plane during these raids as the soldiers explained that it was called the Singer because it sounded like a sewing machine. But not all bombing was as comical as the Singer. One night the airport was bombed by a formation of regular Russian planes. The corner of the building directly under our room was hit, shaking the building and dumping the huge window frame into the room right over us. The raid didn't wake me, but when my friends were shaking me to wake up, I had a hard time extricating myself from the bent-up iron window frame pressing me to the floor. None of us was hurt, but the building was no longer safe to stay in. We moved to another building, but only for a short time. Because of the advancing Russians, I suppose, the unit was ordered to pull back and we were told that we could not go with them. We were on our own again. The night before the unit moved, Budapest was bombed by Russian, or American, or possibly English planes, I don't know which, but it was a spectacular sight. We watched the raid. Occasionally, a searchlight picked up a plane and other searchlights also converged on it. Steady streams of antiaircraft fire created an almost beautiful display of fireworks, as tracer bullets streaked for the sky. We could see the explosions and the fires within the city. The airport was also bombed. I sat in a hole in the ground near the edge of the airport. There were hundreds of these holes dug all around the airport as bomb and strafing shelters. One of the holes nearby was hit and all people in it were killed. My friends and I, though shaken, were unhurt. I have often wondered if my bad hearing could be traced back to this and similar events. The God's Big Book theory made more and more sense to me as people near me were killed while I escaped unhurt. The horrors of war were increasingly evident all around me and I was learning to live with it.

The following morning we helped the planes load up and watched them leave. Then, backpacks piled on our little railroad cart, we were on the road again to Budapest.

* * *

We had no idea where we were going as we were entering Budapest. I expected to see a lot of bomb damage, but only a few buildings were destroyed here and there, not as many as I expected. We were stopped by the police and directed to report to a central military building on Üllői ut for reassignment. The building turned out to be the Killián Kaszárnya (Killián Barracks), a large building in the usual style of military barracks in Hungary. Inside, the three-, perhaps four-story building had wide, arched corridors surrounding a parade ground. We were told to unload our cart and were taken to a room on the top floor of the building. It was a large room about the size of a standard classroom in a high school. There was a guard in front of the door. The room was full of people. I don't know how many were in the room, but it had to be close to two hundred. In spite of the open windows, the room was hot and it smelled. Almost everyone in the room had similar stories to ours. They were mostly young people from defunct labor service units, escaped or deserted like us. Others, including some older people, were arrested on various charges and brought here. They had bad tales to tell. The Nyilasok, members of the Hungarian Nazi Party, were in total control in Budapest. Very few had uniforms, nor did they need any. All of them had military rifles with bayonets, military cartridge belts, and military caps with visors. Their red armband with a four-pointed green arrow cross in a white circle was all the uniform they needed. Most of them were not soldiers. Some were deserters from the army. Others escaped frontline service in the army by virtue of their party membership. In fact, they performed no military duties and activities. Their sole purpose in life was to harass, steal, and kill. In those activities they had carte blanche, and they weren't shy about going overboard. As the people in the room told us, the Nyilasok would round up a bunch of Jews, take them to one of the bridges over the Danube, and either shoot or throw them into the river and then shoot them. Periodically they would raid so-called safehouses, buildings where Jews holding Swedish or Swiss papers were grouped, and haul away and kill as many as it pleased their fancy. Nobody was safe from them. They accounted and answered to no one.

We were allowed out of this room to go to the toilet one at a time. As one would return, another was allowed to go. The line went around the four walls inside the room, but some who had to go urgently clamored at the door. Others just didn't want to stand in line and fought to be next for the latrine. It was chaos. By the time my turn came, it was almost too late. Day and night the line never stopped. I don't remember how long my friends and I were held in this room. People were constantly taken out and replaced with newcomers. When our turn came, we were marched to a building somewhere in Budapest and assigned to a labor service air raid unit.

Life in this unit was quite amazing. The unit was housed in a school building with an individual bunk assigned to most people. Latecomers such as us slept on the floor. No one seemed to have anything to do. Most people in the unit were the typical, sophisticated, smart-aleck Budapest types. This incidentally is not intended to be a derogatory statement. People from Budapest, like people from big cities anywhere, tended to be more sophisticated than us country bumpkins. To my amazement, some of the people in the unit would leave the building at will, without armbands, stars, or anybody's permission. One fellow had a veritable grocery store in his locker. He would cook eggs, beans, other things, and had loaves of bread, butter, and jelly. He was not very communicative and guarded his foodstuff zealously. Some of the fellows in the unit told us about a group of people, some possibly from Pápa, in a safe compound in the Városliget (City Park). Others openly discussed joining the underground. One of these talked to me and Dénes to see if we would want to join the resistance. I said yes, but

Dénes, who must have been smarter than I, said no. A couple of nights later this fellow told me that he was going over to the place where some of the underground people stayed. He told me I could go with him if I wanted to. I went, but Dénes decided to try to find the place in the Városliget. He wanted me to go along, but I decided to join the resistance. Don't ask me why. I probably should have known better. Until then I had heard very little about the resistance, and there wasn't anything I heard which made sense other than the hope of fighting our enemies. My new friend and I left that evening and ended up in the attic of a typical Budapest apartment building. He told us in the afternoon that he was going to get us weapons that night. There were about twenty others in the attic. I didn't know anybody. There were no lights in the attic, and as it was getting dark I decided to turn in. I wanted to know what this group did in way of resistance action, but nobody wanted to talk. I fell asleep. I woke up around two in the morning, hearing all sorts of noises from the street below us. Someone whispered that the fellow who went for the guns must have been caught and the Germans were coming for us. I didn't know what to do, and neither did anybody else. We were all awake, lying under our blankets without words. It was strange that at that moment I remembered Mári telling me as a young child to listen to the quiet. I listened and heard with crystal clarity the noise of armored vehicles, car doors slamming, commands shouted in German, and footsteps coming into the building as the doors were broken down. I was paralyzed with fear. My eyes were open in the dark, but I could see nothing. I heard the noise and soldiers talking in German as they were searching the building. I was certain that I was going to die. We heard shooting below us in the building, but instead of coming up to the attic, some time later the Germans left. No one moved. I was scared even to breathe as I lay in the dark. When the first lights of morning slowly penetrated the attic, one by one we picked up our belongings and left without words or goodbyes. I took my civilian clothes out of my backpack, put them on, and packed everything that even remotely suggested labor service. Then I wrapped my backpack in brown paper and tied it up with string. Coming down the steps by myself was a disturbing experience. The doors to most of the apartments were open, broken, or off their hinges. The rooms were mostly empty and whatever was left inside was smashed to splinters. There was a lot of blood but no people or corpses. There was only one place I could think of to go to. It was the compound in the Városliget. I had no idea how to get there. I knew where it was—my favorite museum, the Transportation Museum was in the Városliget—but I had no idea how to get there. I thought I would just walk until I recognized a landmark, or ask for directions. As I walked I came upon and recognized one of the main thoroughfares, which I knew from my lampshade-making days. It wasn't far from where I stayed with Aunt Manci and Uncle János. The trolleys were running and I got on one going in the direction I thought the Városliget was. The trolley was going very slowly. It was a beautiful, balmy autumn day, and as I hadn't slept much the night before, it wasn't long before I was dozing. Then I woke suddenly realizing that the car wasn't moving. Most everybody had gotten off, but the street was a swirling mass of people. I looked out the window and ahead of my car, as far as I could see, two lines of trolleys like very long trains were standing still. At every cross street Nyilasok (Hungarian Nazis) were blocking the streets. No one was allowed off the main avenue. The sounds of periodic gunshots were heard from the distance. Somebody in the car said, "Megint lövöznek," "They are shooting again." I thought I saw people being asked for papers. I didn't have any. According to stories I had heard, when the Nyilasok caught anyone without papers they would shoot them on the spot. I could tell that's what was happening up the avenue, on both sides. The memory of every split second of the next few minutes is forever etched into my mind in all its most minute detail.

I got off the car and very calmly walked directly up to one of the three Nyilasok blocking the side street. Without any lead-in, I pointed across the street to one of the other Nazis on the opposite corner and said, "That fellow over there told me the Városliget was that way." I looked him in the eye and pointed in the opposite direction to where I knew the Városliget was. He must not have been from Budapest, as he obviously didn't know where the Városliget was, but he turned to one of the others who pointed to the actual direction to Városliget. I said, "That's what I thought, but that fellow over there"—again I pointed at the Nazi on the other side of the street—"is wrong." Both pointed me in the right direction again as I thanked them and slowly walked away. My knees were shaking and it took all my strength not to fall down. I was afraid to look back and expected somebody to challenge me or shoot me in the back any second. When I reached the corner and turned out of view of the Nyilasok, I ran a few steps and threw up. There were very few people on the street. Nobody paid any attention to me. I collected myself and, with my package on my shoulder, started walking. Behind me the noise of a panicked, terrified mass of humanity abated. Some rifle shots in the distance still signaled the tragic, terrible end of another human life. I walked the rest of the way to Városliget, and before evening found the compound.

* * *

It was in the amusement park section of Városliget. Each little building, formerly amusement stands, were jammed full of people—men, women, young and old. After numerous questions, I was directed to an area where I found people from Pápa. Dénes was already there. I was delighted to see him. He took me to a little shack, probably a game stand in prior days, a shooting gallery, ring toss, the type of building one sees in amusement parks. It had the open front with a counter, and in the back portion makeshift tiers of bunks were created to house about fifty people in a space the size of an average room. The tiers of bunks went to the ceiling with just enough space between them to accommodate a prone body. Sitting up would have been impossible. One had to crawl into it. Dénes was next to the wall, on the second tier, and I squeezed in next to him, lying head to toe. Shoulder to shoulder would have been impossible. I guess Dénes was as happy to see my Romanian blanket as he was to see me. He told me that only a few people were there from Pápa. They had no news of my family, or anyone else, other than they were taken to Poland, presumably to a camp. Under the circumstances and in the face of no worse news, this was acceptable, though not very reassuring. By this time rumors were circulating about horrible conditions in German camps—hard labor, starvation, murder, disease—but these rumors were so outrageously horrible that we still refused to believe them. The stories went beyond our wildest imagination and we just couldn't conceive or want to accept that such inhuman cruelty could really exist. I hoped that as bad the rumors were, somehow my parents would pull through and I would get to see them again soon.

Klein Béla and his son, Feri, two people I knew from Pápa, were at this compound. I don't know how they managed to escape the events of Pápa, but they were here, protected against deportation by Swedish citizenship papers. A lot of people in this compound had Swedish, Swiss, or Portuguese papers. With those papers in hand, the International Red Cross, the embassies of those countries, somehow managed to protect a fairly large number of people against deportation. Béla bácsi, as we called Klein Béla, was about my father's age. He told Dénes and me that he would try to get us papers. In the meantime, we were to stay in the little hut. We helped him run a little business enterprise, selling paprikás szalonna, a typically Hungarian food item made from pork. Real paprikás szalonna was a certain type of bacon cut in characteristic rectangular portions covered with paprika. The kind we sold had a really fat back, which has been brined but not processed the way real paprika bacon would have been. We cut the fat back into the usual size and shape slabs, rolled it in paprika, and sold it as paprikás szalonna. We could have sold a ton every hour. Even though everybody who bought it once knew, I'm sure, that it wasn't real paprikás szalonna, they bought it anyhow as it was high-protein food—a little of which went a long way. Besides, there wasn't much else to be had. I don't know where Béla bácsi got his supply, but he had quite a bit of it delivered every day. One thing there was a shortage of was knives. My hunting knife came in handy slicing and cutting the bacon. While I was in the compound, though I cannot recall any mention or discussion of this then, I now believe that this compound was one of the places protected by Raoul Wallenberg. I'm sure all of you know who he was. If not, he was a young Swedish diplomat of noble birth who dedicated his life to saving Jews, homosexuals, Gypsies, and all the so-called "undesirables" from the Germans. He worked tirelessly, constantly rushing from one place to the next, pulling people off deportation transports in the face of the SS and their Hungarian counterparts, the Nyilasok. He saved thousands of people. If it weren't for him, a large population of Budapest Jews would surely have perished. Possibly, as you'll see later, I might not have made it without his involvement. It is ironic that after all he has done for mankind defying German and Hungarian Nazis, and saving scores of human beings, he died at the hands of the Russians. In spite of his protection, the Nyilasok periodically raided the compound. These raids served no other purpose than the personal amusement of the Nyilasok. They would swoop down on the compound on foot or by truck and randomly fire a few shots into the compound, or at times drag a few people away, whom we suspected they killed later. It defies logic that at the time when the Russians already occupied a large portion of Hungary, these hoodlums were committing more and more terrible atrocities. One other danger was the increasing number of air raids. The Russian pilots couldn't have known who the people were in the compound, at least that is what we preferred to believe, and repeatedly strafed and bombed us. During one of these raids a young fellow I knew slightly was badly wounded by a bomb. He was lying on the ground in a pool of blood when I found him. Most of his intestines, stomach, and his mangled liver were lying on the ground next to him. Yet he was completely conscious. His eyes were open and he was talking quietly. I told him that a doctor was coming. It wasn't true and I think he knew it. He could not move, but as we talked and I was telling him that his stomach had a small cut and everything would be all right as soon as the doctor got there, he was making feeble attempts with his left hand trying to stuff his innards back into his body. About a half hour later his voice grew weak and he quietly died. I was shook up of course, but he was gone and I could have been next. The order of the day was survival, self-preservation, which meant not buckling under to these sorts of terrible things. I walked back to my hut to see if everyone else was all right.

* * *

Béla bácsi would disappear every now and then, returning alternately ashen-faced or in better humor. I never knew where he went on these occasions, but it was suspected that he and some others from the compound were making deals with the German and Hungarian authorities, trying to protect the people in the compound. Whatever they did worked, as we lived in relative safety, though completely aware that our existence was from one day, I should say one minute, to the next. We all hoped that the Russians would get to Budapest quickly. We heard that they were getting close. In fact, it gave us tremendous hope when we listened to one of a few radios in the compound and heard the Hungarian news frequently interrupted by a Hungarian voice broadcasted from behind the Russian lines. The Hungarian announcer would say something like, "The combined Hungarian and German armies forced back Russian units all along the front..." at which time the Hungarian voice would break in: "Don't believe him, he is lying!" The verbal duel would go on without the Hungarian announcer being aware of the other voice. It was actually funny, uplifting, and encouraging, but our hopes were smashed early one morning. We heard rifle fire and saw a large number of Nyilasok in the compound. We were told to form up. I had no idea where they were going to take us, but inwardly I knew that time had run out for us.

As usual, my backpack was ready to go. Dénes and I formed up with the group. We were marched, I believe, to the Józsefvárosi railroad station. The dreaded boxcars were there. With the exception of those, like Béla bácsi and his son, Feri, who had very good protection papers, we were jammed into the boxcars and the doors of the cars were closed and locked.

# Chapter 12

# 1944 – OCTOBER | NOVEMBER | DECEMBER
# 1945 – JANUARY | FEBRUARY | MARCH
# A PRIVILEGED LIFE

The cars were so crowded that when the train moved, nobody in the car even swayed. We were jammed one against the other like sardines. Nobody talked. A pall of doom descended over us in the car. Under the circumstances no conversation would have made any sense. None of us had any idea where we were going, but all of us knew that we didn't want to go to wherever our destination was. Though the small, barred, barbed wire–covered windows at each end of the car were open to outside air, the air in the car was almost unbearably hot, humid, and without oxygen. Fortunately Dénes and I were under a window. Occasionally, as the train was moving the wind blasted a gust of fresh air into the car, which was consumed with relish by those who, like us, were close to the window. The people in the middle of the car were less fortunate. There was lots of coughing and gasping for air. The situation was worse when the train was at a standstill in a station. The air was quickly used up and more than a few fainted standing up. When a limp body fell to the floor, getting them up was very difficult. The car's occupants were a mixture of all ages and sexes. When morning slowly came, in the first light of the day we could see clouds of condensation pouring out of the windows of the car into the cool autumn air. The wall of the car was drenched in condensation. Though it was mostly wood, the metal braces were sweating and were ice cold. This was a bit of a relief for those who were leaning against a wall. In spite of the unbelievable conditions in the car, in a strange and naive way I was hoping that we were being taken to some camp, possibly to one my parents might be in. The possibility of this little silver lining was dashed as we saw some of the signs at stations we went through, indicating that our train was heading north-northwest, not northeast. By then we were pretty certain that our parents' train went to Poland via Kassa, a northeast Hungarian city. We were heading up towards Czechoslovakia. My stomach was signaling breakfast time. Fortunately I had enough presence of mind just seconds before we left the compound to stuff my pockets with paprikás bacon. It was now squeezed and flattened in my pockets, but Dénes and I and some of the people near us had a small piece each. We also ate a very small piece of bread, trying to ration our remaining food. There was a bearded Orthodox Jew near us, who prayed most of the time and wouldn't have any of the bacon. The big problem was that we had no water. By the end of the second day, we were parched in the heat of the car. As more and more people were running out of food, I gave more of my bacon away. By the third or fourth day, it was all gone. Dénes and I still had a piece of bread each, eating just morsels of it each day. The train was sitting on a siding somewhere in Czechoslovakia. Troop trains were going by or sat alongside us. We asked some of the German soldiers for water. None of them responded. Fortunately it rained one night. I folded several of my unused postcards into channels and stuck them out the window between the barbed wire. The water trickled in and Dénes and I were able to catch most of it. We had some and doled out the rest amongst the others in the car. I was able to fill my canteen and did this every time it rained. By this time the jammed conditions in the car improved a bit, as we hung most of the packs, bedrolls, and suitcases from improvised hooks and had people sit on others. This relieved some floor space and allowed some of us to alternately sit and doze. One morning, as I was sporadically dozing and waking up, I looked out the window and saw a most beautiful sight, a panorama rising out of the morning mist. It was the city of Nürnberg with its fairy-tale spired buildings.

Strangely, a few years ago while scouting locations for a film in the Washington, DC area, I dozed off in the van, waking up just as we were driving along the Potomac, and across the water I saw the tower of Georgetown University. It was a weird feeling. It was raining slightly, the van was warm, and as I woke up, for some seconds I thought I was back on that train and seeing the towers of Nürnberg.

Even in our miserable situation then, I thought it was a very beautiful sight. What was even more beautiful—figuratively speaking—was the row upon row of damaged and destroyed buildings here and there. Remnants of walls, buildings in heaps of rubble were visible everywhere. I couldn't help wondering why the German people stood by watching their country and lives being destroyed, why they didn't just rise up, get rid of their leadership, and end all the suffering. In fact, some did just that and paid with their lives for trying. The German people, certainly their military leaders, must have known that the war was lost by then with no possible chance of a reversal of the situation. This sight of devastation was repeated in town after town as our train was chugging on its way, going north. The war was lost, yet the Germans still found the time, money, energy, and personnel, all it took to haul us around in Germany to an unknown destination. Their objective could have nothing to do with the betterment of the German people. The objective was clearly the destruction of others. Some, particularly those of us in the car who were near a window and knew geography, traced our progress and knew that in fact we were going back and forth at times, probably because a lot of the railways were damaged by then, and what was left was used by the German Army. At times our train was sitting on sidings for interminably long times before it moved again. Our engine was unhooked, but when hours later the train lurched suddenly, sending baggage flying and us crashing into one another, we knew we were hooking up again and hopefully would be moving soon.

Some optimists reasoned that we were going to Switzerland. They thought—some even claimed to know— that a deal was made between the Germans and the leaders at the Városliget compound to take us to Switzerland for an enormous amount of money. No one knew where this money could have come from, but they insisted that such a deal was made. This theory continued even after the train continued north, ruling out the possibility of going to Switzerland. By this time three people died in the car. All were elderly, including the bearded Orthodox man. Their bodies were moved to a corner of the car and piled on top of one another. The dead were helping the living by providing a little more space. Yet as time dragged, some tempers flared. There were some fights in the car, which indicated how far we'd slipped on levels of human behavior. But there were acts of compassion and generosity also.

I looked at Dénes and realized that he had quite a growth of beard. We hadn't shaved since the beginning of our journey and when I touched my face I felt a good growth of hair also. I decided to shave. Somehow, I extricated my shaving gear from my backpack. I spat on the soap, working up a lather, and without a mirror, being very careful not to disturb people around me, I shaved. It felt good. It reinjected some sense of humanity, which had been steadily ebbing from all of us. A young fellow next to me asked if I could shave him. I said I would, but he wanted to be shaved with a straight razor. He claimed the safety razor was bad for his face. The whole situation was comical. More to pass the time than for any other reason, I agreed to shave him with his own straight razor. He had shaving cream, which he rubbed on his face, and I proceeded to shave him in a lurching train, using a straight razor for the first time in my life. For months after this, even today at times, I chuckle to think that he might have hoped I'd accidentally cut his throat.

As the train was going north, we were beginning to see snow on the ground here and there. Winter was coming. The hunger, weakness, lack of space to move, and air to breathe was almost unbearable. Dénes and I consumed my last tiny piece of rock-hard bread, spreading a thin layer of toothpaste on it to help it go down our parched throats. By this time the number of corpses grew in the car. Urine and excrement was all over the floor and everybody. No one even made an effort by this time to try to squeeze to a door and urinate out of the car through the crack at the bottom of the door. A number of people were sick. I apologize for giving such a detailed description, but without it I don't think I could expect you to understand and appreciate the situation. On the tenth day, the trip ended.

* * *

As daylight was coming up, the train shuffled back and forth, wheels and brakes squealing, and the cars bumped and lurched. We could sense that something unusual was going on. Indeed, a short while later the train came to a stop and we heard the engine's whistle, signaling its departure. We could see SS men outside the train. Some had shepherd dogs on leashes, and in a while the car doors were opened. For the first time in ten days we gasped for the fresh air and tried to keep our balance jumping off the train onto legs which hadn't been used for ten days. The younger ones, like Dénes and me, helped some of the older people get off the train. The German soldiers were yelling, smashing us on the head with thick, heavy walking canes. "Los, los gehen, los," they yelled as we formed up three or four abreast and started walking on a tree-lined dirt road between the SS guards. We were weak, sick, hungry, delirious, but we were off the train and once again breathing the fresh, cool autumn air. The colors of the foliage were beautiful. The sky was gray, leaden, and some mist was falling. There was a strange smell in the air. A pungent, nauseating odor mixed with the smell of smoke, which at first came in snatches on gentle gusts of wind, but grew stronger and more consistent as we marched on. We began hearing music as some buildings came into view in the distance, and fear alternately gave way to hopeful expectation. The music grew louder. It was a waltz, perhaps "The Blue Danube." We were going through large iron gates with the now well-known "Arbeit Macht Frei" lettered on it. A hopeful sign. After all, we worked in the labor service. None of us liked it or would have done it voluntarily, but under the circumstances we did exist while we worked. It didn't come to mind at that time that "Arbeit Macht Frei"—"Labor Liberates You"— perhaps poetically implied liberation through death. The orchestra was now visible. We marched past a sorrowful-looking bunch of musicians, some in strange, ill-fitting striped garments with round striped caps, and others in tattered ordinary street clothes. All looked like lifeless, automated puppets, playing musical instruments like so many skinny ghosts with large, hollow, and glazed-over eyes. The wind was bringing the acrid smell of the smoke directly at us and it was sickening. Yet the compound had some small and large well-kept buildings, some with little beds of shrubs and fall flowers. But whatever hope we had was soon dashed as we were marched through another set of double-barbed wire gates, and as we trudged on the seemingly endless, wide road that was bordered on both sides with barbed wire fences, we saw row upon row of large, identical tar paper–covered buildings. The buildings were separated from each other at regular intervals by single, and in some cases double, lines of barbed wire fences. Large guard towers with searchlights, machine guns, and guards were everywhere. The sights surrounding us were beyond comprehension, beyond belief, and beyond my wildest imagination. Nothing could have prepared us for the horror that greeted us in whatever direction we looked. If someone wanted to forewarn us, this sight could not have been adequately described, nor would any of us have believed it. It defied description, perception, or belief. Heaps of naked corpses, reduced to skin and bones, were piled like cordwood in front of each of the dark barracks. Some of the piles of corpses were neatly arranged. The first corpse sitting on the ground with its legs spread was leaning against the front wall of the building with another, and another, and another corpse sitting between the legs of the corps behind it. All looked like skeletons with skin stretched over the bones. The heads were mostly bald and seemed to be overly large for the diminutive bodies. In most cases their eyes were open and their jaws hanging. It was as though they were shouting something horrible at us, a chorus of screams we couldn't hear. At times it felt as though their eyes were riveted on us, looking at us wondering why we didn't look like them. We passed large two-wheel carts going empty in one direction and stacked with heaps of skin and bone corpses in the other. The prisoners who pushed and pulled these carts looked as bad as the corpses. In fact, they were dead, they just didn't know or wanted to believe it yet. Most wore the striped pajamas, some without shoes, with ice-cold mud caked on their feet. They looked at us with overly large, hollow, lifeless eyes, arms outstretched towards us asking us for food. We had none to give. The road we were on, the main drag of the camp, seemed endless. We could now see as well as smell the sickening, nauseating smoke. There could be no further doubt; it was the smell of burning human flesh and bone. It was coming from a very tall square chimney way in the distance to our right. It had to be a crematorium. We'd heard horror stories about crematoriums, but none of us would have suspected that they were not only for the cremation of those who died a natural death. Till this moment, none of us would have accepted the possibility that if the crematoriums were indeed real, we or our families could have been destined for them. Perhaps it was our own wretched condition, the fear of our own fate, which blinded our senses to fully appreciate the horrors around us and mercifully allowed us to remain sane. Our column was directed into a compound and formed up in front of one of the barracks. We had to take our hats off as the SS guards counted us over and over again. I don't remember how long we stood or what was said; all I remember is that I was weak and unbelievably hungry and thirsty. It went beyond, way beyond, the normal sensation of hunger of having missed a meal or two; it was an indescribable, empty feeling of sharp pain twisting my stomach into knots. Every part of my body was aching and burning. I don't know what kept me and the others standing. Indeed, some couldn't stand. They fell and we were ordered to move and lay them next to the barracks. Finally a young SS officer came and took the report from the guards. Even that took forever.

Once again I have to emphasize that not all of the fine detail of every moment stayed with me over the years. In fact, under the circumstances it is a small wonder that I remember anything. Some of the memories are more like impressions, yet I'm convinced they are factual in detail. The overall account, I believe, is a very close and accurate description of my life during the months which followed, though they are not necessarily in chronological order. In some respects, regarding certain random events and happenings, the memories are very clear and I will talk about them in detail. I did not keep a diary, which doesn't matter, as one day followed another, relentlessly repeating the dull, purposeless, fearful routine which became our life.

At that moment as we were being counted, yelled at, clubbed, we stood in a daze, existing on an unconscious, animalistic will to live. I don't know how long we stood, but eventually we were allowed to enter the barracks so many per building. Inside, Dénes and I staked out a small space on the second level of three, perhaps four tiers of wooden platforms. They were to be our "beds" in our new home, which we found out was called Bergen-Belsen.

* * *

I knew there was a town called Bergen in Norway, but the name Bergen-Belsen meant nothing to me. Till then, I'd not heard of it. As far as I was concerned, it was one of those terrible camps I've heard rumors about while I was in the labor service. I could tell there were thousands of people in the camp, all looking more or less alike. I had no idea what fate had in store for us. All I knew, all I cared about at that moment, though I was weak, scared, hurting with hunger, and was covered with filth beyond description, was that I was alive. Dénes and I decided that one of us would always stay with our packs. Though most of the people had some supplies, blankets, their clothes, like animals we became fiercely possessive of our belongings and didn't trust anybody. I was the first to go outside. The only German presence was the guards in the towers outside the back fence of the compound. Outside the fence was a forest of small pine trees. Behind our barracks was a large latrine. Perhaps as many as thirty to forty holes in a long, bench-like seat over a cement cesspool. White powdered lime and the smell of lime was everywhere. Outside the latrine were several long lines of water pipes, with spigots over long, metal troughs. There were a lot of people around the troughs already, drinking the water and washing themselves. I tested one of the spigots and almost couldn't believe my eyes as water gushed out. Washed my hands and took some sips of water. I knew I shouldn't drink too much or too fast, but it was almost impossible to control myself. It tasted good and I drank a bellyful. Within seconds I had to go to the latrine, but no results. I had a terrible urge, my cramped stomach twisted in pain, but there was nothing in my intestines to eliminate. I went back to tell Dénes about the water. Just as he went outside, there was a lot of yelling. SS guards burst into the barracks, beating everybody with walking sticks who wouldn't jump to a rigid attention or grab their hats off their heads fast enough. It was odd; I thought that they all had walking sticks. I knew that it wasn't part of the SS uniform, and since all of the sticks were different, they could not have been issued. I figured later that they were taken from invalid inmates and carried for the sole purpose of beating people. All of us ran outside and were formed up. The counting started again, after which each of us was given a beat-up half-round enamel bowl, about ten inches in diameter, which was to be our eating dish. I didn't have time to wash mine. Some of the SS with white aprons—cooks— were yelling something I couldn't make out from across the main avenue of the camp as a couple of dozen people were led across the road by one of the guards. They picked up some large, heavy containers, our dinner. Lines were formed as the containers were brought into our compound and the food was doled out. On several folding tables were loaves of bread, cut into roughly one-inch-thick slices. Each of us was given a slice. It looked almost like the Kommissbrot I liked so much in labor service, but it had more sawdust on it and, as I found out, in it. I couldn't figure out if my tongue was shriveled up or swollen, but it was sticking to the top of my mouth. It felt like I was salivating as I saw the bread, but no saliva came to my tongue or lips. When it was my turn, a small cup of the food was sloped into my bowl. It was some kind of a soup I had never seen before. The color of it was a brownish gray, with a few small pieces of unpeeled potatoes and what looked like chunks of raw beets in it. It was tasteless and disgusting looking, but it was warm. It was supposed to be food, and I was incredibly hungry. But when I took the first mouthfuls, I felt mud still on the obviously unwashed beets and potatoes, and even the smell of the soup was nauseating. But I knew I had to have something in my stomach. It had been ten days without food except for the paprikás bacon and small pieces of bread with toothpaste on it.

I don't know if it was my remaining sense of humanity or my stomach that in reacting to the soup just about made me retch. I noticed a young kid in the compound next to ours, standing on the other side of the fence. He was skin and bones. His expressionless, large hollow eyes were riveted on me. I went over to the fence and tried to talk to him in Hungarian, but he didn't understand me—he was Polish. I tried German and asked him what this soup was called. "Vie heist ist dieser suppe?" "Gemüse," he said, meaning "vegetable soup." He was thrusting a bowl, just like mine through the fence at me. "Bitte... bitte..." he kept repeating. ("Please... please...") I didn't think I could have eaten any more of this foul-smelling, foul-tasting stuff, but the kid looked like he was half dead and I poured what was left in my bowl into his. It was gone in seconds. He lapped it up before I could fully realize how hungry he must have been. I gave him a piece of my bread, which he gobbled up equally fast. I asked him what he had for lunch. He shook his head. "Kein mittagessen," he said. ("No lunch.") "What did you eat yesterday?" I asked. He answered, "Gemüse."

The gentle mist kept falling and the awful smell of the smoke was stronger than before as I finished the rest of my bread and went inside the barracks. The stench we brought with us from the train was strong in the crowded space, but all of us ignored it. At that moment there wasn't much we could have done about it. Besides, all of us were spent. Evening came as I fell asleep on the hard wooden boards, lying down for the first time in ten days. Loud and frightening whistles and yelling woke us. It was still dark as SS guards were once again clubbing people to get outside and line up for formation.

* * *

As I look back on this phase of my life, it seems as if we were treated and trained like animals. We were not told how to react to commands or how to do anything. We were yelled at and beaten till we did what we were supposed to do, the way we were supposed to do it. There were fewer beatings as we figured out what was expected of us, and phases of our daily lives settled into a routine. The counting lasted for hours. We stood shivering in the cold, hoping that it would finish and we could have breakfast. But there was no breakfast to have. We learned that from then on we would be given one meal a day, consisting of a slice of bread and a cup of Gemüse. There would be no variation. Always Gemüse and bread. Always the same amount, sometimes hot, sometimes cold, and never at the same time of the day. I don't know if this was by design, but wouldn't be surprised if the cooks purposely gave us our Gemüse one day in the evening and the next day very early in the morning. Then the following day we wouldn't get our soup till late evening, which meant that we would spend the better part of two days without food. By the end of the second day I ate all my Gemüse, every drop of it, and with every passing day was hoping to get a little extra. Such as it was, it was the only food I, or any of us, had, and I was going to eat it because either it or the lack of it was going to kill me. Mentally I could not accept the possibility of me looking like the people in the neighboring compounds. I was never going to look like them, and I was not going to die.

We started cleaning up. Though it was very cold and raining most of the time, I washed and cleaned every item of my clothing. I shaved every day, which became the joke amongst my friends. They thought it was funny that I shaved every day, standing half naked at the trough in the cold or in the rain with my small mirror, shaving. But I thought it was wonderful and I knew that in spite of our low-grade existence I was improving my situation. I looked and felt clean and orderly, thinking that my father would be proud of me. My supply of razor blades was running low, as was the case with everyone else who shaved. I started sharpening my old blades on my wide leather belt, which made an excellent strop. I even sharpened razor blades for others, which helped occupy some of my time.

In all other respects our lives became a dull, repetitious existence, without any purpose other than survival. There was nothing to do but form up for head count in the morning or at any time the SS thought it would amuse them. Other than that, we waited for our food, knowing it would be the same as yesterday but hoping it would be more. As we settled into this routine, a new activity was added. Trying to get rid of lice became the most important daily chore. Within weeks, perhaps days after we got to Bergen-Belsen, we became infested with lice. It was revolting at first, but the human brain and body will adapt to anything. The most prevalent of various species was the body louse. Though we had lice in our hair as well, the body lice multiplied at an incredible rate, occupying every seam, fold, and crease in every article of our clothing. Most of our time during the day was spent with the futile task of trying to get rid of the lice. No effort was to any avail.

Getting rid of the lice was impossible. We kept after it but accepted it as an unalterable fact of life all of us had to live with.

* * *

Friendships were formed as each individual found a group he or she fitted into. There were all kinds of people in our group. A fellow, perhaps twenty years older than I, a young industrialist from Budapest, became a very close friend. Even under the circumstances he maintained a good sense of humor. Because his expression reminded me of a frog, I called him Frogface, or some Hungarian word I long ago forgot. He had a large nose, big eyes, which seemed to come out of the side of his face, and his lips seemed to go around almost to his ears, giving him a perpetual smile. I don't know how he found out about my being a fencer, but he called me Dr. Kabos, after the Olympic gold medal–winning Hungarian saber champion. Dr. Kabos was one of my idols. He perished, I found out later, at the hands of the Nyilasok in Budapest. It is sad that I no longer remember Frogface's real name. He was a good friend, though some time later he and I found ourselves opposing each other. More about that later.

As a child and young student I loved to read travel and adventure books. One of my favorites, which gave a vivid, fascinating account of the author's travels in India, was written by Lukács Pál, who was in one of the barracks next to ours. He was also the editor and publisher of the leading Hungarian theatrical magazine, *Színházi Élet*, or *Theatrical Life*. (This is the magazine I mentioned earlier that featured Uncle George during his visit to Pápa in 1936.) When I finally met Mr. Lukács, a gentleman much older than I, I was awestruck. I was even more surprised to hear that he never visited India. In spite of this, I found it fascinating to be around him. I have no idea of his fate.

The head coach of one of Hungary's best soccer teams, Ferencváros—the team I named my button soccer team after—was also in our compound. Every time I think of him, a name like Frankfurter wants to surface. It could have been his name. He was a tough individual who exercised every day and at one point put a group of people together for daily calisthenics. I was one of them. I recall doing jumping jacks at our first get-together in the rain. I wanted to be the best of the group, but after a few minutes it became obvious that we didn't have the strength or the stamina for calisthenics. Nor

193

did I think it wise to burn up energy I could ill afford to give up. Most of the group must have thought so, and the group dissolved a few days later. I don't remember the coach's fate either.

The people I mentioned above, as well as others, made life in camp a bit more bearable. But there were some lowlifes with us also. Some would steal, cheat, fight, behaving in ways that did not help us retain the little dignity we still had as human beings.

* * *

As winter came we occasionally had snow. Those who knew our exact location explained that due to ocean currents, this part of northwest Germany never has severe winters with lots of snow. In a way this was good, though damp, cold temperatures, rain, and deep, icy mud made our lives miserable. I wondered how the unfortunate creatures we now called Mussulmans, in the skimpy striped pajamas and without shoes, could cope with the winter as they pushed the carts loaded with corpses in the deep, cold mud. The sad truth was that one day they pushed the carts, and the next day they were on them. I don't know for sure where the name "Mussulman" came from. In comparison to the Mussulmans, the group in my compound did remarkably well. We had our own clothes, our own shoes, toiletries; some of us still had basic medicines such as aspirin and iodine, and we didn't have to work. For most of the time we were left alone. We had no Kapos. Let me explain.

As we had some limited contact with people in adjoining compounds, we were amassing quite a bit of information about life in other parts of Bergen-Belsen. For instance, in the compound on one side next to us, where I saw the hungry kid on my first day at Belsen, were people from Slavic countries. All of them wore the striped garments, no underwear or coats or sweaters, and all had a number tattooed on their left arm. They were brought from slave labor camps, which had no exterminating facilities, as they became too weak and could no longer work. They were brought to Belsen to die of systematic starvation and disease within weeks after their arrival. In fact, hundreds of fresh corpses were stacked in front of each of the buildings we could see from our compound every morning. As people died, new captives arrived in never-ending columns. The situation was the same in most other compounds all over the camp. All these compounds were run by Kapos. The word "Kapo" is an abbreviation of "Kaserne Polizei," German for

"Barracks Police." Most of these Kapos were Ukrainian. They were prisoners themselves, petty and major criminals who, because of their well-known brutality and antisemitic tendencies, the SS put in charge of the compounds as Kapos. Most were typically round-faced, rosy-cheeked, burly, cruel, and sadistic individuals. Some were known to club prisoners to death daily. They lived in the barracks in a relatively well-furnished private room with all the food they needed. Besides extra rations of better-quality food than what the prisoners got, they were also in charge of the prisoners' food and sold all the portions which would have gone to prisoners who died to other prisoners, provided the prisoner had something of value, such as gold teeth. The Kapos were perhaps more feared than the SS. Our compound did not have Kapos. The administration of our food was done by some of the elders or those who, like Frogface, were elected by the people in our barracks.

We found out that there were also Russian prisoners of war held at Bergen-Belsen. They were as badly treated as any of the other prisoners. In fact, probably every nationality from Europe and other places of the world were represented amongst the prisoners at Belsen. There was even a large number of Germans suspected of being communists, liberals, intellectuals, homosexuals, criminals, and many other classifications of "enemies of the state." Some mark or the other methodically identified each person or group. Some had large squares cut out of the backs of their coats, replaced with striped or other colored material. Even the shape of these patches had particular significance. Some were small triangles of different colors on the front of the jackets, denoting homosexuals, Catholics, and so on. We had none. None of us could understand our obviously different status, except those who still insisted that we were being held to be eventually taken to Switzerland. Believing this rumor helped our morale, and the more we learned about the fate of other prisoners of Belsen, the more we wanted to believe it.

\* \* \*

One morning after head count, instead of being dismissed we were marched out of our compound and told that we were going to the Brausebaden, "showers," to be deloused. By this time we have heard lots of rumors about the showers in other camps such as Auschwitz. Most of us thought that this was the end, except the Switzerland advocates who believed that we were indeed going to be allowed to shower in preparation for the trip to Switzerland. At the so-called Brausebadenand delousing station, we were told to undress and hang all our clothes from hangers with numbers on large racks. We saw these racks being pushed into a steamy room, surprisingly, by SS men. We were then given soap and razors to shave off pubic hair. The small cakes of soap, the size of hotel bars, all had three letters, RJF. Later, rumors circulated that the soap was made at the crematorium from the body fat of cremated prisoners, and RJF meant "Rein Jüdisches Fett," meaning "Pure Jewish Fat." I understand that after the war this rumor was substantiated, proven to be a fact, and played a part at the Nürnberg War Crimes Tribunal. We fully expected to be gassed, but instead, hot water came out of the showerheads, and we scrubbed and laughed and enjoyed the hot water. There was even a claxon horn signaling the end of the shower before the water was turned off. There were no towels. We dried off as best as we could. Our clothes were waiting for us, having been deloused, still warm and steaming. As we marched back to our compound, we passed the never-ending, unbroken line of ever-present carts of corpses, and we couldn't help feeling that, indeed, there was something special about our group. At the same time, there was, I found out later, a feeling of guilt in all our hearts of being privileged and so much better off than the others. As one of the carts passed us, one of those who were pushing the cart called out my nickname, "Bandi." We couldn't stop or speak with anyone, but I turned and saw one of the Mussulmans looking at me. Whoever he was must have known me well enough to call me by my nickname, but I didn't recognize him. He looked just like any of the other walking skeletons reduced to skin and bones. Even today, I shiver as the thought gnaws at me that he could have been Sándor, my brother.

For the next couple of days we were relatively free of lice. We knew it wouldn't last, as all the barracks were infested. But we were moved out of our barracks into a stone and cement building, which at one time, we figured, was some sort of a hospital. This type of building was less prone to have lice than the wood and tar paper barracks we left behind, giving encouragement to the optimists, who insisted that the Germans were living up to the bargain of taking care of us while waiting to transport us to Switzerland. We even had bunk beds, and, best of all, our food rations changed. Instead of Gemüse, we were given red beet soup with slivers of some kind of meat. We were given a small portion of liverwurst, margarine, and cheese. One of the older SS guards actually talked to us. We called this guy Popeye. He looked like Popeye, one eye squinting, having a protruding jaw, and always smoking a pipe. He only said a few words and didn't tell us anything of course, but the diehards interpreted even this as another indication that we were on our way to Switzerland.

Just about this time I started to resent that my friend Frogface played favorites with the food. He would give extra helpings or just a little extra to his friends, myself included. But I thought this was wrong. I told him and he was obviously offended. He accused me of trying to take over the food distribution. I really wasn't, but at the same time I didn't want his practice to continue at the expense of some who might have been afraid to speak up. When I spoke up, others echoed my feelings. I was appointed to distribute the food. That afternoon I fashioned a ladle from my canteen cup and a piece of a bed board. The following day we were given a thick soup of some kind of shredded pumpkin or radish. I carefully measured each portion. The container the food came in was marked with the number of liters it held, and I divided this by the number of people. The canteen cup ladle was to be just the right measure for equal portions for all. It didn't work out that way. As I was getting to the bottom of the container, I knew I was going to run short. Not getting one's food portion was the worst thing, which could have happened to anyone. Fortunately the only one who didn't get food that day was I. Frogface gave me some knowing looks, but I honestly don't think he was happy about my situation. Basically he was a very nice man.

While I am on the subject of food, let me tell you that food became an obsession. There were women in our compound, though none in our barracks, yet the conversation, as it would happen when a bunch of men congregate, was seldom about women. Even when we started to talk about women, within a short time the subject matter would switch to food. Food was the premier subject matter, and thinking about food became an obsession. We salivated as someone talked about a particular dish or eating experience. All of us related cooking and eating experiences. We visualized, talked about, dreamt, and thought about food constantly. Then suddenly we were moved back to our old barracks, and our menu switched back to Gemüse, day in and day out, as before. No one was able to figure out why we were given different and somewhat better food for a few days. Some speculated that the Swiss Red Cross inspected the camp, but if true, none of us saw any signs of that. One more thing about food. Some claimed that the Germans put something into our food that suppressed sexual desires and stopped the menstrual cycle in women. But I think that it was the lack of food and the awful quality of it that did not allow our bodies and our brain to function properly, and had all sorts of ill effects on us. All of us lost weight; we were all weak, yet I, for one, wasn't sick for a single day. It could have been psychological, but aside from the effects of the lack of food, I never even sneezed. Our hair thinned out, looked stringy, and lost its luster and color. One could see one's scalp right through the hair. Yet our hair grew, if a bit slower than usual. We had barbers in the group, but no scissors. At various times during the past ten months, we were told to turn in knives, scissors, straight razors, anything which could have been used as a weapon. It could have been and probably was due to stupidity on my part that I never turned in my hunting knife, which truly was a weapon. Nor did I turn in a small pair of scissors I had in my sewing kit. Close to a hundred people had their hair cut with those small pair of scissors in our barracks.

* * *

Even though it was obvious that for some reason or other we did enjoy a privileged, somewhat better treatment than most in camp, we were by no means living the good life. We were starving, weak, ridden with lice, and covered with sores. There were sick people most of the time. My precious supply of iodine and aspirin was gone, having doled it out to whoever needed it. Diarrhea was plaguing us almost constantly. At other times our stomachs were twisted in cramps by hunger, and we were so constipated that by the time one had a bowel movement it was a very painful experience. Those who had some serious illness, mostly the elderly or anyone who by this time were very weak, would not be able to get off their bunks and died quietly. Death and the smell of death surrounded us. The pile of corpses grew every day, and the faces of the dead were unforgettable. Most of the eyes were open or half open, as were the mouths, as if the corpses were screaming in silent agony. Rumors went around that some in the piles of corpses weren't dead. They were thrown onto the heap, as they no longer had enough strength to move or talk. Some of these probably lived through the ride under a heap of corpses on the carts on their way to mass graves or to the crematorium, where they were cremated or buried alive. We saw men and women clubbed to death by the Kapos in nearby compounds. We saw thousands of new prisoners brought into camp, most of whom we knew would be dead in a matter of weeks, even days. We had our own deaths in our barracks. Teams of Mussulmans collected the relatively well-dressed corpses, at times as long as a week, even longer, after they died. When someone died, people amongst us wrote down the individual's name and whatever else was known about them. It was also an accepted practice to take some items of clothing if one needed it, a gesture, if you will, of the dead helping the living. I never took anything. Perhaps I really didn't need anything, but mainly because the very idea was hard for me to accept.

\* \* \*

We entered 1945 and we were no closer to Switzerland than the year before. But the diehards steadfastly maintained that our privileged situation was due to the fact that a deal was made and the Germans, terrible as they were, were living up to their end of the bargain. They just didn't have enough transportation to get us to Switzerland, the diehards reasoned. Surely, as bad off as we were, it was obvious that we were in better shape than the Mussulmans or any other prisoners in eyesight. Though we had no up-to-date news of any sort, we speculated about the war, where the Allied forces might be. But by all visible indications, there was no change in our or the SS's lifestyle within the camp. The SS still strutted around in polished boots, they still looked well fed, and as far as I could tell, we might be in that camp till the end, one way or the other.

\* \* \*

One day we saw a large group of women herded to a compound across the main avenue of the camp from us. They were all in regular clothes, some even wore fur coats, and didn't look as bad as most new groups we saw arriving. Most of us crowded around our front fence to see if we could recognize anybody. I did. It was an awful shock to see my Aunt Alice in the compound directly across the road from us. I yelled at her, but as everybody else was yelling, she couldn't hear me. Then she saw me and broke down crying. I wanted to know why she was there. Since our last correspondence months ago, I believed that she, Uncle Miklós, and their son, Jancsi, were still in Pápa. Now she was in Bergen-Belsen asking me if I knew anything about Uncle Miklós and Jancsi. There was so much yelling going on that I couldn't understand most of what she was saying, and I'm sure she couldn't understand me any better. We were chased from the fence by the SS guards, as were the women across the road. For the next couple of days I tried to catch a glimpse of her, but she was not to be seen again. She perished in Bergen-Belsen.

* * *

On the twelfth of January 1945, I celebrated my nineteenth birthday. My last year as a teenager, perhaps my last year. It wasn't much of a celebration; I probably never even mentioned to anyone that it was my birthday. But I was nineteen years old, going on sixty-five.

* * *

It could have been in January or perhaps February when we were taken to be deloused and to shower again. It was a new reprieve and once again the Switzerland rumors became rampant. There were new analyses and explanations. The war was being lost and the Germans wanted to prove their humanitarian side to the world. Any day, the diehards claimed, now that we've been cleaned up again, we would be taken to the train and be on our way to Switzerland. We wouldn't be any good to the Germans, they reasoned, if we weren't in Switzerland before the war's end. It made sense. We knew the war was coming to an end, though we had no hard information; we just knew that it had to. One day, a lone aircraft flew low over the camp and some claimed it fired at or dropped a bomb on the crematorium. We saw the plane, but thick smoke continued to curl uninterrupted from the huge square stack, which was visible from our compound. The smell was as awful as ever, and I didn't think the attack was true. But one night we heard a consistent low, distant rumble, which reminded me of the noise made by the large formation of planes I saw flying over Pápa and Kolozsvár, and we heard the noise again a few nights later. The brains, our analysts, figured that it was a bomb attack on one of the nearby large cities, probably Hannover. During the next couple of days, a very large formation of American planes, their silver bodies pulling contrails, flew over the camp. We were elated, though nobody gave any indication of our feelings other than a suppressed smile. The SS were shooting at and clubbing the prisoners to go inside the barracks.

This was the first visible proof in a long time that the Americans were bombing Germany, and the war we all hoped would soon be over. But how soon? Every day thousands more starved to death, or were killed by clubs, shooting, and disease. Even a day would spell the difference between life and death for thousands of people. The SS behaved as if they had no connection to the war. Their only concern seemed to be the murder of multitudes. That day, perhaps as punishment for being hopeful for a few seconds, there was no food brought to our compound.

\* \* \*

There were a few babies born in our compound. The miracle was that, as I understand it, some survived, at least for then.

\* \* \*

Winter was slowly giving way to spring. I don't remember the day, one day was like any other, but I remember the sun coming out for the first time in months. It warmed us and filled us with renewed hope. More sunny days followed. Though the temperature warmed somewhat, most still walked around with blankets over their head. We were always cold. Mercifully the breeze carried the smoke and the smell away from us at times, and the usually gray skies gave way to blue. One morning, it must have been in early March, I noticed a larger-than-normal contingent of SS in our compound. We were counted with more meticulous care than in recent weeks and were told to get ready to leave the compound with all personal belongings. Despair and hope alternated. We were going to Switzerland; we were being taken to an undisclosed place and would probably be killed. We got ready.

As we formed up again, an even larger contingent of SS guards with bayonets fixed and dogs on leashes were waiting for us. We marched out of the compound in the direction we came from when we first arrived at Belsen. The devastation all over the camp was worse than I ever saw before. There were mountains of corpses everywhere. Other compounds were full of people, walking slowly and aimlessly amongst hundreds of corpses all over the ground. The carts were an endless procession slowly heading in the direction of the crematorium with their dead cargo. The wheels of the carts cut into and churned the axle-deep soft clay mud. Our feet were covered with it by the time we marched through the barbed wire gates separating the barracks section of Belsen from the shops and the well-kept SS quarters

201

and administration buildings. Soon we went through the massive iron gates as the pitiful, sad band of musicians played a happy tune. The guards at the guardhouse outside the gates exchanged jokes with our escort, and as we walked, the guard towers, the huge smoking chimney of the crematorium, the images and stench of death, the worst forms of mental and physical torture, the purgatory on earth that was Bergen-Belsen slowly faded into the distance behind me. I was alive, but I knew that the horrors of the past few months would remain with me for life, unless I did something about it.

## Chapter 13

# 1945 – MARCH | MAY
# GOING TO SWITZERLAND

We couldn't walk very fast; some could hardly walk. Dénes and I had somebody—I have no idea who—hanging off our shoulders between us. His weight added to my backpack made walking in the mud very difficult. But it was a beautiful day. Spring was bursting open in the countryside, and the first of the wildflowers were coming up along the road. The air was fresh, pure, and sweet and we were walking away from the camp, which at that moment seemed like an unreal, gigantic freak show, a horrible, twisted nightmare. The waiting train of boxcars reminded me that the nightmare, in fact, was not over. I was surprised to see a flatcar at the end of the train with two huge cement rings, in each of which were two double-barreled antiaircraft guns. Then came the next surprise. We weren't jammed into the cars in the usual manner. There were fewer of us in each car, still a lot, but not as bad as the conditions were in the cars on the way to Bergen-Belsen about five months before. But the biggest surprise was that the doors of the boxcars, though they were closed, were not closed all the way, and the latches were not locked. In fact, the first thing we did, as the train started moving and there were no SS guards by the doors, was to see if we could unlatch the doors from the inside of the car and slide them open. To everybody's amazement, we could! Most of us couldn't explain this, except the diehards who were now convinced that we were finally on our way to Switzerland. Even I began to believe it. The problem was that the train was going east, not south. The diehards had an explanation. The tracks and stations were destroyed in most of Germany. We saw that all along the route our train took, and they reasoned that we had to go east to get south. They were convinced that the train would eventually turn south.

I was actually beginning to believe and look forward to arriving in Switzerland. About this time I noticed and became very conscious of my and all of our pitiful shapes and conditions. It was demoralizing. We lost a lot of weight in Belsen. As the loss was gradual, we adapted and tried not to notice it. Our tattered and dirty clothes were hanging off of us. We were still wearing as many layers as we had against the cold, shirts on top of shirts, and in my case a beat-up, dirty white towel, which I wore as a scarf. Some had the soles of their shoes tied on with string or wire, or had no shoes at all and had their feet wrapped in rags. All of us were covered with sores. During our stay in Belsen our skin became very dry and scaly. This and the sores were due—those who knew told us—to lack of vitamins and to the lice infestation. We were constantly scratching and the sores became larger, got infected, and festered.

The joy of our newly found "freedom"—not being locked in—soon went sour, as by the second day we realized that we hadn't been given any food since our last portion of Gemüse in Belsen. At the rate we were going, Switzerland was days, perhaps weeks away, and I didn't think we could make it without food. The next morning it was raining hard, and as daylight was coming up I realized that our train was sitting on a siding in a station next to a freight train that was loaded with potatoes in open freight cars. The station and the potato train must have been bombed some days before. A few fires were still smoldering and some of the wooden sides of the freight cars were burnt. At the risk of their lives, a few of the adventurous ones jumped out of our train and collected some of the half-burnt potatoes. Even though by this time they were cold and soaked with rainwater, it was manna from heaven. We stockpiled some in our car and lived on them for the next three days. Three days later our train came to a halt in a station and the engine was unhooked. By this time we realized that the SS did not stop us from getting off the train. We could get off to relieve ourselves and even wander away from the train. When a new engine hooked on, the signal was several long and short blasts of the whistle, with two long blasts just before the train started to move. As we explored near our train we found out that we were back at the same station where we found the potato train three days before. For three days and nights we went around in a circle, obviously not able to find an open route to get us to wherever we were going. We collected some more of the half-cooked, burnt potatoes, as well as some unburnt ones, hoping to be able to cook them sometime. This opportunity came the following day when our train stopped somewhere in open country and our engine was taken away. We dug a hole in the ground with my hunting knife, put some rocks in the bottom, filled the hole with potatoes, and built a fire over the hole. Without the matches I carried with me for almost a year, we could not have done this. The fire burnt for about an hour. As we sat around waiting for the potatoes to cook, we salivated and talked about the feast we were about to have. Baked potato stories were endless. I remembered and talked about the potatoes we used to roast in our large ceramic stoves in our home on Eszterházy Street. At that moment, Eszterházy Street, my youth, seemed like it was eons ago and didn't even seem real. When the last of the fire flickered out, we scraped away the ashes and uncovered the potatoes. The top layer was almost completely burnt solid charcoal. But even that tasted good. In fact, some claimed that the charcoal was going to have beneficial effects for those who had diarrhea. The next layer of potatoes were half burnt on the top and half steam boiled on their bottom side. They were absolutely great! The layer underneath these was just steam boiled, and the bottom layers were hardly cooked. It didn't matter; all were gone in a matter of minutes. The only one who offered criticism was Lukács Pál, who thought that we the cooks, myself included, botched the job and the potatoes were not cooked the way they should have been. Nobody agreed with him. We were starving. We would have eaten anything that even remotely resembled food, and the potatoes then seemed like the greatest gift from God. We devoured them and couldn't understand why Lukács Pál was so critical, in spite of the fact that he also had his share.

Frogface and I were friendly again. He, Dénes, and I went exploring the countryside. There was a farmhouse not too far from the train and we went to see if we could find some food. There was a woman in the house alone. She must have been frightened to death by our appearance. I'm sure she thought we came from another planet or were possibly dangerous criminals, but she gave us bread and milk and some sausage. I didn't realize that I lost my taste of real food. Biting into the bread and the sausage, drinking the milk was a strange experience. My taste buds must have been hibernating, if not completely dead. The taste of ordinary food was an almost totally new experience. Every taste seemed exaggerated and overly strong. Even the milk had a strong taste to it. The woman watched us, horrified, as we devoured and gobbled the food, and was surprised and relieved when we thanked her and left with some of the bread and sausage.

The train sat without an engine for about a day and a half. We baked the rest of our potatoes and stretched out on the ground, on soft, lush, fresh grass, and dozed in the spring sunshine. Occasionally an SS man walked by without paying attention to us. I often think about this, as I or any one of us could have just walked away from the train and escaped, but nobody did. Why? There must be a simple explanation, though psychologically the real reason might go very deep. But at this phase of my life, I didn't act on the basis of sound reasoning. It was instinct. Looking back on it, where would I have gone had I escaped from the train? I had no idea where I was, much less where I would have gone. How far would I have gotten in a country which, for the past decade, had been trying to kill me? There was no doubt in my mind that had I been caught I would have been killed instantly, or perhaps returned to Bergen-Belsen in a striped suit. I realized that there was comfort, if not security, being amongst the people I spent the last half a year with. They were my family for now. I belonged with them. Furthermore, though I still didn't believe it, the possibility of Switzerland loomed ahead more plausible than ever. On top of everything else, I knew I was better off at that moment than I've been for the past five months. I stayed with the train, as did everyone else.

The weather was exceptionally nice for this time of the year. I still couldn't grasp the significance of the antiaircraft guns at the tail end of our train and couldn't get comfortable with the idea that the Germans, who till this time went to great lengths to kill us, were now protecting us. But the guns were there, big as life, pointed at the sky.

\* \* \*

We were on our way again. Just as the diehards predicted, the train turned south someplace near Berlin. It was late afternoon when we were hit. As the train was chugging along I heard an explosion and a tremendously loud, hissing sound. The train was braking, wheels locked and screaming as the train slowly skidded to a stop. I looked out of the open door and saw a huge cloud of steam enveloping the engine. That was when the first bullets hit my car. It was like a shower of metal, ripping holes in the roof and splintering the sides of the car. Five planes were strafing the train, one zooming down out of the sky following and being followed by another in an

206

unending circle. I, like most of us, panicked and jumped. There was a long, rock-strewn embankment on my side of the train and I was tumbling down it, unable to stay on my feet. The planes were on top of us, and the bullets were kicking up dust and rock fragments in my face. I kept running. Frogface was shot in the neck next to me, his head grotesquely twisting, bouncing along his body, trying to separate from the rest of his lifeless torso rolling down the embankment. People were dropping everywhere as the planes came relentlessly again and again. They were so low that I could see the faces of the pilots and the flashes of the machine guns at the forward edges of the wings. I was running towards a row of trees at the far end of the open field. The planes were shooting; people were running, screaming, and dying. I made it to the trees and a ditch at the far end of the field, but instead of jumping into the ditch I grabbed onto one of the trees, both arms hugging the tree, unable to let go. There I was, hanging onto the tree, fully exposed to the bullets, which were hitting all around me, penetrating trees and killing people. Finally, after what seemed like eternity the planes flew over the field, rocking their wings without firing, and went away. I couldn't let go of the tree for some time. Just hung there, horrified, scared out of my wits, unable to do anything. When I finally collected myself and let go of the tree, I could not believe the devastation around me. I have no numbers, but there must have been over a hundred dead and wounded. There was nothing I or anyone else could do to help the wounded. My brain must have switched off, as I don't remember what we did with them and the dead. We could not have helped the wounded and could not have buried the dead. There were too many and we had no shovels or picks or anything to dig with. If we collected the bodies, I don't believe we put them on the train. I have no recollection. We tried to help those who could walk. Frogface was at the bottom of the embankment. I recognized his cap, which somehow stayed on. His eyes were open and he seemed to be smiling his ear-to-ear grin. A macabre, sad, grotesque, and frightening sight. It was a helpless, wrenching feeling as I walked away from him. I had become accustomed to death and insensitive to human suffering. My interests were self-centered with the primary objective of survival. But his death affected me strongly, and I made up my mind then that I would not make any more new friends.

The train was a disaster. Hundreds of jagged-edged holes in the sheet metal and splintered wood everywhere. We hauled some dead bodies out of the cars. In one of the cars a man was sitting on the floor with his back against the side of the car. His head was hanging to one side, eyes closed. He was surrounded with dead bodies, blood, remnants of clothing, and hundreds of holes where the bullets hit. But when he was about to be taken out of the car as one of the dead, he woke up. He was asleep during the entire raid, and a living testimonial to proving my mother's God's Big Book theory. Strange things happen under strange circumstances. Those who jumped out of the train on the other side of the cars fared better. They found themselves on the uphill side of the tracks in the woods. Perhaps because the pilots saw all the people in the clear on my side, the other side was not strafed. Those of us who were spared were now the only occupants of a shot-up, half empty car.

It took a couple of days to take away the destroyed engine and hook up a new one. I wondered if we were going to be hit again. I speculated about other freight trains having similar guns, and if they would have been manned if the cargo demanded it. I wondered why the antiaircraft guns didn't fire. It dawned on me that our guns could not have fired. There was no personnel to fire them, probably no ammunition either, and even today I wonder if the guns were attached to our train to make an ordinary freight train appear to be a target for the Americans to shoot at and to kill us.

* * *

We were going south-southeast away from Switzerland. The remaining diehards still clung to their beliefs, still holding to the "have to go east to get west" idea. The problem was that we were now somewhere in Czechoslovakia, shunted onto a siding, this time with the doors of the cars closed and locked. Though it was a sunny day, we weren't too uncomfortable, as there were fewer people in the car than we had started out with and the air was circulating through the many bullet holes. Even before the doors were opened we heard shouting, and through the bullet holes in the side of the car I saw SS men all over the place. I wondered if I should have gotten away from the train while I had the chance. The doors were unlocked, and as they slid open we were once again ordered off the train amidst blows of walking canes. I knew we were at our new home. I had no idea what our new home was or where we were, but it was a safe bet that it wasn't Switzerland.

* * *

You are right to think that I tried to inject a bit of humor into the sentence above. Over a half a century after this event took place this is not particularly difficult, but even then, as unlikely as this may seem, humor played a part in our lives. Self-effacing as it was most of the time, it helped us cope with the horrendous aspects of our existence. Getting off the train and heading for our new home, which I found out was Theresienstadt, called for all the sense of humor I could muster.

* * *

I don't know why I do not have a better recollection of events at Theresienstadt. As I think of those events so long ago, I wish there was some way of replaying them and bringing up long-forgotten details. Just recently I was talking with a friend, Mary Kaufman, who was also from Pápa and spent some time in Theresienstadt while I was there. She reminded me of something I told her in Theresienstadt a half a century ago about our train ride during which we were badly shot up by American planes. As she talked about this, my brain kept clicking, and with her help an episode that I had forgotten surfaced. After the attack on our train, perhaps to save their miserable lives or hoping that it would prevent further attacks, the SS allowed me to paint a large red cross on top of several boxcars.

Perhaps because I did not spend a long time in Theresienstadt or because I was not physically and mentally up to it, my brain might have switched into low gear, refusing to store some aspects of my situation. Don't get me wrong, I wasn't giving up. My father's philosophy about not being defeated till one gives up stayed with me and helped me go on. The day we got off the train I vaguely recall standing for hours in the midday sun, somewhere in a compound, surrounded by stone or brick buildings. We had no food or water. From the distance I heard screaming and anguished yelling, which never stopped. Then we were marched out of the compound into what appeared to be a normal, pretty town with a park, large trees, and two-story buildings. There were no people anywhere. We came to a street with three-story military barracks on both sides. There were SS men and women around, most with heavy walking sticks. We were led into one of the buildings called Hannover Kaserne, "Hannover Barracks." The building, which looked deserted on the outside, was teeming with the most wretched-looking humanity on the inside. Once we were all inside the SS just abandoned us. We weren't told where to go or stay; they just left us standing in the middle of the large courtyard surrounded by the huge building and, it seemed, thousands of other prisoners all in worse shape than us. There were dead bodies all over. Some of us, including Dénes and me, found a room on the ground floor which was not too crowded and dropped there. There wasn't much available space in the room, but just as we walked in, some dead bodies were being dragged out. The people who were lying on the floor were all sick. We knew they had typhus. By this time we learned about this disease, carried by lice, and knew that it struck without notice. The first sign of having it was losing control of one's bowels, followed very quickly by losing consciousness. The majority, those who were in very poor condition before the disease hit, never regained consciousness. Others woke up one, two, maybe three days later, only to die then of malnutrition or some other disease altogether. A small minority miraculously did not die, and although no one was immune, some escaped getting this dreaded disease. There were other diseases also. Besides standard illnesses and malnutrition, there was cholera, which produced a lot of bloody excrement and vomit all over the place. The barracks had indoor plumbing. The problem was that each building, designed originally for six or seven hundred soldiers, now had as many as five thousand or more people in it. Most of these people, those especially who had cholera or typhus, could not have made it to the latrines, and even if they could, it wouldn't have mattered, as there was no water and the urine and the excrement could not be flushed away. There was no point to go to the latrines. The entire place was a gigantic cesspool. In some areas excrement, old and new, covered the ground. Unburied, uncollected corpses were everywhere. The smell was not to be believed and couldn't possibly be described. There was no food, and water would be turned on at irregular intervals for varying short periods on most days. People would fight for water. Some lapped up the muddy water from the ground after the water was turned off. I tried to recall how I lived during this period, but aside from the general situation which I described above, I have no recollection of most detail.

* * *

Typhus hit me at about this time. When I woke up, lying in filth, I was hardly able to move. The disease robs the body of almost all strength and we didn't have much to start with. Dénes was asleep. I didn't know if he also had the disease or if he was alive, but when I shook him he gave some feeble signs of life and I left him alone. Somehow, I got hold of some water. There was a pipe with a spigot in a small yard near the room. The water was on when I got to it. Perhaps the news of the water being turned on didn't get around yet, as surprisingly only a few people were near the pipe. It was amazing how drinking some of this water returned some of my strength. I took some to Dénes, who woke up shortly after. Some food was brought into the barracks; I think it was wagons full of beets or turnips. I seem to recall several large mounds of it, attacked by hordes of half dead prisoners. In spite of the lack of food, my strength was slowly returning.

\* \* \*

Some adventurous young guys, those who somehow escaped health problems, found ways through underground passages (all military buildings of this era were connected by underground tunnels as part of their design) to venture out of our barracks and into others. Whenever they went, they tried to get information on who were in the other barracks. One of these young guys who knew Dénes and me came to see us and told us that he came across people from Pápa in one of the other barracks. He didn't remember who they were but told us that one man from Pápa was a lawyer and the other had the same first and last name. I think my heart stopped at that instant. No one I knew in Pápa other than my father had the same first and last names. It was as though someone hit me on the head with a sledgehammer and at the same time injected strength into my veins. I wanted to go see my father immediately. The young guy who brought the news agreed to take me. He led me across the courtyard to a corner of the building and down some steps into a cellar. We had to grope along in the dark with some light filtering through small barred street-level windows way above us here and there. There was rubble everywhere in the tunnels, which probably hadn't been used or cleaned for decades. There was a long stretch of darkness where we went under the road between the buildings. Then we came into a large room in a cellar. One small barred window way above us allowed in some subdued light over a heap of bricks and rubble in the middle of the room. My guide told me to stay there while he went into the building to see if he could find my father. I also wanted to go, but for some reason he didn't want me to go with him. I waited for what seemed like an eternity. Then I heard noises, feet shuffling, footsteps climbing over the mound of bricks. Out of the darkness came my guide and two men in the familiar striped-pajama-type clothes, with round striped caps. I recognized my cousin Imre, but I wasn't sure if the other man was my father. He didn't look like my father. He was small, extremely thin, and bent over, both his hands pressed against his lower stomach. His facial features were that of a hundred-year-old man, but he was my father. I ran to him and embraced him. He completely broke down, cried and sobbed uncontrollably. I tried to comfort him, but it was a long time before he regained enough of his composure to talk to me. As a child my father represented authority to me. He was the master of our lives, powerful, unafraid, and unbending. His image, the last time I saw him standing erect at the railroad station in Pápa as my train pulled away, seemed like centuries ago. That image was etched into my mind, but now that big, powerful, and proud man was reduced to a bent-over wreck of a human being, perhaps on the verge of the last moments of his life. He was a devastating sight. As he regained some of his composure, perhaps to explain his terrible condition, he said, "Nagyon megvertek." The statement struck me like lightning, as it means, "They beat me terribly." As a child I wouldn't have thought that anybody would have dared to lift a finger to my father. Now here he was, beaten to perhaps within an inch of his life. I've seen some of these beatings. Two or three Kapos mercilessly beating a weak person with clubs, until they would tire and stop the torture, or the person died. In fact, very few ever survived such a beating and I wondered how my father did. But he was alive, and that was all that mattered to me. I also suspected that he might have been beaten for his defiance, or for standing up for or helping others. Imre told me later that my father was overworked doing not only his own work but also the work of those who could not have done their quota and would have been killed. This must have been the reason behind his double hernia, which is why he had to press his hands against his stomach as he walked. During their death march to Theresienstadt he had carried a man, Bodó Imre, also from Pápa, who was too weak and could no longer walk. After some hundreds of miles the man died. My father was exhausted and probably robbed of the last vestiges of his strength. I was outraged and felt utterly helpless. At that moment I would have liked to kill every German.

My father wanted to know if I had information about Sándor. I did not. I told him about Alice néni, which at the time was probably a mistake, as it seemed to shake him. He told me that my mother and most of the family, who were taken away from Pápa almost a year before, were separated on arrival in Auschwitz and were probably murdered within hours after they got there. He told me he didn't know for sure, but I sensed that, as most of us, he was still deluding himself. In retrospect, the thought occurred to me that perhaps he didn't want to believe it. We sat on the heap of rubble for a long time. Imre was quiet most of the time. Strangely, he was in much better shape than my father. We decided to meet every day in this place about the same time. The young fellow who was responsible for this unbelievable reunion sat quietly while we were talking. I wish I'd found out his name or where he was from, but at that time I don't think I even said thanks to him.

Walking away from the cellar, I knew that I was going to make it. I had to. Now that I knew my father was alive though in terrible condition, I had to make it to look after him.

* * *

Finding out that my father was alive was perhaps the most momentous event in my life. Yet seeing him in the condition he was in filled me with sadness and anger. At the same time it gave me renewed strength and a will to live. My mother's death was not unexpected, though I had hoped against hope that someday I would see her again. Now that I knew she was dead my heart was filled with grief, yet strangely I was relieved to know that she was spared the unbelievable agony and suffering of slowly and painfully dying over a long period. Aside from the sadistic, inhuman treatment, the tortures, starvation, and disease, her anguish for us surely would have killed her. At that moment I was grateful to know that her suffering mercifully did not last too long.

There were no others in my father's barracks from Pápa. Though I slept little that night I woke early, revitalized and grateful to God for my father's return. I got out some of my clothes to give him and waited impatiently to go see him again later that day. Though I went through a bout with typhus, until this time I didn't fully realize how bad my own condition was. I had no way of weighing myself, but it would be safe to assume that my total weight was around forty, forty-five kilograms, or about ninety pounds. Lacking all other nourishment, the body, I suppose, consumes itself. I also noticed that Dénes, I, and just about everybody around me walked hunched over, taking small, shuffling steps. My guide came to see me later and told me that the SS sealed off the barracks and it would be very dangerous to try to go over to my father's armory. He also told me that the Russians were within days from reaching us. I recalled my experience waiting for the Russians in the woods in Romania after my train was shot up. I wondered if they would take their time again. I didn't think we could hold out much longer. We no longer had the luxury of measuring time in months, weeks, even days. Every hour or minute that passed brought us closer to death, and the clock was ticking faster and faster. The mounds of turnips were gone and people were dying in large numbers of starvation and disease. I was determined and knew I was going to make it, but I wondered how much longer my father could hold out.

* * *

About two, maybe three days later the Russians got to Theresienstadt. We didn't know that the war was over for two days by then. It was May 8, 1945, when we heard the rumble of tanks. One drove right through the massive gates of the Hannover Barracks. I don't suppose they knew who was in the barracks and could not comprehend the sight, which greeted them inside the armory. Some of them, battle-hardened veterans, got sick and were vomiting. Thousands of dead, in twisted, grotesque positions, lay all over the grounds. The situation was the same in the rooms, in every conceivable place a man could drop. The smell of decomposing bodies, vomit, blood, urine, excrement, and disease was overwhelming. Flies covered the dead, the sick and those who were still alive. Some of the latecomers such as us were in better condition than most. Some were brought to Theresienstadt by marching from great distances, as much as a thousand kilometers. They were the worst off amongst the prisoners, and most of those who survived the death marches did not make it in Theresienstadt. But I was liberated and well enough to believe that I was going to make it. I went through the main gate out of the armory looking for my father. Just outside the gate was a formation of SS women. I was still spooked and was startled to see them before I realized they were held by Russian soldiers. I was hoping they were going to be shot. When I found my father amongst thousands, he seemed about the same as before, barely alive.

* * *

The events of the following days and weeks are more vivid in my memory, though there are still gaping holes as I try to recall some of the detail. As the Russians weren't prepared for the massive cataclysm, the cleanup, the removal of the dead, medicine for the dying and the sick, food for the starving was slow in coming. There was a large contingent of German SS women at Theresienstadt. Their hair was shaved off and they were the first group put to the task of removing the dead. They had to be heavily guarded, as they would have surely been killed, probably torn apart, if the prisoners were not restrained. Some military ambulances arrived. Soviet soldiers in white smocks took the near dead and the sick away, ostensibly to hospitals. The Red Cross arrived and food started trickling in, but not enough to feed everybody. Only the strongest could fight their way to the food, and unfortunately the weak and the sick still got little food, if any, and still went hungry, or died. But slowly more and more food came, and the kitchens in each barracks were cleaned up and put back into service. Regular meal service started, but the clamor by the voraciously hungry was still creating riots for meals. I volunteered amongst others to try to help contain the crowds fighting for food. It was an almost impossible task. Food was an obsession, a most urgent necessity, and the fear of not getting it turned most of us into animals. But slowly it became obvious to all that there would be enough food for everybody. The portions were getting larger also, and the crowds were slowly returning to a more or less human sort of behavior.

Because I helped out with the crowd, I was near the kitchen and got to know all the kitchen people. I was getting ample food, too much, in fact, but I was able to get some of it to my father and Imre. With my strength returning, my adventurous spirit got me out of the barracks exploring the outside world, once again a free man. By the time I got into a nearby town, full-scale looting was going on all. Most of the residents hung white sheets of surrender hanging from their windows; others, most likely Germans who had something to do with the camp, fled, abandoning their homes. Those were the houses hit worst by the looters, myself amongst them. It made no difference at times whether we needed certain things or not; we took whatever we found for the sheer pleasure of taking it, or psychologically perhaps as punishment of people who we believed were responsible for our suffering. We looked upon the Russian soldiers and the Russian nation with gratitude as our saviors. But we were at war with the rest of humanity around us. I don't remember exactly what sort of loot I came up with. Whatever it was was most likely trivial, and it probably hurt the people I took them from, less than it helped me. I remember grabbing a belt somewhere, which I gave to my father. Looking back on this experience, at times I wonder if I should have a feeling of remorse. While I don't think that the looting was right, I do not have any guilty feelings about having done it. I went even further. One day as I was venturing further and further from the barracks, a group of Hungarian soldiers, disarmed of course, came through the area. They had horse-drawn wagons; all of them were in uniform and undoubtedly on their way back to Hungary. Some of the Hungarian ex-prisoners from the camp attacked these soldiers. I joined them. We beat the soldiers with whatever we could lay our hands on. Some were badly hurt as they were trying desperately to get away from us. I was too weak to pursue them, but it gave me satisfaction and filled me with joy to know that now it was my turn. On one of my excursions away from the camp, I spotted a young German officer on a bicycle. He could not have been much older than I. His khaki uniform was almost spotless. As he came towards me I grabbed the handlebars of his bike and told him to get off. It may have been my frightening physical appearance or the club in my hand, or my hunting knife, which by then I wore on my belt again, but he did get off the bike and smiled at me without trying to resist. I couldn't believe it, but he had a pistol in a holster. I motioned to him to give me his belt, holster and pistol. I took the pistol out of the holster. It was loaded and I pointed it at the young German just inches from his face. He held his hands up and started backing away. I could not get myself to pull the trigger.

I have often thought about this incident over the last half a century. When it happened on that beautiful sunny day in 1945, I was disappointed with myself for not being able to pull the trigger and avenge the death of my mother and so many of my family. But looking back on it, I now believe that had I pulled the trigger, it would have been murder, which would have haunted me for the rest of my life. The war was over, the killing was supposed to have stopped, and the young German was unarmed. I had his gun. Had we met as enemies in opposing armies under conditions of war, had he been shooting at me and I at him, I probably would not have hesitated to shoot and kill him. But at that moment, as I held the gun on him at point-blank range, I now know would have been murder. Thank God that even in my animalistic state, with rage filling my heart and calling for revenge, I was not capable of it. As it was, he was going home to his mother, his family, his wife perhaps, though I doubt he was old enough to have one. As I yelled and waived the pistol at him, his smile turned into a grimace of fear and he turned and broke into a run. I'm glad I did not pull the trigger. But I kept the gun. It was a small symbol of a minor, meaningless victory over my enemy without easing any of my terrible losses.

I hung the gun in its khaki canvas holster from a nail in our room, which by then had been cleaned up. Most signs of the terrible times of only days before were gone. The room was as clean and as organized as we could make it. A young Russian soldier who befriended us stopped in now and then. When he first came into our room, at the time when it was still in shambles, he kept pointing to his chest and repeating the word Jevrey, Jevrey. We found out later that the word Jevrey meant "Jew" in Russian. One day he brought us some Russian tobacco and showed us how to make a cigarette, wrapping some of this black, coarse, and awful-smelling tobacco into newspaper. We smoked some to make him feel good, but it made us very sick. I think it would have made the strongest smoker sick, and we were neither smokers nor strong. He was scared to see my pistol hanging on the wall. One of the Polish guys in our room explained to him that I took the gun from a German officer. He was very pleased and kissed me on the lips. Don't worry, that was and still is an accepted practice in Russia and some other middle European countries such as Hungary. But as grateful as we were, meeting the Russians was disappointing in some ways. I couldn't believe how ill equipped and badly clothed some of them were. I thought that a mighty nation would have an abundance of everything. But they didn't.

\* \* \*

I became a cook. My help keeping the crowds in line, now that everyone knew there was going to be enough food, was no longer needed. But they needed more help in the kitchen. By then all the cooks knew me and one of them asked if I wanted to help out. I said yes, and found myself standing on an elevated stand which encircled a gigantic vat, stirring beef soup with a paddle big enough for a canoe. The vat cooked hundreds of gallons of soup, or goulash, or whatever was on the menu. It was probably the best beef soup I've ever had, not just because I was hungry, but also because it cooked huge amounts of beef and beef bone with marrow. It was hard work in the hot kitchen, as the stirring for some reason could never stop. On the other hand I learned that one should not stir peas. If peas are stirred, they will burn. Every day, after the meals were served I'd fill several mess kits with whatever food was prepared that day in my kitchen, get on my bike, and take the food to my father, Imre, and some of their friends. By this time I found an abandoned apartment in town—probably some fleeing Germans lived there before—and moved my father, Imre, and friends into it. I was also able, though I no longer remember from where or how, to get some clothes for my father and Imre. For the first time in almost a year, my father slept in a bed.

* * *

During my wanderings and exploration of our surroundings I found a piano in a shed. It was an upright. The keys worked and I remembered that one of the people in our group was a pianist. His name was Fejér György. In spite of his youth, he was by then a well-known and highly regarded pianist in Hungary. I went searching for him and when I found him, my friends and I went with him to the shed with the piano. Funny, how some unimportant details make lasting impressions. I clearly remember the anticipation on Gyuri's face on the way to the piano. I remember his parted curly hair, the long strides he walked with, cracking his fingers, and his overcoat that was way too big and hung from his shoulder. I think he was frightened as he sat down at the piano for the first time, and I suspect he was apprehensive of his fingers possibly having lost their dexterity and skills and if his artistry might have been affected by the long absence from his music. But the sounds that emanated from his keyboard filled the air with beauty, humanity, and an indescribable joy of being alive. He played some scales at first, some variations on the scales, improvising as his fingers came alive.

I'm not certain, but he might have had tears in his eyes. One of the songs he played was a favorite of mine. This American song, "Smoke Gets in Your Eyes," became popular in Hungary just before the truly bad times started. His music helped us return to humanity by a giant step and we just couldn't get enough of it. But Gyuri's fingers gave out and to our regret the impromptu concert came to an end. We heard Gyuri play again during the subsequent days. Years later I met him in New York. He was playing at one of the fashionable clubs in the city, and we reminisced about the day he played the piano in Theresienstadt. He remembered and played "Smoke Gets in Your Eyes" for me again.

* * *

The International Red Cross and some other relief organizations came to Theresienstadt. All the survivors, my father, Imre, Dénes, and I, were registered amongst thousands. We eagerly sought lists, hoping to get information on family members. But the lists were short and incomplete. I hoped that just as we were registering, others were registering elsewhere, and soon we would have more information available to us. The Red Cross also assured us that we would be repatriated as soon as transportation became available. Until then we were to remain under the protection of the International Red Cross and the Soviet Army with all our needs to be provided for. I think most of us were still confused, still hadn't sorted out our newly found freedom, and did not know what our next steps were to be. We stayed in camp in relative comfort, free and far removed from the daily tortures of previous days under the Germans. We were visibly getting better. I was gaining weight and getting my strength back, feeling more and more human every day.

I was proud of myself for bouncing back so quickly, and for being able to provide the most needed necessities for my father. Little did I know that bringing him food every day under the circumstances was possibly the worse thing I could have done. Though it was consumed voraciously, my father's weak stomach could not tolerate the rich, spicy foods such as goulash. After showing some signs of improvement at first, my father became ill. I didn't know what was wrong. He lay down in obvious discomfort and didn't talk. The following day when I got to his house he was in bed, motionless. He looked at me, but I didn't think he recognized me. His eyes were glazed, and I don't think he knew where he was, and didn't respond to my questions or when I told him I was going to get a doctor. I feared he had typhus. The epidemic was still going on and many died of it even after the liberation. I was desperate and knew that I had to get him medical attention. Imre and I managed to get a hold of a Russian officer in the administration office of the camp, and within a couple of hours an ambulance arrived. Some soldiers in white lab coats over their uniforms put my father on a stretcher and put him in the ambulance. One of the people who came with the ambulance was an officer also in a white smock, with a thermometer and stethoscope in his pocket. I thought he was a doctor, though he probably wasn't. He was very friendly, spoke a few words of German, and appeared to be reassuring. As the ambulance drove away, I tried to follow it on my bike but couldn't keep up. It disappeared in the distance down the road. Imre assured me that we would find out where the hospital was and I would be able to visit my father in a couple of days. I didn't believe him. I wanted to hope for the best and I wanted to believe Imre, but in my heart I knew that I would never see my father again. Long after I left Theresienstadt I heard that the Russians were horrified of all the raging diseases in the camp, and collected the very ill and, regardless of their illness, took them to some remote place where in most instances the sick died slowly without even minimal medical attention.

This part of my life still haunts me. I cannot be certain if the food I brought daily to my father was the sole cause of his illness and subsequent death, or if it even contributed to his death. All of us ate the same food. I have been assured by many, such as Imre, who spent the entire time with my father since they left Pápa, that my father would not have made it under the best of circumstances. He was extremely weak, sick, mentally and physically depleted, and kept alive only by his stubborn determination. Imre reasoned many months later that my father, knowing his wife was dead, being aware of his own terrible condition, probably wanted to die. Imre also thought that seeing me in relatively good shape and recovering fast relieved my father's anguish and provided him with a peaceful death. I would like to believe this, but the gnawing suspicion that I'd contributed to his death never left me. I felt then, as now, that I didn't make enough of an effort to find him after the ambulance took him away. As I recall those times filled with anguish and anxiety, I distinctly remember that in spite of my displeasure with myself my actions must have been based on the unconscious, helpless belief that he was dead. Watching him being put into the ambulance, unresponsive, wordless and motionless, I would not be surprised if he didn't make it to the ambulance's destination. But I don't know that, and not knowing has haunted me to this day, and I do know that it will continue to haunt me for the rest of my life. Perhaps thinking about it, recalling it in detail, talking about it here for the first time in over fifty years, will help ease my grief and sorrow over his death. He was not an old man. He was only two months shy of being fifty at that time. But it does give me some peace of mind to think that seeing me, as Imre said, might have relieved his anxiety over the fate of at least one of his children and helped him die peacefully. Imre assured me that in a couple of months I could return to Theresienstadt, by which time my father would have recovered, and bring him home. I knew he was saying this only to comfort me as by then he must have suspected, perhaps even known, that my father was dead. I did. I didn't want to believe it then, but deep down in my heart I knew that it was so. Perhaps because my senses were still not functioning at normal human levels, emotionally I was not able to react to his death in a "normal" manner. Having seen death in its most horrible manifestations, my senses and emotions were dulled possibly to the lowest levels of human awareness. Perhaps this was merciful, as not having to watch him suffer spared me agony, and I hope a quick death might have relieved him also. The sad fact was that he was gone. After miraculously finding him and spending a brief but wonderful few days with him, he was gone in a matter of seconds. Having survived the war, the indescribable horrors of Auschwitz, Birkenau, Buchenwald, and Theresienstadt, being alive and with me after our liberation filled me with hope, which was now dashed. My remorse is not so much over his death as it is over not knowing when, where, and how he died, and what I could or should have done to prevent it. Though I hoped against hope and talked about seeing him again, deep down I knew he was gone. It must have been so written in God's Big Book.

It was time to go home.

# Chapter 14

# 1945 – 
# GOING HOME

Summer was coming on. The weather was beautiful and the large horse chestnut trees in the park were flowering. Our conditions were improving, though very slowly. The Red Cross was still registering survivors, but we still lived in the same barracks surrounded with ghosts and bad memories. We had more and more food, more clean clothes, but the lice infestation was still not completely eliminated. Though there was still typhus, the sick were now receiving some medical treatment.

We kept discovering people we knew, some from Pápa, some from the labor service, and heard that some others were leaving camp to go home on their own. I was also anxious to leave. I wanted to go back to Pápa to see if any of my family, particularly my brother, Sándor, had possibly returned. I hoped that my Uncle Miklós and his son, Jancsi, were still there, in spite of seeing Aunt Alice in Belsen. But the Red Cross was still unable to arrange transportation for anyone. We were told that the railway operated at minimal capacity, and for the time being mass repatriation was out of the question. No one had any estimate when we might be transported home. A new bulletin appeared one day, announcing a plan for those who wanted to leave on their own. They were to be given a safe conduct pass and a thousand Czechoslovakian koruna for expenses. Imre, Dénes, four or five others, and I decided to take advantage of this and signed up. The "safe conduct passes," small, gray books, were printed in five languages, I believe: Russian, Czech, German, French, and English. It simply explained who we were and asked for the assistance of the authorities of the countries one had to travel through to get home. We got the passes, but the Red Cross had no money. We were told that if we could get to Prague, the Hungarian Red Cross would give us the money. Prague, we knew by then, was only about sixty miles from Theresienstadt. We didn't give much consideration to how we were going to get to Prague, but I started packing. I had more stuff than any of us. All my gear was more or less still in acceptable condition, as clean as I could make it, and I also had the pistol and the bicycle I took from the German officer. The bike turned out to be our ticket to Prague. A local man who had a truck was going to Prague and agreed to take us in exchange for the bike. I was still working in the kitchen and stocked up on food for the trip. With a heavy heart, grieving for my father and feeling very guilty about leaving without him, we left early one morning. Probably less than two hours later the fairy-tale spires and castles of Prague, like the Emerald City, loomed in the distance ahead of us. The truck let us off somewhere in the city, and after getting directions and much walking, we arrived at the Hungarian Red Cross office. It was on the second floor of an ordinary apartment building across from a large park. The park was full of refugees from every country in Europe, all trying to go home. There were lots of Hungarians, some of whom told us that the Hungarian Red Cross, as the International Red Cross in Theresienstadt, didn't have money either. Just the same, we went up to register and to see if they had information about our families. In the front office we were given a questionnaire, a single sheet of paper to fill out. The woman who spoke Hungarian gave us the forms and explained that it was for the purpose of compiling survivor lists, though they only had a few short lists for us to see. We didn't find anyone we were looking for. The figure *1000* with a *K* in front or after it at the bottom of the questionnaire caught my eye. The questionnaire, incidentally, was in the Czech language, which none of us could read or understand. The woman told us where to write our names and personal data, and where to sign the questionnaire. I wondered if in fact the piece of paper was a receipt for one thousand koruna, which we didn't get. I questioned her about it. She left us and in a little while returned with a small, bald, and slimy-looking character who introduced himself as the director of the Hungarian Red Cross in Czechoslovakia. He invited us into his office, which was small, most of the space taken up by a big desk. He sat behind the desk as all of us stood facing him. He explained that the Hungarian Red Cross had no money, but he felt sorry for us and was going to give each of us twenty koruna out of his own pocket. Twenty koruna probably would not have bought us a meal, yet I wondered if this guy gave twenty koruna to every refugee who came into his office how long would it be before he went broke. Behind me in one of the corners of the office was a safe. Oddly, I should say stupidly, its door was slightly ajar and I could tell that the safe was stuffed with stacks of neatly bundled money. The situation was quite clear. This guy was ripping off the refugees who would sign for one thousand koruna but got only twenty. My pantlegs were stuffed into my boots and I ripped the pockets open. While Imre, Dénes, and the others were talking to this little son of a bitch, I stuffed my pantlegs full of bundles of money. I think I even put some in my shirt. We then each took the director's twenty koruna, thanked him, and left the Red Cross office. It was hard to walk with my pantlegs full of money, but we made it to the park. I had no idea how much money or what denomination I had until I emptied my pantlegs onto the grass. The heap of money was thousands and thousands of koruna. Even though there was staggering inflation in Czechoslovakia at that time, it was still a very large sum of money. My first instinct was to get going before the loss of the money was discovered and the Red Cross chief had the police after us. Imre didn't think this would happen. Instead, we distributed a lot of the money to some of the other refugees, mostly to the Hungarians, and explained that if they signed the questionnaire without getting a thousand koruna, they were gypped. We encouraged them to go back and demand their money. We then left the park on our way to somewhere to find shelter for the night. Without knowing it we walked into a convent somewhere, I think on Castle Hill. The nuns fed us and allowed us to spend the night sleeping on the freshly scrubbed floor in a large, empty room.

The rest of our stay in Prague is hazy. Perhaps the details of the time I spent there weren't important. I wasn't there for sightseeing, wasn't a tourist, and I didn't care about anything other than getting home as quickly as possible.

The thought of not having a home occurred to me. A year ago my family and I were put out of our home and undoubtedly someone would've moved into it. The same thing would be the case, I was sure, with my grandmother's house on Bástya Street, our ghetto home. I wasn't too concerned. I even thought of chasing people who might be living in our home out at gunpoint. We decided to go to the main railway station in Prague, hoping to find a train to Hungary and Pápa.

As in the case of my stay in Prague, only the more interesting events of our trip stayed in my memory. There were no scheduled passenger trains from anywhere to anywhere. Some passenger trains, at times mixed with freight cars, were coming into the station and leaving Prague. The important thing was to know which direction a train was going. Trains leaving for points south were the ones we were hoping to find. All the platforms along every track were teeming with huge crowds, waiting and hoping to get on the right train, trying to go home. When we got to the tracks said to be for trains to Hungary, the crowds were mostly Hungarian and largely ex-concentration camp inmates like us. When a train slowly backed onto the tracks, there was a mad scramble for any available space on the train. The roofs of the cars were so crowded that there wasn't a square inch of space available. The trick was to get on and hope that the train was going in the right direction. When the train stopped at a station and we heard it wasn't continuing in our direction, we got off to wait for the next train. The scene was the same at every station. Immense crowds of refugees, all anxious to get home. There was a freight train on a siding at one of these stations, and I realized that the boxcars were full of people and the doors were locked. Armed Soviet soldiers guarded the train and I shuddered as the sight brought back bad memories. Then I realized that the people in the cars were German soldiers. I was elated at first, but in a short time I felt guilty about rejoicing and realized I felt sorry for them.

The trip from Prague, which under normal circumstances takes less than a day, took, I believe, five days to the Hungarian border town of Pozsony, now Bratislava. We slept wherever we could, ate whatever we had or could get a hold of, and hopped on any train that left the stations in the right direction. A train left Bratislava on the way to Győr. It was already dark when we arrived at Győr. We got off, as the train was continuing east towards Budapest. There were no other trains at the station, which had surprisingly few people around. We unrolled our blankets on the platform and Dénes and I were about to spend our last night sleeping under my Romanian blanket, which was now almost in shreds. The following morning we woke early, as a gentle spring rain was falling. There were still no trains in the station and the stationmaster told us he didn't expect any for a while. We went looking for food. There was a bakery near the station. It was open and had rolls, salt sticks, and bread. We still had a lot of Czechoslovakian money, but the woman in the store wouldn't take it. I told her that I had some old Hungarian money from before the war. I was sure that the prewar money with Admiral Horty's picture would no longer be good. She wanted to see the money. I cut some of the stitching in the shoulder straps of my backpack to extricate one hundred pengő notes, which before the war were worth a lot, but I didn't think would be worth anything now. Surprisingly, I was wrong. Though the money wasn't worth as much as before the war, it was still the currency in circulation. When she saw the money the woman in the store offered us milk and eggs, which we ate with gusto. I was delighted that the money was still good. Even after we paid for breakfast I still had quite a bit of money left, and some more hidden, still sewn into various places in my backpack.

* * *

Frankly, I don't remember the trip from Győr to Pápa. I do remember arriving at the Pápa railroad station before noon. It was a very emotional experience. Just a few weeks short of a year after I left Pápa and the ghetto, seeing my mother, brother, and most of my family for the last time, I was home again.

Or was I?

# Chapter 15

# 1945 – 1946
# HOME AGAIN

Aside from one or two people, the railroad station was deserted. The building looked as I remembered it, but it was in bad shape. To my left the bridge was still there over the tracks, bringing back images of a young kid standing in the smoke, and my father's image standing erect on the platform cane in hand came back to me—ghosts of bygone days. The linden trees on Eszterházy Street were giving off their sweet scent as Imre, Dénes, and I walked towards the center of town. It was a gray, damp day. There were very few people on the streets anywhere. I remember one woman walking on the other side of Eszterházy Street with hurried steps, eyes riveted on the walk in front of her. She had a grave expression on her face. It occurred to me that I didn't know where we were going. When we passed our house on Eszterházy Street, I thought of my father standing behind the window puffing on his pipe, but the shutters were closed. The carriage gate was lying on the ground, its metal bars bent, all twisted up, and some of the trees around the house had been cut down. I remembered this end of Eszterházy Street on summer evenings as boys and girls promenaded. There were ghosts everywhere. Every street corner we turned reminded me of something or someone, but the town was almost completely deserted. Russian women soldiers stood on some of the street corners, directing traffic with red and yellow flags. Even the main square had only a handful of people. Uncle Miklós's store was closed, but none of us commented. A few people stopped to gawk at us before going on their way. A lot of the stores were closed, boarded up, or abandoned. A ghost town. Going under the archway into Kossuth Street, passing Saint László Street on the right, I expected to see the burnt skeleton of a German car, but it wasn't there. My cousin Klári's husband's store was open. We went in. No one was in the store besides the one clerk. There was hardly any merchandise on the shelves. Imre talked with the clerk for a few minutes. He was a former employee of Klári's husband. We went on towards Uncle Miklós's home. My heart was pounding as we went up one flight of stairs. The door to his apartment was locked and no one answered the bell. None of us spoke. None of us wanted to admit our fears. "We'll come back later," Imre finally said. I knew from my father that my mother and many others of my family were gone, but I was desperately hoping to see my Uncle Miklós and of course my brother. Dénes home was just across the street. He went upstairs as we waited on the street. Less than a minute later Dénes was back, telling us that their apartment was locked also. We turned left onto Deák utca, Deák Street, past the movie theater towards Józsa néni's store. The store on Main Street was open. Jolán, the oldest employee who had worked for my aunt, was in the store. There were no customers and very little merchandise. Jolán, who was a very nice woman, seemed scared and broke down crying on seeing us. She told us that she has been running the store, which was assigned to her by the authorities after my Aunt Józsa was taken away with the rest of the family. She had no information of Uncle Miklós either, other than that he and his son, Jancsi, were still in town in October. As far as she knew, no one from the family came back. Imre told her that unless we found a place to stay, we would be spending the next few nights in the store. I divided the rest of my money amongst the three of us and we decided to meet in the store that evening.

I headed down towards the Tókert and our last home before moving to the ghetto. The gate was locked and nobody answered the bell. I waited for a bit. I could see some of our outdoor furniture through the iron bars of the fence and the gate, a long wood and iron bench, chairs, and the round table I used to "fly" as a child. After a while I left towards Jocó's house. I was very hesitant. I haven't had any information about Jocó in almost a year. I didn't know if he was home or even if he was alive. Walking towards his house I noticed again that the streets were deserted. Pápa was a ghost town. It didn't feel like the city I grew up in and I felt as though I was in a strange town for the first time. When I got to Jocó's house the wooden gate to his house was locked, but that was not unusual. They always kept the gate locked. I rang the bell. Jocó and I had a code. When he came to my house he would ring the bell two short and one long rings, repeatedly. Everybody in my house would know it was he at the door. At his house I always rang one short and two long rings, repeated several times. It was our signal. I rang one short and two long rings, twice. In seconds the gate flew open, Jocó standing there. We hugged each other. His mother (Juliska) and father (Jóska) came running. She hugged me and his father shook hands with me. It was wonderful to see them, particularly Jocó. They couldn't believe how bad I looked, though by this time I thought I was well on the way to my former shape. The first thing she wanted me to do was to eat. I knew I shocked them, telling them that I didn't want to go into the house, as I was still infested with lice. She heated some water in their wash-kitchen in an outbuilding for a bath. Jocó brought out some of his clothes. I emptied my pockets—there wasn't much in them besides some money—then I emptied my backpack. I took my tools out. Jocó was surprised to see the pistol still in its khaki canvas holster. I told him the story of taking it from the young German and that I wanted to get some more ammunition. He didn't ask why but told me that under the Russians, guns were not a good thing to have around, though he told me he also had a pistol hidden in the house. My hunting knife was on my wide leather belt. The backpack and the clothes I had in it were in pretty bad shape. After I scrubbed down I shaved and put Jocó's clothes on, I felt like a new man. Though he was always smaller and skinnier than I, surprisingly his clothes fit. I took all my things, the Romanian blanket, my clothes, and backpack, behind the building, put them in a pile, and set fire to them. In a way it was like a funeral pyre, saying goodbye to the recent past I didn't want to remember. At the same time I was sad to see my backpack, which became part of me, burn. I recalled making it, making the hardware for it, sewing money into the seams, and how well it served me during the hard times. In a matter of minutes it was all gone, lice and all. Juliska néni had some food waiting. Noodles and salad. They watched me eat it all and I could tell they were shocked at my hunger. We talked. They wanted to know about my family. I told them about my father, Imre, and Dénes. They had nothing to add to what I already knew about Uncle Miklós and Jancsi. All they knew was that they were taken away at one point the previous fall. Jocó told me he was drafted into the army by the time Hungary was almost totally occupied. The army didn't even have a uniform to give him. Somehow, he just came home even before the war ended. His brother, Big Jocó, was in an American prisoner-of-war camp, happy as a clam. He was a pilot officer in the Hungarian Air Force and somehow managed to be captured by the

Americans, the dream of every Hungarian soldier in Germany at that time. I mentioned some of my experiences, but judging from the expression on their faces they had a hard time comprehending or believing what I told them. They wanted to know what I was going to do and where I was going to live. I had no answers to either of the questions. Jocó's father told me that I would be welcome to stay with them. I accepted.

Jocó and I decided to walk around town. On the way up towards Fő utca, Main Street, a tall man passed us. He had a Hungarian military cap, a pistol belt, and a red armband. He was Závory Zoltán, an artist and art teacher who, Jocó told me, was now the chief of police in Pápa. Seeing him from a distance startled me a bit, as he looked the way the Nyilasok did during the war. Even more frightening was a guard in front of the temporary town hall on Main Street, looking exactly the way the Nyilasok did in Budapest when I got off the trolley car on my way to Városliget. He had the characteristic military cap with a visor, a cartridge belt, and a rifle with a bayonet, civilian clothes except for his red armband. The only difference in his appearance from one of the Nyilasok was the missing green arrow cross in a white circle on his red armband. Shockingly, I recognized him as one of the former Nyilas members of the local Arrow Cross, the Hungarian Nazi Party. Now he was a guard at the town hall under the new communist regime. The only thing that was different was the armband. I couldn't understand how this ex-Nazi could be a communist now and why he wasn't in jail.

\* \* \*

Over the next few days I explored the town. The first place I went to was my grandmother's house on Bástya Street. The house was occupied by people I didn't know. They were hesitant to let me in even after I explained who I was, but I didn't take no for an answer. I went into every room asking questions. I knew they were scared of me. There was nothing of any interest in the house for me. I recognized a few pieces of furniture but had no use for them. Still, I told the people that I was holding them responsible. The secret compartment I built but wasn't able to finish was broken open. The people in the house claimed no knowledge of who broke it open. I couldn't have cared less about what was in it—none of it had any value for me—but I wanted to know if it was discovered by the gendarmerie, in which case I know my father would have had some unpleasantness on account of it. The people in the house didn't know. Walking around town, here and there I saw people I knew. Some recognized me; others obviously wanted to avoid me and acted as though they didn't see me. It became a game. I pursued and caught up to them as they tried to hurry away. Invariably, everybody had a story. With the exception of a few, almost everybody had a story about helping Jews. I knew most were lying. The ones who looked sorry or shocked and had no story were the ones I wanted to talk with. Unfortunately no one had information of any value.

Some survivors like me who returned to Pápa before us had no information of any kind about my brother and other family members. The disappearance of Uncle Miklós and his son, Jancsi, remained a mystery. Imre went to the police station, but no one there seemed to know anything. It was as though the memory of a whole town was completely erased about one single aspect of the last year. Over three thousand people disappeared and nobody knew anything about it. I went to see our elderly neighbors, the retired judge and his wife who lived next to us on Pozsonyi Street. He had a horrible story to tell. When the first Russian troops came into Pápa, they tied him up and gang-raped his elderly wife repeatedly. They ransacked their house, cut the leather furniture up, ostensibly to have boots made out of the leather. They smeared jelly from their larder onto the walls with brooms, cut open the pillows and quilts, and tossed the feathers onto the sticky walls as a lark. It was sad to see these old people in the broken shape they were in. She didn't speak at all, and judging by her catatonic stare, I thought she had probably lost her mind. He and I went out to their garden to dig up my tin can. I already told you what happened to its contents. The tablecloths my mother gave them, he told me, were looted from them by the Russians, but he gave me seven gold coins (Swiss francs) that I didn't know my father had given him. I felt very bad for these elderly people. The fellow in our old house came after me with an axe when I demanded our outdoor furniture. I told Imre about it and also told him that I was going back for the furniture, and if the man was going to get nasty, I was going to shoot him. I would have done it, but Imre talked me out of it. As a lawyer, he quite logically explained that it would not have made sense to live through the German camps, then go to jail for killing the dumb son of a bitch.

Naively, I expected a different reception in Pápa. I thought that the people would welcome me back and try to help. With the exception of Jocó's family and a few others, the opposite was the case. Most people avoided me. I despised the ones who were trying to be friendly. Days later, a man stopped me on the Main Square. He looked familiar. He explained that he used to be one of the gendarmerie. He also told me how much he admired my father, Uncle Miklós, and my whole family. He even told me how he tried to help them while they were in the ghetto. I knew he was lying but didn't know why he was telling me this. He told me that he found my bicycle and wanted to return it to me. As we walked towards his house where the bicycle was, he winked as he told me that he knew it was my bike as it had my name in the saddlebag. As far as I remember I never wrote my name in the saddlebag. Surprisingly, the bike he had was brand new, and as expected, it wasn't mine. It looked like no one had ever ridden it. He winked again when he showed me my name scratched into the flap of the saddlebag. I still don't know why he wanted to give me this bike other than possibly trying to get on my right side. I detested him, yet I took the bike mostly because I didn't want him to have it. I knew it didn't belong to him. He might even have taken it from my uncle's store. I asked him if he had anything else that belonged to me. He tried to give me some long-winded account of how he came by the bike, but I didn't listen. I took the bike and left him mumbling to himself.

The first place I went to on the bike was Celldömölk. On the way a Russian soldier wanted to take the bike from me, but I outran him. In Celldömölk I found out even less than in Pápa. No one from my family or friends was there, and as in Pápa, no one knew anything. The only information I got was about Mári, which broke my heart. It was late at night when I got back to Pápa and to Jocó's house.

During the next few days I went to our old house on Eszterházy Street. The Russians occupied it as a sort of headquarters office for one of their units. As I told you, the carriage gate was torn of its hinges, lying on the ground. A tank must have driven through it. Alongside and behind the house, most of the trees were gone as I found out, used for firewood during the past winter. The parquet floors, gilded window frames, whatever wood there was in the house suffered the same fate. All the toilets were stuffed up, as the initial troops who occupied the house didn't know that these kinds of toilets had to be flushed. One of the young Russians spoke Yiddish. I didn't speak Yiddish, but between my limited German and his Yiddish I managed to explain who I was, though I didn't tell him that the house used to belong to my family. Their officer in charge, who incidentally didn't look like an officer and was just as shabbily dressed as any of them, told me to have lunch with them. They had some kind of a stew and very hot tea they drank from glasses. A few days later I went back to take their picture. Jocó had my camera and even some film, and all my darkroom equipment and chemicals. The Russians became good customers. Word got around and more and more of them came to the house to have their picture taken. Jocó's backyard became the studio. We put an old table out there with an empty wine bottle and glasses. The favorite pose was holding the glass high, caps pushed back on their head. Rightfully, Jocó's parents were at first very apprehensive of Russians coming to their house. The Russians were a pretty bad bunch. Almost every night there were burglaries, looting, rape, murder, and so on. Every now and then some of my customers got out of hand, particularly when there were women soldiers around, or when they had too much to drink. But I managed and we never had any major problems. Most of them didn't have much money, but we still built up a good amount of rubles, which was more readily accepted than Hungarian money. We could buy black-market goods with it, even exchange some for American dollars. The Russians could also get film for me, which they probably stole. My old contact, the large, heavyset photographer, and her diminutive husband became my source for chemicals. My life was slowly coming together. When Imre and I went to Uncle Miklós's store with the police, a locksmith opened the locks on the shutters and I found a length of a drive belt, which at that time was still used in Hungary to drive harvesting equipment and other industrial machinery. It was good, thick leather, ideal for shoe soles, a commodity almost nonexistent then. There was quite a bit of merchandise in the store of assorted machine parts, a couple of new bikes and bike tires. We locked up and had the police seal the store shutters, hoping for Uncle Miklós to return and resume his business.

Within the next couple of days I bartered part of the belt for a couple of small pigs. Jocó and I were going to fatten the pigs, which were priceless but illegal to have, as we hadn't registered them with the local government. Food was very hard to come by. Incidentally, I could not have cared less about the legality of something like having pigs. I felt that this godforsaken town and country owed me a lot. With the money Jocó and I made photographing the Russians, we also managed to get some good foodstuff. At times we were even paid with exchange goods, which were most likely stolen the night before.

Jocó and I went over to the Kollégium. The school, which during the last months of the war was converted into a military hospital, was in bad shape. Some of the old professors were back, amongst some new faces. I found out that within a couple of weeks the first érettségi, the comprehensive examination, was going to be given to those who were around to take it. Both Jocó and I signed up. I had no idea how I was going to pass it, as my school days seemed far in the past and I didn't think I would remember anything. I managed to get hold of some books, but I didn't spend much time studying. Studying for the érettségi was far down on the list in the order of my priorities. The first order of things every day was to get together with Imre and Dénes to see if there was any new information. There were a few people trickling back to Pápa. One showed up one day, two, maybe three the next, or weeks would go by without anyone returning. None of the returnees had any information other than their personal stories. Whenever I brought up the subject of returning to Theresienstadt for my father, Imre evaded the issue. I sensed that he knew that my father was not alive. Mary Kaufman, who after returning to Pápa became a good friend of Imre, also told me recently that Imre knew that my father died shortly after the ambulance took him away but for some reason didn't tell me. Deep down I also knew, but talking about going back to Theresienstadt kept my hopes alive. My anxiety over ever seeing my brother grew.

One night I woke in a daze. Jóska bácsi, Juliska néni, and Jocó were standing, horrified, by my bed. I didn't know where I was for some time. Juliska néni was trying to hand me a towel, but it was sometime later when I realized that I was drenched in perspiration. I had a nightmare. In a way it was a simple dream, but at times simple dreams can have tremendously shocking, devastating effect. This dream did.

In the dream I was at my grandmother's house on Bástya Street. There was no one else around and I knew I was alone in the house. The doorbell, a small nonelectric bell that was activated by pulling on a handle outside the massive doors, rang incessantly as I walked through the garden and the archway to the gate. It's interesting how clearly some details of the dream are etched into my memory. The quality of the light was identical to the morning I left the house for the last time. It seemed like early dawn on an overcast, gray day without much color. When I got to the gates, I remember how hard it was to pull them open. In the street facing the gate stood my brother, ashen-faced and motionless. "I am your brother," he said. I looked at him and said, "You can't be my brother, my brother is dead." As I said that I closed the gate. Then I must have screamed and kept screaming, waking and scaring everybody in Jocó's house, before I fully woke up and slowly returned to reality. This dream had a devastating effect on me for days. Days later I had it again and again and again, just about every night. I was afraid to go to sleep. But as time went by, the dream returned less frequently. I don't know when I had it last, certainly not for years, but I still remember it in all its simple yet terrifying detail.

Imre reclaimed his mother's apartment on Main Street. He opened an office and started practicing law again. The effort I made to prepare for my érettségi was very halfhearted. First, my activities of trying to find relatives and friends took a great deal of my time. The photography business also kept me busy, but most importantly the idea of studying under the circumstances was not realistic. Sitting with a textbook, as I would have done only a year before, was not the same. Under the experiences of the past year I must have matured further than I could have in years under normal conditions. My mind was occupied by far more important things than calculus or ancient Hungarian history. On top of everything else there were some disturbing factors about my life in Hungary. Conditions in Pápa were bad under Russian occupation. My life, like everyone else's, was a day-to-day existence, offering very little encouragement for a future. Why should I even bother with taking the test, I asked myself. It gave me no additional preparation for a future, which under the circumstances I couldn't even visualize. Further, I was disturbed by the attitude of the acting dean of the school, one Vásárhelyi Károly, I believe, who took a very hard-nosed position about having me pay the tuition before I could take the test. The simple son of a bitch didn't take the fact into consideration that his society kicked me out of my home, took everything I and my family had, conscripted me into labor service, and shipped me off to the German death camps, which was the reason I didn't have enough money to pay the tuition. I didn't like him, yet I had to deal with him on his terms. The Hungarian mentality didn't change much during the past year, and this man acted in the same, archaic, and unreasonable manner he would have behaved a year or so before. Imre was finally able to bribe him with a sack of flour, promising to pay the tuition as soon as I was able to, if he allowed me to take the test. The tests, during three or four days towards the end of June, perhaps early July, were not that hard. Under the circumstances, I suppose the requirements were eased to allow the few of us who returned from various aspects of the war to graduate. I recall taking pictures of my class at the completion of the tests and receiving our diploma, but I no longer have the picture.

Jocó's older brother returned from Germany with glowing stories about the Americans and the treatment he received in the American prisoner-of-war camp. He brought back some American cigarettes, chocolate, even toilet paper, which he used as cigarette paper. He talked about the food, which he said was better than he had in the Hungarian Air Force before he was captured. His young wife joined him. She was a very beautiful young woman, and now both of them were added to the already overcrowded, small Sinkó house. It was time for me to move out. I moved in with Imre but still spent a great deal of my time at the Sinkó house, where Jocó and I turned the wash-kitchen into a darkroom for our photo business.

As the conditions in the country, trying to recover from the devastating effects of the war under Russian occupation, were slowly improving, I decided it was time for me to venture a trip to Budapest to look for family. My letters to Aunt Manci and her husband, Uncle János, were not answered, and in fact some were returned weeks later. We did receive correspondence from Uncle Matthew and his wife, Margit. They and their son, Gyuri, were alive, living at their old address in Budapest. They had no information at all about the family. More people returned to Pápa, but they had no information either about my family. I found it very hard to believe that Uncle Miklós and his son, Jancsi, could have just disappeared from the face of the earth without a trace and without anyone in a town of sixteen thousand knowing anything about their disappearance. The police, ex-members of the gendarmerie, the neighbors, all claimed to know nothing. Some claimed to "have heard" that they were taken away to somewhere, as it was not safe for them in Pápa.

Beyond that, neither Imre nor I was able to come up with anything. I was getting very fed up with Pápa. I felt as though I was living in a foreign country where most everybody regarded me with disdain, suspicion, and fear. It was as though everybody expected me to go after them and to take revenge for the events of the past. Even Kovács Lajos, my old fencing master and gym teacher whom I had idolized, behaved in a way which I found difficult to understand. I had rushed to the Kollégium when I heard that he was back in town. By then I'd heard that he, as almost every other male person in town, young and old, was called into the military in the last days of the war. Some of the officers such as he were harshly dealt with by the Russians. I wanted to assure him of my help in case he needed it. Naively, I believed that the injustices committed against me and my family earned me some sort of privileged status and that I could be of help. He was wearing military britches and boots, perhaps the only things he had, when I caught up with him in the teachers' room at school. He was never a big talker, but at this time he hardly said anything. He acknowledged my offer of help with hardly more than a faint smile and a nod of his head, but other than that, and a few questions about my father and Uncle Miklós, said nothing. He seemed much older than just a year before. I was very disappointed, as I thought he would have been happier to see me, but even he acted as though he was afraid of me.

\* \* \*

Big Jocó, my friend's older brother, and I decided to go to Budapest. He had some cockamamie ideas about making fortunes on the black market and was looking for some of his cronies from the air force as potential partners. I of course was trying to get information about my family. Train travel those days was an uncertain and risky way to go from place to place. One had to find trains going in the right direction and be able to get on. The trains were unbelievably crowded. Every inch of space, including the roof, was occupied. There were trains taking prisoners to Russia occasionally in almost every station in the country. These trains, such as the trains I was in as a prisoner, would stop and spend hours at times in a railroad station, waiting for trains coming from the other direction to pass. While in the station, the prisoners managed to throw messages out, as I have done, to friends or relatives in town. When such a message was received, the friend or relative would come to the station and try to have the prisoner released in exchange for alcohol, money, or some other things of value given to the Russian guards. Once the prisoner was released, he would be gone in seconds, but the guard now would have to come up with a replacement so that the head count in the car would tally. When a guard released a prisoner, the usual practice was that he would pick some person at the station and force him into the car at gunpoint. The head count in the car would tally, the guard would be off the hook, but the innocent civilian would most likely wind up in Siberia and never be heard from again. These practices were well known, and Imre as well as the elder Sinkós were very much against our going to Budapest. We went anyway. At one of the stations a Russian guard, who undoubtedly was looking for replacements for released prisoners, accosted us. By then I spoke a few Russian words, which I learned from my photo customers, and also had my safe conduct pass with me from Theresienstadt. The Russian left us alone and in a couple of days we arrived in Budapest without further incidents.

The city was in ruins. All the bridges were destroyed and we walked from some place on the Buda side to a pontoon bridge, the only way to get to Pest. My first destination was Aunt Manci's apartment. The entire top floor of the building, where their apartment used to be, was blown off as a result of either artillery or aerial bombardment. The owner of the building had a silversmithing business on the street floor, and he told me that my uncle and aunt might have been killed in the apartment at the time the top floor of the building was destroyed, but he didn't know that for a fact. No one in the building had any information.

My next stop was Uncle Matthew's apartment. I wrote them that I would be coming to Budapest, though I couldn't say when. All three of them, Uncle Matthew, Aunt Margaret, and their son, Gyuri, were home. It was wonderful to see them, but they seemed very blasé and sat quietly as I told them about my father. When I talked about my own experiences, Aunt Margit insisted on telling me how they suffered during the siege. I heard about the terror of the Nyilasok, of having to do hard labor such as digging tank trap trenches around Budapest, and how hard it was for them to get food during the siege. On one occasion, she told me, they had to eat horsemeat. But it turned out that they managed to sleep in their own beds, except when there was an air raid and during the long siege of Budapest. All of them had some sort of protection papers, which more or less guaranteed their safety. No doubt they had suffered, but at this point they looked healthy, pretty much as always, though their clothes weren't as crisp as usual. I don't think they had any understanding of what my father and most of the people in the camps went through.

They had a bowl of fruit on their table. I was hungry and as I kept looking at the fruit, Uncle Matthew finally told me to have one. I picked a peach. It was wonderful, and as I finished it I took a pear. I was about to take another fruit when from the corner of my eye I caught Aunt Margit signaling Uncle Matthew to take the fruit away. As he picked up the bowl, he asked if I wanted another one. I don't think I would have taken one if he had held a gun to my head. I might even have said something to the effect that I have probably taken too many already. I stayed a bit longer and told Uncle Matthew that I was looking for work and will try for a job at one of the two movie studios in Budapest. He told me he knew someone at one of the studios and promised to inquire. I think they were relieved when I left. Maybe they were afraid I wanted to stay with them.

I had one more stop to make. My Aunt Alice's younger sister by the name of Darvas lived in Budapest, and I had been corresponding with her. I was to spend the night at her apartment. She put together a meager dinner and was extremely happy and at the same time very emotional to see me. I already wrote her about having seen Aunt Alice in Bergen-Belsen and that I hadn't seen or heard of her since. She had no information about anybody. Somehow, she escaped deportation, hiding in Budapest for almost a year. Physically and particularly mentally she was a wreck. Throughout the entire night she alternately wanted to talk and cried. I didn't know what to do. The next morning I told her that I would probably be coming back to Budapest and would help her with food from Pápa. Food incidentally was a bit easier to come by in Pápa than in Budapest. There was food in Budapest also, but it was mostly black-market goods and very expensive. She told me that an elderly aunt of hers who died during the siege had a small apartment, which she still continued to rent, and if I wanted it, I could have it when I came back to Budapest. We went to see the apartment. It was near where my Aunt Manci used to live, on the sixth floor of an apartment house. It had a small living room/bedroom, a toilet, and a very small kitchenette separated by a curtain from a bath. The furniture was old, broken down, and smelled. But

241

the prospect of an apartment in Budapest, at a time when apartments were at a high premium in that devastated city, was something to look forward to. I agreed to take it and she gave me the keys, one to the apartment and one to the entrance gate downstairs. I told her I wouldn't need it yet, but she told me to hold onto the keys anyhow, in case I decided to come up to Budapest again and needed a place to stay. I think she wanted to encourage me to come back. I had some money, not much, but I gave her some, which she didn't want to take. I knew she needed it and I insisted.

Big Jocó and I met later at the pontoon bridge and we crossed over to Buda, hoping to find a ride or a train to Pápa.

* * *

I passed the érettségi with a "B" average, which even surprised me. I now had a diploma, which under normal circumstances would have assured me an opportunity to enter just about any university of my choice, become an officer in the army, and a gentleman in society. But at that time my diploma was no more than a fancy piece of paper. I couldn't afford to go to a university and support myself for four years without a job, after which I probably would have had another diploma and not much else. I couldn't see myself spending my life taking pictures of Russian soldiers, living at somebody else's house, and wearing old, hand-me-down clothes. I was tired of life in Pápa.

The only item from our old house that I found was our large, carved walnut and veneer dining room sideboard. I found it by accident when I went to a shoemaker's house to have a pair of shoes repaired. Walking through this man's house to his shop, I spotted our sideboard in one of his tiny rooms with a dirt floor. There sat this magnificent piece of custom-made furniture, surrounded by the lowest level of poverty. How they managed to get it into that room is a mystery. I asked the man how he came by the sideboard. He must have recognized me, though I didn't know him, and told me somebody gave it to him, he didn't remember who. I told him the sideboard was mine and held him responsible. I think he was too scared to answer or even look at me. But I never claimed the sideboard. I had no place for it, and if I took it, it would have just reminded me of the past, which I was desperately trying to forget. It was another ghost in a town full of ghosts, and I wanted to get out.

Fall and winter were coming, and if anything, the future looked bleaker now than it did when we were on our way to Pápa from Theresienstadt.

I was living from one day to the next. Whatever work there was in and near Pápa, I didn't want. Taking pictures of drunken Russian soldiers was getting to be a pain. When Uncle Matthew's letter came and told me that I could have an apprentice position with a movie company called MAFIRT (short for Magyar Film Iroda, Reszvény Társaság, meaning Hungarian Film Bureau, Inc), I was elated.

* * *

I immediately started to prepare for moving to Budapest. It wasn't hard. I didn't have much. One of my prized possessions was an overcoat, which Uncle George had sent me from America. It had a history. Uncle George bought the fine wool fabric for the coat in London on his way to his 1936 visit in Pápa. He had it made into an overcoat in Budapest by one of the best tailors and took the coat with him to New York. Now the coat was back in Pápa. It was too big for me, but at that time fit or style was not a consideration. The initial contact with Uncle George came actually very soon after we returned to Pápa. He knew an American colonel who was stationed in Budapest with the American Military Mission. This colonel forwarded to us a number of letters from Uncle George, each addressed to a different member of the family. No one whose names were on the envelopes was alive. All the letters were given to Imre and me. After this initial contact I corresponded with Uncle George regularly. He encouraged me to come to America and offered to help. By then I'd been thinking about leaving Hungary but had no definite plans. As I was very interested in the filmmaking process, Budapest and the Hungarian movie studios were a good prospect for the time.

A number of entrepreneurs with trucks ran occasional lorry service to Budapest. It was expensive since benzin, as we called gasoline, was available only on the black market at astronomical prices. But the trucks were jam-packed, and even at the price they were preferable to taking a chance on the trains, particularly as one traveled with luggage and a bicycle. I corresponded with Aunt Manci's sister and knew that the apartment was waiting for me.

The trip in the open truck was cold and uncomfortable, but in those days comfort was not expected. I arrived at the pontoon bridge on the Buda side, which just then had traffic coming from the Pest side. The bridge was open in each direction for four hours before the direction of traffic would be reversed. I had a long, cold wait. When the traffic was finally reversed, I pushed my bike across the Danube on the undulating bridge, balancing my suitcase on the bike's luggage rack. Fortunately my apartment was not too far from the Pest end of the bridge. Still, by the time I got to the apartment house it was near evening and almost completely dark between the tall buildings. It was a good feeling as I got to my new home. The future looked a bit more promising. I had a job, an apartment, and a brand-new bike for transportation. Somehow I managed to work the bike up a flight of stairs to the wire gate by the elevator cage. I could have taken the elevator, but in order to do that I would have had to ring for the janitor, who would have had to be tipped. I didn't want to spend the money. Instead, I put the bike on the inside of the wire gate and lugged the heavy suitcase to the sixth floor. By the time I came downstairs to get my bike, it was gone. How about starting a brand-new career with a blow like that? I was really depending on the bike. The studio was miles from the apartment. Though sporadic trolley service was available by this time, it was slow, not reliable, and, for me, expensive. Reporting the loss of the bike to the police under the existing conditions, I knew, would have been utterly useless. I went back upstairs to unpack.

* * *

Uncle Matthew and my Aunt Manci's sister, whose first name I unfortunately have forgotten, were very happy with the food I brought for them from Pápa. I saw them on occasion, but I made it a point of never going to see Uncle Matthew at any mealtime. My cousin Gyuri, Matthew's son, who by this time was back to his medical practice, treated me with tolerance and basic civility without much else.

My job situation was not much better. My work hours were from seven in the morning to three in the afternoon, with a few minutes allowed for lunch at the commissary. The lunches were usually some thin soup, bread and jelly, or at other times some overcooked stringy meat prepared as goulash. The work was equally without interest. There was no film production to speak of in Hungary at the time. Some prewar foreign films were subtitled and processed. Besides sweeping the lab, my job was to put the undeveloped roll of film in the machine and take the developed print off at the other end.

At times, I was allowed to see some of the movies, and I remember seeing *Gunga Din* and *Beau Geste* several times. I usually went up to the studio on my own time after my shift was over at three o'clock, but there was very little going on. The studios were looted by the Russians and most equipment such as cameras and lights were gone. Some newsreel coverage was going on. On one occasion I was allowed to ride with the newsreel people to photograph the unearthing of a mass grave, somewhere near Budapest. More ghosts from the past.

On my way home from work I would stop off at one of the street corners where some village people were making a fortune selling either cooked corn on the cob or baked pumpkin. It was usually a mob scene, but I would manage to get a few ears of corn or a couple of slices of pumpkin for dinner. Even that depleted my meager income. Major expenses—the apartment, commuting, and food—left me with practically no money for anything else. I was learning very little about film production and knew that the movie business was not going to happen in Hungary for years to come. I was now twenty years old and the thought of emigrating to America became more and more the only viable consideration for my future. I decided to put the movie business on hold and go back to Pápa.

* * *

Imre liquidated Uncle Miklós's old store and the proceeds were divided between Aunt Manci's sister, Imre, and me. I don't know how Imre was able to keep Uncle Matthew out of the deal. I also recovered some linens, some of which I gave to Imre and some of which I sold for a fraction of their real value. The gold coins returned to me by our neighbor, some rubles from the photography business, some dollar bills I bought for rubles, and the few dollars Uncle George sent now and then were beginning to make the idea of going to America seem possible.

In the early spring I worked for the Eszterházy estate for a while as a manager of a railroad tie-making operation in the Bakony Mountains. I lived in a small peasant house near the woods and slept in a bed with wooden slats and a burlap sack filled with straw for a mattress. The house had no kitchen or bathroom, nor indoor toilet, and the job was a waste of time. The government was breaking up the large landholdings and I didn't think it would be too long before I would have been out of a job anyhow. I went back to Pápa. Though Jocó was no longer interested, I continued to take pictures of Russian soldiers for a while, collecting more rubles, jewelry, goods, and items of almost any description—most of it probably stolen—which Big Jocó fenced for cash. I even got some American dollars from some people for the food the Russians brought me. Almost everyone in Hungary who had a relative in America was hoarding old dollar bills. One dollar at this time represented a large sum of money, one of a few types of currencies one could buy black-market goods with. There was a big black-market operation growing in Hungary. Big Jocó got involved and was helpful to me by converting some of my Russian junk into money. On today's terms the sum total of my loot in gold, dollars, German marks probably wouldn't amount to beans, but in Hungary then it represented a small fortune.

More people returned to Pápa, amongst them two young women, one of whom was a classmate of mine in elementary school. Her name was Deutsch Emmi, the other her younger sister, Márta. Though twenty years younger than Imre, Emmi started going with Imre, and after a while they planned to marry. I moved out of Imre's apartment to a small attic room in the modern apartment house where Klári, Imre's sister, and her husband used to live before the ghetto days. Aside from a convertible bed, I had no furniture. The recent returnees brought news of large camps called Displaced Persons Camps developing in Germany, populated with thousands of people who were taken to Germany during the war but didn't return to their homeland after the war. The majority of the people in these camps expected to go to America. The UN and various relief organizations, I was told, would help people emigrate. One of these relief organizations was called the JOINT, or the Joint Distribution Committee for the Displaced Persons, or something like that. It was believed that if one could get into one of these camps, going to America would be just about assured. I decided to go. Uncle George wrote, recommending the same thing also. He sent some papers, one of which was an affidavit stating that he would assume all responsibility for me; therefore, I would not become a "ward of the state." Such a document was a prerequisite to being admitted to America. I started getting ready for the trip. I sewed some of the gold coins and dollar bills into various items of my clothing. Everything I had fit into a small backpack. Several others from Pápa decided to leave also. We thought it would be smart going in a group—more ears hear more, more eyes see more. It was a good decision. The problem was that by this time, the new Hungarian government under the Soviet occupation didn't want any military-age men leaving the country. Exit permits were required, which were only given in rare cases or for very large bribes. But we kept hearing about people who left the country by simply walking across the border to Austria. That is what my group collectively decided to do. There was one hitch for me personally. I was falling in love. Horvát Hajnalka came back from Germany. I don't know why she was in Germany or how she got there, but she was now back and we spent a lot of our time together. It was becoming a big dilemma for me. I liked her a lot and she was probably the only person who could have prevented me from leaving, but I knew I had to get out of Hungary. I let everybody know that I was going to leave. In a way this was a bit reckless, but there was a method in my madness. A lot of people were talking about leaving, but I didn't think one would get in trouble for talking. I didn't mention anyone else's name in my group; in fact, I wanted to give the impression that I was going to leave by myself. As this got around, there was one other young woman whom I knew from dancing school and the Nátus who asked me to take her with me. I didn't know her too well nor did I care for her, and I didn't want the responsibility and burden of having somebody attached to me. But I told her that I would think about it and would let her know. I also told her that I was leaving on a certain date, which in reality was about three weeks after I really planned to leave.

My group left Pápa one by one over a period of a couple of days to meet in Szombathely, a fair-sized town near the Austrian border. Though he wasn't in favor of the trip, Imre did not discourage me. In some ways I might have become a burden, and I believe he thought of that also. He was about to get married and start a new life. I wanted to get on with my own life also. One precious possession I knew I couldn't take with me was my pistol. I gave it to Imre. Some time later, as firearms were against the law and became dangerous to have, I heard he threw the gun into the Tapolca River. I said goodbye to no one other than Imre and the Sinkós. On the given day Jocó and I bicycled to Mezőlak, one station down the line from Pápa towards Szombathely. We said goodbye for the last time. I got on the train and he took the bikes back to Pápa. As the train was leaving Mezőlak, I made up my mind that I would never return to Pápa and Hungary. All of my family was gone; everything we ever had was gone, as though none of us had ever lived there. I thought of my past life, the early trips to Celldömölk on the same train, and the sad and happy memories of my childhood and my family. I was filled with hope and expectation for a better future, as I was on the road once again on my way back to Germany.

\* \* \*

My group met in a churchyard in Szombathely as planned. By the time I got there, someone in the group made a deal with a Russian soldier to take us across the border into Austria that night. A friend of mine, Beke Gabi (Gabriel Beke), who was part of this group, recently reminded me that we each gave seven US dollars to this soldier. We waited in the churchyard all afternoon and evening, and it was already dark when the truck finally showed. We climbed into the back and crawled under a greasy, oil-spattered, smelly tarp. Gears grinding, the truck left the churchyard. We kept going, stopping, the sharp turns tossing us around in the back, without any idea where we were. Every now and then the truck stopped, we heard Russian conversation, and minutes later the truck would move on. We knew we had to be in the mountains. The engine of the beat-up truck was laboring, gears grinding as the truck was going up long slopes. Then we started coming down, breaks squealing, and shortly after the truck pulled off the road and stopped. Under the tarp we heard the front door of the cab open and felt the tarp being lifted from over us. It was totally dark. The slightest light defined the ridges of distant mountains and we could make out some pine trees along the road, but not much else. The Russian soldier explained that this was where we had to get off. He assured us that we were in Austria, and all we had to do was to follow the road and we would come to the first Austrian village shortly. I wondered as he pulled away why we could not have stayed aboard if the Austrian village was just ahead. Maybe the Russian was afraid of getting caught. But we decided to walk very cautiously. We couldn't have walked very fast in the dark anyhow, but I sensed that something wasn't exactly right. Our Russian driver either got cold feet or outsmarted us by telling us we were already in Austria. We had to take his word for it as we were in no position to argue. That was the deal; he was to take us into Austria, no further. Sure enough, some distance ahead of us we saw a light on the road. It looked like a kerosene lamp attached to a makeshift barricade. There was a lone Soviet soldier sitting on something, probably half asleep. We decided to go into the woods. I, for one, thought that if indeed the barricade was the border, we could get up on the hillside, walk parallel to the road, and come back down to the road some distance past the sentry. All of us thought this was a good idea. But it was very hard to walk in the woods in total darkness. Yet we knew we had to get away from the road and kept climbing. I don't know how far we got, or how long we walked, but when we came to a clearing we thought it would be safe enough to spend the night there. We were very tired as we bedded down and went to sleep.

* * *

Daylight woke us the following morning. We must have come a lot further than we thought, as we were in a clearing near the top of a mountain. Below us on the side opposite to where we came from was a curving road leading into a small village in the distance. As we were about to get going, a Jäger showed up. Let me explain who and what Jägers were. Jäger, with two dots over the *a,* is the German word for "hunter." On the large feudal estates, such as Eszterházy's estates, Jägers were employed as gamekeepers and wardens to keep out poachers. Though it wasn't a uniform, all these Jägers wore characteristic clothes. All wore small, green velvet Tyrolean hats with a brush of boar hair on its side. Their jacket was of a particular cut, gray wool with green silk braids and antler buttons. They wore britches either with high boots or wool knee socks and heavy walking shoes. All carried a double-barreled shotgun, a cartridge belt, and a leather shoulder satchel. All had well-trained hunting dogs. The Jäger who materialized at the clearing that morning told us that he knew who we were and that we wanted to get out of Hungary. Every day, he told us, he helped and guided several groups of people like us across the border into Austria. He explained that the border was very heavily patrolled by the Russians and we could not get to Austria by ourselves without knowing a safe route. He said he could guide us but wanted an astronomical amount of money. We told him we didn't have the money, but he said to think about it and he would be back. We really didn't have the money, but even if we did, there was something fishy about this character and we decided to jump him when he came back. He came back about twenty minutes later but wouldn't come close enough for us to grab him. Instead, when we told him we wouldn't pay him, he started blowing a very loud whistle, waving his arm as though signaling someone. We stood thinking that we would be arrested any second, but nobody came. He kept blowing the whistle as we walked past him down the slope towards the road and the village. The truth of the matter was that we were already in Austria. We had spent the previous night in Austria without knowing it. His game was to rip off people like us, making them believe that he was taking them into Austria.

The rest of this trip is not clear. I guess nothing really noteworthy happened, but by midday we were in Vienna, and after a night in Vienna we moved on towards our destination, a displaced persons camp in Ulm, in Southern Germany.

# Chapter 16

# 1946 – 1947
# GOING TO AMERICA

We registered at the Displaced Persons Center in Ulm. The camp was in a huge ex-military complex of large, multistory barracks buildings surrounding parade grounds. There were thousands of inhabitants, all homeless ex-concentration camp inmates. The majority were Jews. I made no mention of having returned to Pápa when I registered, as I thought this would have disqualified me from the Homeless Displaced Person status. My safe conduct pass from Theresienstadt qualified me without questions. Our entire group was billeted in a relatively large corner room on the second floor of one of the buildings. It had some rudimentary comforts such as bunk beds with blankets, a table in the middle of the room, four benches, and some lockers. Food and basic personal items were supplied, though all I remember about the food was that it was pretty bad. Aside from picking up rations of bread, most of the time I didn't take the food. Within days we made contact with the local black market for food and other necessities. My first letters went to Uncle George in New York and Imre, Dénes, and Jocó in Pápa, notifying all of my new address. Lists of concentration camp survivors were posted on endless bulletin boards, which for me unfortunately held no new revelations. In a way I believed that even this was preordained, written in God's Big Book. I was much bothered by not returning to Theresienstadt to look for my father. If my brother's name appeared on one of these lists as having returned to Hungary, I would have gone back immediately. But by this time I was reasonably certain that my brother was not alive. I didn't give up hope of course, as I heard many stories of people having not been able to return or communicate from camps in the Soviet-occupied territories. I continued to hope as long as there was no proof of his death. I talked to as many people as I could; all of us did, asking about our own as well as the relations of our friends. This way, we felt, we could cover a much broader area by multiplying our inquiries.

The daily activities soon became routine and boring. We walked into town, shopped on the black market, which was openly flourishing. All of us were given an ID card called Kenkarte with our photographs. Other than establishing our hopefully transient status and entering us on a list of intended émigrés, Displaced Persons, it had no other purpose. I found that my finances were in surprisingly good shape. I knew I would be able to sustain myself for quite a long time with my gold coins, dollar bills, and German marks. This was reassuring, as I had no idea when my request to emigrate to the USA would come up or if it would be approved. Single dollar bills were the most sought after on the black market in connection with any small transaction, as they were easiest to deal with. At times larger denominations were sought, raising the exchange rate or the value of the currency and signaling big black-market deals requiring large amounts of American money. I was actually able to buy some new clothes, summer shirts in stores, which accepted German marks provided that one had ration cards. I could buy ration cards on the black market, and with them and German currency, I bought items of clothing and some foodstuff. I also made contact with a photographer in town, who occasionally hired me to do darkroom work for him. The pay was almost nothing, but it replenished some of the German money I spent. By far the most sought-after commodity of exchange was American cigarettes. Very few people smoked them, but everybody used them as a commodity of barter. All of us had a small ruler, ten centimeters long and calibrated in millimeters, as at times a portion of an American cigarette paid for certain merchandise. In that case, the cigarette was measured and cut with a new, sharp razor blade, so as not to lose any of the tobacco in the cigarette. I remember buying a hat for one-seventh of a Chesterfield. At this time I did not yet smoke but bought black-market cigarettes to buy certain items with, which would not have been available for any other exchange. Though it was highly illegal, chocolate bars, coffee, anything that was not available in Germany showed up on the black market through American GIs, who purchased them for next to nothing at the PX. Some weeks later I started receiving packages from Uncle George. I asked him for cigarettes, which cost him little but were extremely valuable for me. In fact, within weeks after I arrived in Ulm, I bought a big motorcycle with a sidecar for seven cartons of cigarettes, which I knew was more than I should have paid for the bike. Some of my friends who were active in the black market criticized me for paying so much, but I wanted the bike very badly. For a few more cigarettes, I had the bike cleaned up, serviced, and tuned, with new oil and parts as needed. It was almost like new, and liberated me from the daily monotony and boredom of doing nothing in the dreary camp. At times I took one or two friends to swim in the Danube, or just go ride around in the country. Other times I took some of my black-market operator friends in search of food and items that by this time had risen in value on the black market near our camp. I bought black-market gasoline for the bike. It was against occupation laws to drive a vehicle without proper permits attesting to the necessity of operating a motor vehicle. I had some phony documents, I don't remember where they came from or how I got them, but they even helped me buy a very limited amount of legitimate gas for the bike. The bike was an NSU 500cc single-cylinder bike, with a spacious and fancy sidecar. It also had a buddy seat over the rear wheel. On one occasion I drove all the way into Austria to the Mauthausen concentration camp. Though it was deserted and devoid of most of its former horrors by then, it still filled me with dread and hatred.

The bike helped me make new friends, particularly of the female gender, which helped make my stay in the camp a bit more enjoyable. There were some downsides to our stay at the camp in Ulm also. On one occasion when I returned to my room from one of my trips, I noticed that my belongings in my locker seemed to have been rearranged. I have always been a creature of habit and kept my things—shirts, underwear, socks—arranged in a certain way, and I was always able to tell if anyone tampered with them. My locker had a padlock, which seemed intact, but seeing my things rearranged gave me a foreboding feeling. The first thing I checked on were my gold coins. They were gone. I suspected one of my roommates, Weisz Karcsi, a fellow from Pápa who in the past had been suspected of stealing things of value from other roommates. He first denied taking the coins when I confronted him, and then became belligerent, and I sensed it was he who took them. I told him I would call the camp police, which one of my other roommates already did while I stayed in the room keeping an eye on him. The police found the coins in his locker. He claimed they were his, but when questioned about them he didn't even know what they were—I mean, Swiss, French, Austrian, or what. I got my coins back, but unfortunately I also found out that one was a counterfeit. It was a gold-plated lead coin and I have no idea where it came from. It might have been in the original batch my old neighbor had given me in Pápa, or it might have been a counterfeit my father had given him without knowing it was a counterfeit. Incidentally, on today's scale the six coins would be worth between twenty-five and twenty-eight hundred dollars. Then, though their exchange rate in American dollars was far less, their buying power in Germany was immense.

I don't know what happened to all the pictures I took in Germany. Besides the ones included here, a half a century swallowed them up. They might be in one of the many boxes in our attic, and one of these days I'll look for them.

While my existence in the displaced persons camp was very unproductive, I managed to make the best of it. I registered for emigration to the United States under the Yugoslav quota. Before leaving Hungary, Imre suggested I list my birthplace as Sombor, Yugoslavia. It could have been that this town and the area it was in were part of Hungary prior to WWI, near the area my father's family were from, but I don't think so. I realized at this time that I never really knew where I was born, as until this time I never needed to be concerned with my place of birth. I had always assumed that my place of birth was most likely Pápa or Bikolypuszta. But the records in both of those places, particularly in Pápa, were not available, lost, misplaced, hidden, or destroyed at that time just after the war. Besides, registering under the Yugoslav quota was a stroke of luck as it was larger than the Hungarian quota, and as Yugoslavia was allied with the Western powers, Yugoslav emigrants received faster and more favorable treatment. Sometime during August I believe, I was notified about my case being processed and I was directed to go to Frankfurt for an examination. Actually, there were two examinations. One, a personal history interview, and two, a medical exam. My friends and I had heard that these examinations were extremely thorough. On passing a tough personal interview, a thorough medical had to be passed. All serious illnesses, TB, VD, intestinal disorders, even bad teeth would be scrutinized and could be the basis of rejection. I could not even consider rejection. I didn't want to return to Hungary and possible retribution for leaving the country illegally. Besides, I wanted to go to America very badly. I had my teeth fixed. I always had very good teeth, but the neglect of two years and the time in the camps took their toll. I found a very good dentist in a bombed-out building whose office could only be entered through a neighboring building and a makeshift wooden passageway built over the destroyed innards of the building. But the work he did was outstanding. Some of his fillings are still holding. I started an exercise program to put myself in good physical shape. Every morning I would do an increasing number of push-ups, sit-ups, running in place, jumping jacks—the sort of exercises I used to do in Mr. Kovács's class. As a result I passed the medical examination without a single hitch, while some had to return several times.

My case history was a crucial part of the process of being approved for emigration. Lots of ex-Nazis, SS men, German Army officers, and enlisted men, those who were sought by Allied and local authorities for war crimes and other reasons applied for emigration under assumed identities. In cases where they claimed to have come from an area where documentation was not available, this personal history examination was the only way to ascertain whether the applicant was legitimate or not. Everybody had to fill out a long questionnaire containing detailed personal information. Even the smallest slip-up could, and most likely would, have resulted in further investigation and, in some cases, rejection and arrest. I understand that many war criminals were apprehended this way by the American authorities. When my turn came, I was asked about my preference of a language for the examination to be conducted in. As I didn't speak English and Hungarian was not listed as a choice, I chose German. Because of that I asked a young woman friend whom I went to grade school with and whom I had unexpectedly met in Germany to come with me as my interpreter. The rationale behind this was that I would have additional time to think about the questions and the answers while she was interpreting. I did not want to slip up. Breiner Éva, my friend and interpreter, and I arrived at the specified building in Frankfurt at the time designated for my examination. I was very nervous but tried to appear calm and self-assured. After about a half hour wait the two of us were finally seated in an office facing a man behind a desk, dressed in a crisp uniform but without military markings or rank. The letters US, in a blue triangle, were embroidered on his shirt collar. There were several other similarly dressed men, sitting behind other desks and in armchairs around the room. One was smoking a pipe and was reading a newspaper. It amazed me how well Americans, from the lowest-ranking privates to officers in the military and people such as these men in the room, were dressed and looked, particularly as I compared them to the

Russians I had met in Czechoslovakia and Hungary. The man sitting across from me smiled, extended a hand in a handshake, and introduced himself as my examiner. I was beginning to relax. In front of him was a file holder with my name on it. He asked in German who my friend was and why she was there. I started to explain but my friend cut in and explained that I didn't speak German well enough and she was there to help with the translation. The examiner smiled and told her that he thought I understood well enough, and told her to wait in the outer office. He said he would call her if I needed help. The examination started as soon as she left. The examiner opened my file box. In it were all the forms I filled out, as well as documents such as the affidavit from my Uncle George, my high school diploma, etc. The examiner started reading the first sheet: "First name András, last name László, born January 12, 1926," and so on. As he was reading off my personal data I kept nodding my head, but he didn't ask me any questions. It took about a half hour for him to read through all the documents in the file, make a notation here and there, but throughout all he didn't ask me a single question. When he finished the last document, he closed the file folder, slammed his hand on it, and smiled at me. "Alles ist in ordnung," he said, meaning, "Everything is in order." He then stamped the top cover with a large *OK*, which by then I knew meant "okay." That was the examination and I obviously passed. At least that's what I thought. The man who was smoking a pipe and reading a newspaper put the paper down and talked to me in Hungarian. "I couldn't help overhearing," he started. "Was there a math teacher in the Reformed Church Kollégium of Pápa named so-and-so?" He asked. There was, and I told him so. He asked about others in the school, some I didn't know. He asked many questions about Pápa, as well as other questions of seemingly little significance. I don't remember them specifically, but he seemed to have good and bad information about Pápa. Some of his questions could only be answered with yes or no, or "I have never heard of so-and-so, or never knew or saw such-and-such," or "Yes, I knew of him, or knew him personally," and so on. Some of his other questions required longer explanations and descriptions. Judging by the way he spoke the language, he was obviously Hungarian or of Hungarian descent. The conversation ended with handshakes and smiles, but as I left the room I wondered what it was really about. To this day, I'm convinced that it was this casual conversation that was the real examination. Had I given hesitant or wrong answers or information about what the railroad station looked liked, or where the three movie theaters were located when there were only two in town, if I'd said I knew a professor who didn't exist, I'm sure the large *OK* on my dossier would have been meaningless. I knew I had passed when I was told I'd be notified when and where to report for my physical. It was a great day—I was on my way to America.

* * *

During this time, I met up with a fellow from Pápa by the name of Stockner Laci. We knew each other from Pápa, though not very well. But it was wonderful to see him. He was older than I and was also hoping to emigrate to America. He had a young wife, Ibi, also a survivor of Bergen-Belsen, whom he married after the war. Our petitions to emigrate were approved at about the same time. We were going to America together. It was early fall when the news came that permission was granted for me to "land in America." Needless to say, I was overjoyed. It would be totally useless to attempt to describe how I had felt at that moment. A new chapter of my life was about to start, holding out hope for a future. Once again I was heading north in Germany in the fall, but this time I was traveling in a passenger car on a regular train, with a ticket and an assigned seat. I knew the doors of the train would be unlocked and there would be no SS with dogs and clubs waiting for me at my destination.

In preparation for my trip to New York I decided to have a new suit made. A friend of mine, a fellow displaced person in the camp, was a tailor. I had seen some of the suits he had made for others out of black market–bought or stolen US Army blankets. The blankets were usually died dark brown or black, as those colors hid the blankets' original khaki color best. After the large US letters were removed from the center of the blanket, it would be cut into the parts of a suit. One blanket was just barely enough for my suit, but this young tailor was a genius and the suit turned out to be really handsome. I bought gloves on the black market, and shirts and underwear with German marks and ration cards.

It was sad to leave some of my friends and even sadder to say goodbye to my motorcycle. There would have been no point in trying to sell it. I didn't want cigarettes or German money and had no time to try to sell it profitably or even reasonably. None of my friends wanted it, so I just left it where I parked it last, hoping that whoever was going to wind up with the bike would take good care of it. The notice to check in at a demarcation center in Bremerhaven gave me very little time for anything but to pack one suitcase and write my last letters from Ulm to Uncle George, Imre, Dénes, and Jocó. I was on my way. The train trip must have been very uneventful, as I don't remember any of it. Several people from the camp were with me. I knew some, though not very well, and till this trip had never seen the others amongst the thousands of people at the camp in Ulm. I was wearing the overcoat Uncle George sent me to Pápa, not because it was cold but because it still had some dollar bills sewn into it. My remaining gold coins were in a special pocket sewn into the inside of my pants by my tailor friend. I vaguely recall arriving in Bremerhaven and being taken to the departure center in a dark-green-colored US Army bus. The soldier who drove the bus was friendly, though I couldn't talk to him. Just as when we arrived in Ulm, our hair, the clothes we were wearing, and everything in our suitcases were again liberally sprayed with DDT. We were issued blankets and bedding and were shown into barracks-like rooms with double-decker bunk beds. I knew that my friends, Stockner Laci and his wife, Ibi, were already there and went looking for them. This must have been sometime in October or early November. We were given tickets to depart by ship from Bremerhaven on a given day—I don't recall exactly when, but probably no more than two weeks after arriving in Bremerhaven. My friends and I were trying to figure out what to do with our remaining German money. We didn't want to buy anything in Germany, and I didn't think that German money would be any good in the US. Someone's birthday was coming up. Laci and I though we would go into Bremen and try to buy some liquor to celebrate the birthday as well as our departure. We knew there was no use trying to get booze in stores and hoped to find some individual or the local black market to make our purchase.

The trip into Bremen was unbelievable. Though some of the main routes were cleaned up and some trolley cars were running by this time, the city of Bremen was in ruins. No building stood intact along miles of the route into town. Some were totally demolished; others had walls, but no floors or roofs over them. There were some strange sights. One that stands out in my memory was a seemingly intact bathroom high above street level on a section of floor that no longer existed in the rest of the building. Some chimneys stood pointing to the sky, rising out of the rubble without the rest of the building around them. In some areas the buildings were in better shape, though most obviously not habitable. There were large, hand-painted messages on most of these buildings: ALLE TOTEN, ETLICHE LEBEN, ALLE LEBEN—EVERYONE DEAD, SOME ARE ALIVE, ALL ARE ALIVE—and so on. I wondered how the multitudes of the German people who not too long ago attended Nazi rallies with outstretched arms and tears of joy in their eyes felt now? I wondered if they felt remorse for the past, or felt hatred for their conquerors. One thing I had found out would be interesting to mention here. During this period in Germany I had many occasions to ask German individuals of all social levels if they were Nazis, party members, or sympathizers. None owned up to Nazi Party membership, and most denied any involvement, connection, even leaning towards the Nazi ideologies. Just as in Pápa, some claimed to have opposed the Nazis and quoted all sorts of activities of helping Jews. I don't doubt that there were some decent people in Germany, but having lived through that era, having seen the newsreels, read the papers, and witnessed the atrocities, not finding a single Nazi in Germany less than a year after the war was over was an irritating, though predictable, joke.

Strangely, the inner city, at least the area where we got off the trolley, was in fair shape. Though lots of the buildings were damaged, most were standing with people coming in and out of them. There were people on the street everywhere. Though I have little recollection of this, Stockner Laci recently reminded me of going into a bar and buying drinks for some American soldiers. He also recalled that one of the people who came to Bremen with us that day was a pianist who played the piano in this bar, mostly popular American tunes, to the obvious delight of the American soldiers. I do recall talking with some people who were chipping mortar off bricks from bombed-out buildings, salvaging them. Some were pulling old nails out of destroyed lumber and straightening the nails on small anvils. One of these people knew where to get black-market booze. We followed his assistant for many blocks and waited for him as he went into a small building with some sort of shop in the back. In a little while he came back with a man. This man said he had very good schnapps and would sell us as many bottles as we wanted for an astronomical price. We attempted to bargain, but he held to his price, and in the end we bought several bottles. Schnapps was the national drink in Germany, second only to beer, and probably one of a few kinds of hard liquor Germans drank. It was relatively easy to make if you had the right ingredients and equipment, such as a still. Both of us, Laci and I, had several bottles of homemade schnapps in our arms. I spent most of my German money, but it didn't matter, as we were about to have our last celebration in Europe before going to America. We followed the young fellow back to his workplace. The rest of the crew was still chipping mortar and straightening bent nails. I opened one of the bottles to taste it and offered a drink to the man who sent us to the source of the booze. He had a leather cap, which looked exactly like an SS cap without the skull and braid, except it was made of leather. I asked him how much he wanted for the hat. He shook his head, indicating he didn't want to sell it. When I offered him more marks than he probably made in several months, he took his hat off and gave it to me. I paid him and he thanked me, but he became bewildered as I proceeded to tear the hat to shreds. Though it wasn't a real military hat, it looked like one and I tore it to pieces. We had just enough money left for the trolley and train fare back to Bremerhaven. I offered a drink to the conductor, who took a good swig out of the bottle, and we sent the bottle around in the car, from person to person yelling, "Hoch!" as the people drank. I wished my German had been good enough to make a toast to leaving Germany—the hellhole of the universe. By the time we got off the train near the center all of us were well on our way to being totally drunk. Ibi and some of our other friends were waiting for us. A cake materialized and we started celebrating. The booze went fast and I remember very little else of the evening, other than spending the night fully dressed in an empty bunk, completely smashed and dead to the world. I spent almost the entire twenty-four hours that followed sleeping, and woke in the afternoon the following day with the headache of the century. The headache didn't go away even after I washed my face in cold water. It became even worse when one of my friends informed me that due to a long shoremen's strike in New York, our departure was postponed "indefinitely." There I was, in Bremen "indefinitely," with the world's worst headache and hardly any German money. It took several days for the headache to clear, and weeks before the strike in New York was settled. During this time I must not have done anything worthwhile or of particular interest, as I have no recollection of any detail of this period. Weeks later I was told I had been rescheduled to embark on the last day of the year and leave for America the same day on a ship called the SS *Ernie Pyle*.

* * *

The *SS* I found out stood for "Steam Ship," and Ernie Pyle was the name of an American war correspondent who became famous for reporting on the American foot soldier during the war. I, and many others, arrived at dockside on the afternoon of December 31, 1946. As we went aboard, luggage and all, we again faced the predictable DDT guns. We were dusted and were assigned bunks by numbers. As the SS *Ernie Pyle* was a Liberty class troop ship, it didn't have all the comforts of home. The bunk areas were deep in the hold of the ship, packed tight, five tiers high. But the bunks were not too uncomfortable. They had sheets, pillows, and blankets. Getting to them was another thing. While en route—and I'll tell you more about the trip later—when we were in a storm and the ship was heaving and rolling, climbing up to or down from the bunks was somewhat of a gymnastic achievement. Because of the community-type accommodations, men and women were separated.

Shortly after we were situated, bunks made up, luggage stowed, we all congregated on deck watching the dockside activities. I believe, though I'm not sure about this, that everybody was given a small amount of American money, something like seven dollars, by, I believe, a Jewish relief agency. With this money in hand—or was it my own?—I headed for the ship's store, which we were told was open for a short time only each day. The "store" was a tiny, closet-sized cubbyhole. One could not go into the "store" but had to stand outside the door, the bottom half of which was closed and formed a sort of a counter. But the little store was full of marvels. It had candy, chocolate bars, soap, toothpaste, shaving cream, everything of the best quality I had ever seen. The first part of the American dream was turning out to be true. Cigarettes, which on the black market not too long ago could buy gold and silver, were selling for pennies a pack. Aboard ship they no longer had black-market value, and from here on they were bought for smoking only. I was smoking by this time. Somehow, it was a visible expression of one's privileged status as a future American. It represented abundance of worldly goods of the finest quality at affordable prices. The hand-to-mouth existence was finally over, hopefully forever. We were free to explore, go anywhere on the ship, except areas marked off limits, such as the bridge, the engine room, and the like. We watched the dockside activities from the deck of the surprisingly small ship. Until this moment I had never seen an oceangoing ship, or the ocean, for that matter. Perhaps on the basis of pictures of ocean liners, I had always thought all ships were gigantic. But the *Ernie Pyle* was very small and very crowded with refugees like me.

Lights were coming on all over the dock as night fell. The moisture in the air, a light drizzle, reminded me of Bergen-Belsen, which at this point almost didn't seem real. The dinner bell rang and all of us headed to the large mess hall. Even this was a never-before-seen marvel. Cooks in crisp white uniforms dished out new and fantastic-looking food. We helped ourselves to bread, a kind of bread I had never seen before. The slices were square, not unlike the Kommissbrot, but it was soft, white, and smelled wonderful. It had no sawdust in or on it, and we could take as many slices as we felt like. There was soup, fried chicken with biscuits and gravy, fried potatoes cut in long sticks—my introduction to French fries—and all kinds of desserts and fruit, and the best ice cream I have ever had. There was milk and orange juice, tea and coffee in unlimited quantities. My first dinner aboard ship was an unforgettable experience. Even the stainless steel trays with compartments for the different kinds of food were amazing. I had never seen anything like it, and it, like every new thing that surrounded me, exceeded, underscored, and proved my expectations of the high level of American life. Even lining up for the food, observing the expressions on the faces of the ship's personnel who served us the food, indicated that they saw nothing out of the ordinary about the abundance of all the good food that suddenly was ours. I'll never forget watching after dinner as the leftovers were unceremoniously dumped into garbage cans. It was shocking, but it was a powerful indicator of abundance and a dream about to come true.

It was completely dark when we went up to the deck after dinner. My stomach was full for the first time in a year and a half. There was lots of commotion on the dock as the ship's lines were released and the ship slowly eased away from the dock. It was a strange feeling as we got underway. Just recently I was talking with a friend, Joe Fóti, who was on the ship with me, and he told me that leaving the European continent behind at that moment was a very emotional experience for him. For me, it was the beginning of the fulfillment of a dream, though also emotional, knowing that my life up to this moment—including the good and the bad—was finished, and I was heading into the unknown. Behind us the lights of the harbor and the buildings were slowly swallowed up by the darkness and the mist over the North Sea.

\* \* \*

By the following morning hardly anyone came for breakfast. During the night the gently undulating motion of the ship gave way to almost violent pitching and rolling. The ship seemed to be moving in all directions at once. Most aboard were seasick, but my friend Stockner Laci and I were not. We had a huge breakfast of eggs and bacon, and waffles—which were completely new to us—with lots of butter and syrup. Going to the toilet, known as "the head" aboard ship, was quite an experience. The men's head was located at the bow of the ship. The seats were built onto the hull on the inside of the curved bow. Each seat was separated from the others by a metal partition. There were two handholds on either side of the seat on the partitions, and it didn't take long to find out why. As one sat on the toilet and the ship's bow alternately rose and then slammed into the water with force, one would have been catapulted if there were no handholds to hold onto. It took some getting used to the ritual of going to the head. The head and topside were the places where most people became vulnerable to getting seasick. In the head the motion of the ship, coupled with the smell of vomit, made people sick suddenly, without warning. The situation was even worse topside. There, added to the ship's pitching and rolling, was the sight of the rapidly rising and sinking horizon, the gigantic waves, and a strong smell of diesel exhaust from the ship's engines. What none us knew was that we were in a storm, which according to the *New York Times*, I found out later, was the worst in the recorded history of the North Atlantic. In fact, some days later we heard that the engines of the ship were shut down as screws (propellers) came out of the water when the ship heaved and the engines would suddenly speed up. In order to avoid possible damage to the engines, they were shut down. We bobbed up and down like a ping-pong ball in the vast ocean, at times on the bottom of a huge canyon of giant waves towering over us on all sides, the next moment sitting on top of a wave. Lacking nautical backgrounds, only few of us could appreciate the immensity of the storm. Some of us thought it was a more or less normal part of the trip, while others who were seasick felt as though they were about to die and didn't care. Most of the ship's personnel seemed to take the storm in stride, which was reassuring, until we saw one of the officers bending over the rails, heaving. For some unexplained reason I didn't get seasick. Perhaps the enormity of going to America did not permit such unpleasantness as seasickness to spoil the fun for me.

I recall one experience, which looking back on it over a half a century later I could only classify as mean. Then I had thought it was fun, though mischievous. Stockner Laci, who until this time also escaped seasickness, and I went to lunch. Besides the cooks and us, hardly anyone was in the mess. Lunch was roast chicken. Each of us took several portions and took it up on deck. We ate the chicken sitting on the railing of the ship, rising and falling with the waves, and inducing new attacks of seasickness in those who no longer had anything in their stomachs to heave up. Seeing us eat with gusto, gnawing on chicken legs, wiping our greasy, bulging mouths, made them run to the railing over and over again. Though it won't redeem me, I only did this once. I did do one other thing, which might be of interest to a doctor or perhaps to a psychologist who deals with seasickness. The friend Joe Fóti, who had told me about his emotional experience of leaving Europe, was so sick that he no longer got out of his bunk, which I believe made the extent of his illness even worse. I told him that I had read about a Russian remedy for seasickness, which was drinking strong hot tea with salt in it. I have to confess that this was a complete fabrication on my part. Unbeknownst to me, Joe dragged himself up to the mess and drank some hot tea with salt in it. Almost immediately and miraculously, as he related to me later, his seasickness stopped. He came topside for fresh air and was all right for the rest of the crossing. Mark one up for the power of suggestion. The joy of coming to America permitted such foolishness, even under the stormy conditions. The crossing and the storm continued for two weeks.

On the twelfth day of the voyage I was going up to the deck as the ship heaved unexpectedly, and I bumped my head on the massive metal door frame. Almost immediately a large bump developed on the top of my head, and my friends thought I should go to the infirmary. I went, and on receiving an ice pack, the medic asked for some personal information to put down in his log. On giving my name and age I realized it was my birthday, January 12, 1947. I was twenty-one years of age.

\* \* \*

Five days later, seventeen days after leaving Europe, all of us woke early realizing that the ship no longer rolled and pitched. In fact, it wasn't even moving, and the noise and vibration of the engines turned into a pleasant hum. The night before, we were told that the following day we would be arriving in the United States. The anticipation was electrifying and obviously we slept very little. Most of us stayed up talking, and shortly after we did go to sleep we woke to the stillness of the ship. I dressed quickly and headed for topside. Many people were already on the deck. It was still too dark to see anything. The sea around the ship was calm and the ship was standing still. Shortly afterwards, a small boat pulled alongside and people in uniforms came aboard. We were told to get our papers ready for our final check before being admitted to the United States. All of us lined up in the mess as the lines quickly moved up to small tables where the uniformed customs people stamped our papers. As expected, we were all admitted.

The Stockners, Fóti, and some other friends and I went back on deck just as the ship started moving again, gliding smoothly and slowly through the darkness. I knew a lot about America. It was always the land of my dreams, and bits of information I collected, such as that there were more telephones in the Empire State Building than in the entire country of Hungary, always fascinated me and filled me with wonder and admiration. I'd seen pictures of the skyscrapers of New York, of shiny, large American cars, and so on. I had expected to see all these wonders as soon as daylight came up, but as the sky was slowly getting brighter and the leaden-gray morning gave way to the rising sun, and the shoreline became visible, I could see nothing but barren countryside and an occasional little white cottage here and there. A few electric lights pierced through the semidarkness, a couple of headlights silently curving down distant roads, and deep-throated blasts of distant ships were the only indications that I had passed through the storm of the North Atlantic and the storm that was most of my former life. I had no idea where we were. Neither did anybody else, but we all knew we were going to New York, to a new life in freedom. I realized that the whole ship was strangely quiet as it slid into the mist over calm waters. I could hear the muffled thumping of the engines and the cries of seagulls that seemed to have followed us all the way from Europe. Nobody talked. We didn't have to. As I looked around, the expressions on the faces left no doubt about the inner feelings of any of us. The deep and overpowering solemnity of the occasion would be impossible to describe. All I could think of was I was free, about to be born again. I wondered if my friends, my companions and comrades throughout the long journey since leaving the ghetto almost two years before, had the same thoughts and sentiments. I, for one, realized that my journey was about over and dawn was breaking over the first day of my new life in the new world. As the memories of hunger, the images of torture and disease, the stupor of acceptance of the inevitable, the cries of anguish and pain, the deafening silence of fear were fading rapidly, further and further into the past, I wondered if Uncle George would meet me. I wondered if I would recognize him and if he would be glad to see me. The anxiety of starting a new life, in a new world, hit suddenly, and with force. Within a short time I would set foot in a new world with two dollars and sixty-three cents in my pocket, and unable to speak the language. What if my uncle wasn't there to meet me? Where would I go? What would I do? Those and a million other questions filled my thoughts. The ship continued moving slowly as daylight became stronger, bringing into view distant shorelines, buildings, and finally the realization of a dream, the skyscrapers of New York City rising above the mist, glittering, sparkling in the warm light of the rising sun. We passed the Statue of Liberty on our left and the bustle of New York City became more and more visible. Laci and I speculated about all the yellow cars, hundreds and hundreds of them, driving at the bottom of the deep canyons of the city's streets. We continued up the Hudson River, slowly passing the Empire State Building, the Chrysler building in the distance, and the other famous landmarks of New York City, which on first sight exceeded my wildest expectation.

Tugboats took control of the *Ernie Pyle*, gently easing her into berth. Within minutes the gangplank was lowered, and as if nothing had happened in the past decade, people started getting off the ship. I was wearing my new suit; my necktie was meticulously tied in a Windsor knot as I carried my cardboard suitcase filled with pitiful reminders of my former life down the gangplank. My mind was racing, trying to lock out the past and trying to look only to the future.

Uncle George was waiting for me. I think there were tears in his eyes, but otherwise he was cheerful and very friendly. Aunt Edna, a very beautiful woman who at this time was still not married to Uncle George, was standing next to him. She smiled and said something that I sensed was friendly and welcoming, but I couldn't understand her words.

Laci's sister and her husband were there to greet them. Within minutes I said goodbye to Ibi, Laci, and all others, and found myself sitting between Edna and George in one of the many enormous yellow cars, a taxicab. My journey was over. The future, my new life was about to start!

# EPILOGUE

The preceding is intended to be an overview of those parts of my life you asked me about so many times and which I did not talk about until now. This account is not accurate or complete in all of its details. One hundred percent accuracy would be impossible after all these years. Memory faded by the passing of years and the natural process of aging, warped by the mind's ability to shut out unpleasant, unwanted reminders of the past, makes it impossible to present an altogether accurate account. Talking with others who also experienced and survived those horrible years proves that their accounts of the same events, at times warped by their losses of memory, tend to come up differently or not at all. The preceding pages are my best recollections of long-ago events and experiences. By and large, I believe them to be as accurate as my memory can conjure them up after all the years.

Now you know! At least part of everything I didn't talk about till now. Had I kept a day-to-day diary throughout those years, I probably would have a more accurate chronology and more information to pass on, but most of that information probably would have been trivial and very likely unimportant. More detail would have made this account overly long also. As it is, I hope the preceding will give you a flavor of my childhood, a sense of where I grew up and how my family and I lived. I hope it filled you in on the void of the good and the bad aspects of my life, and I hope you now understand why I've been reluctant to talk about it in the past.

Lack of information in certain areas is due mainly to two factors. One, to my recollection as a small child and young man—very few family matters were discussed with me or, for that matter, with anyone. Two, finding information to fill in the gaps just after the war was very difficult, as there were few who survived and could have provided information. Documentation was almost nonexistent or very difficult to find, as government papers were either destroyed during the war or were in total disarray.

The events of those years have been recorded in history books; but fifty years ago I made only a minimal effort to research details, dates, names, and so on. Instead, I relied on my recollection, though at times it is supplemented and reinforced by discussing certain events with friends who were also part of it. I quoted from one of the history books earlier in this account, simply as an illustration of how some historical events are at times flowered up or minimized, and bent to the sentiments of the historians. Quoting further from the same book, *Studies From The History of The City of Pápa*, on page 420 is the following account:

> On June 29, 1944, the people were herded from the ghetto to the Fertilizer Factory. At dawn, on July 4, they were jammed into boxcars and taken to Budapest, then Kassa. They arrived in Auschwitz on July 13. Only three hundred returned.

Thus, the fate of 3,300 Jews of Pápa and the vicinity were entered into a finely printed 670-paged history book, in four short sentences.

"Bitterness and self pity is the medicine of the weak." My father made this statement many times. In a way, I think it helped me cope with the events of those bad times. I hope it helped him live long enough to see one of his sons again. His other son, my brother, Sándor, perished during this terrible time in history. The place and circumstances of his death are not known. None of his group survived to give testimony. It is almost certain that my beloved mother perished in or on the way to Auschwitz. So must have my grandmothers and twenty-five other family members. Some of my aunts and uncles could possibly have survived Auschwitz, only to perish under unbelievably cruel circumstances in one or another Nazi death factory. Likewise, the younger members of the family, eleven cousins, with the exception of Imre and my cousin János from Magyaróvár, all perished no one knows where. Another recently published history book describes my Uncle Miklós's and his son's deaths as follows:

> A Pápai zsidóságnak két olyan tagja volt… együtt kivitette az utcára és…mindhármukat agyonlőtték…

Translation of the full account (staying as close to the original Hungarian wording and grammar, as possible):

There were two amongst the Jewish population of Pápa to whom the fascist, anti-Jewish orders did not apply: László Miklós, a machine-parts dealer, and Frimm Pal. Both were 75 percent disabled veterans and recipients of the Hero's Gold Medal. Both lost one leg during the First World War. Neither of these two individuals had to move to the ghetto or to the fertilizer factory, but, as exempted ones, remained in their own homes. His thirteen-year-old son remained with László Miklós. Until the fifteenth of October—though in constant fear—they lived in Pápa. After the Szálasi rule, Dr. Horwáth János, police official and a Lotz Pal, ordered the two exempted ones and the thirteen-year-old boy to be sent to an internment camp in Komárom, after robbing them of money, clothing, and jewelry. But the commander of the internment camp at Komárom honored their exempted status and ordered them returned to Pápa with instructions that because of their exempted status they were not to be deported. When they arrived back at Pápa and checked in with the police, the two police officials ordered both disabled veterans and the thirteen-year-old boy to be taken to the street and... all three of them were shot to death...

The above account makes no mention of Uncle Miklós's wife, Alice, whom I saw briefly at Bergen-Belsen.

This seems to be the most probable of a number of versions of Uncle Miklós's and his son's deaths. According to one other story—who knows which is true—the Nyilasok took Uncle Miklós and his son from their apartment in Pápa one night, ostensibly to transport them to Budapest as "it was no longer safe for them in Pápa." They made them get out of the car in a field just outside of town and shot them in the back. Their remains were found accidentally years later and interned in the Jewish cemetery in Pápa. In the postwar years after I left Pápa, a monument was erected in his honor and a street was named after him.

My fervent hope is that all who died had died quickly, escaping at least some of the indescribable cruelty of a perverted nation and her willing collaborators.

* * *

The question, why there was no resistance, why we didn't fight back, comes up often in retrospect. The answer might be very complex, but to my way of reasoning it can be expressed with a single word: hope. Let me explain. Had the events of the forties come up suddenly without warning, there might have been resistance. But distant events in remote areas, Germany, Poland, Czechoslovakia, and in other countries, over a long period of time signaled the hard times to come, and as they were not happening with the same severity in Hungary, the distance numbed one's senses into a false security and hope, believing that by the time they might reach Hungary, the war would be over and the danger would pass. Hope was the all-important factor. Disbelief of news and rumors, which reached us, went far beyond any imaginable limits. Everyone hoped that what eventually did happen couldn't happen. Having heard of the unbelievably cruel reprisals at Lidice, at the Warsaw Ghetto, seeing pictures of Russian partisans hanged from piano wire dozens at a time, had a demoralizing effect and was a powerful persuader that resistance would be of no avail. The knowledge of torture and of instant, brutal death to all of one's family and to many innocent people was traded off for hope instead of resistance. Uncertain as hope for the future was, it seemed to buy time. Had I been caught, for example, trying to burn the German car, there is no doubt in my mind that I would have been shot or hanged with my entire family. Hope was the only acceptable course of action and not unreasonably so, as from every indication it looked as though the war was going to be over in a very short time, bringing the madness to an end. Few of us ever considered the extreme hatred of a large segment of the Hungarian nation and, with the exception of a few, the cowardice of the rest. There is no doubt in my mind that of all the quislings and collaborators, the Hungarians were the worst. Between March 17, 1944, and the end of July of the same year, in a time period of ten weeks, Hungary managed to do more to and against its Jewish citizenry than Germany did in over a decade.

It may not be hard to understand that in spite of my parents' teaching, there is bitterness in my heart. Of my large family I'm the only one left to tell the tale, and I'm grateful to you for encouraging me to do so. But I didn't write this account solely for you. I wrote it as much for you as for myself.

It is a relief for me to know that I no longer conceal secrets from you. It makes me feel good to have relived those events and to know that as adults, your lives would no longer be affected by my past, which until now you were not aware of. Mom, who in later years shared these secrets with me, deserves the most credit. When I fretted over the possibility of this account possibly driving a wedge between us, she assured me that it would not. Now that the account is finished, I know she was right. This account was over fifty years in coming. Perhaps it is fifty years too late. Though it will undoubtedly have an effect, I know you will accept it as an unalterable fact of the past without allowing it to affect the future.

I note with sadness that I am the sole survivor of the László clan, but still hope that I won't be the last to bear the László name.

* * *

And now it s time to close this book. Now that you've read and know all that has been shrouded in a veil of mystery and secrecy for so long, the important thing is to close this book and go on with life as though nothing has happened.

As I indicated at the end of chapter twelve, I knew even then that I must do something so as not to let the events of those days, the past, affect and possibly destroy the future. I firmly believe that one must not ignore the past. We must call on and learn from the past, and not allow past mistakes to repeat themselves but use those mistakes to create a better future. At that time I made up my mind not to allow the tragic, horrible aspects of my past to take over, possibly affect my future and, therefore, yours. My solution then was to take all that which was unpleasant, put it in a strongbox, and lock the box away. So, once again, close the book, lock it away, and go on with your lives as you have till now.

* * *

In closing, I want to dedicate this book to you, my new family, in the sacred memory of my mother and father, brother, and old family, and the events, which stand alone in history. Though these pages were never intended to be more than a simple account of my early life, I hope that in some way they might help prevent anything such as the events I talked about from happening again.

I would like to pass on some of my thoughts and feelings to you.

Let me start with that principle which can be traced back to my love for my mother, whose Big Book theories, I am convinced, helped me pull through. The Big Book theory is valid. Had my life been ordained differently in the Big Book, I, and all of you, would very likely not be here today. Considering the circumstances as related on these pages, my life would not have turned out the way it did without the Big Book. My mother also believed that one must never look back with hatred, "for revenge is not sweet, nor satisfying, and never, never just," she used to say.

Though there is no vengeance in my heart, in a way I resent and at the same time feel sorry for the Hungarian nation wallowing in a "glorious past" that is built largely on a flowered-up, trumped-up, twisted, and falsified thousand-year-long history which is full of blemishes, none worse than the events of the 1930s and the '40s.

At the same time, my eternal gratitude goes out to my new country, America, and its wonderful people. I'm grateful to this country for accepting me without conditions. I will never be able to repay an indebtedness I owe to the American people for their supreme sacrifice so that I and so many others may live. My heart is filled with gratitude and sorrow as I think of the over ten thousand American and Allied soldiers who died during the first hours of the Normandy invasion, and the many thousands more before the end of the war. The Americans who came from thousands of miles, leaving their homes and families in a peaceful, unthreatened country, deserve the most credit. They did not fight for themselves. They fought against tyranny and for the freedom of all mankind. The glory belongs to them and to those who fought and died for humanity, and not to any who followed the banners of evil.

* * *

You noticed, I'm sure, the four-line verse written in Hungarian on the cover-leaf. It is a thought which came to me shortly after I started writing this account. Here it is again with translation:

**Nem tudom hol alusztok,**

**Nem tudom hol haltatok meg,**

**Tudom menyit szenvedtetek,**

**Emlékeid örökre szivemben van.**


*I know not where you sleep,*
*I know not where you died,*
*I know how you suffered,*
*Your memory is in my heart forever.*

\* \* \*

I still strongly believe in the theory of God's Big Book, and shave every day.

\* \* \*

Should auld acquaintance be forgot...

# PHOTOGRAPHS & CORRESPONDENCE

The postcards and letters are translated to the best of my ability. In some instances, the fading of the originals and the difficulty of reading the handwriting, added to my limited retention of the Hungarian language, resulted in untranslated text indicated by dots or blank spaces. In all instances I tried to stay as close to a literal translation as possible, hoping to retain the flavor of the originals.

The photographs on the following pages provide glimpses into my and my family's life till the day I was inducted into the Hungarian Labor Service (page 290). The correspondence following these pictures rounds out the events from then on, and ends with a page from a book of survivors of the Theresienstadt concentration camp. The two pages of photographs that follow relate to my life after the war, until leaving Europe in December of 1946.

(The originals of these photographs, letters, and postcards are available for scholars and researchers at the United States Holocaust Memorial Museum, Washington, DC.)

Your Grandparents, early 1920s

*Top left:* Mom and me inside Bikoly house; *top right:* Backside of Bikoly house; *right center:* Remaining detail of Bikoly house; *bottom right:* In front of Bikoly house; *left center:* Chapel detail.

*Top:* Our house on Eszterházy Street, 1993;
*bottom:* One of the stoves in the house.

WORLD WAR I

*Top:* My father with his unit; *center:* My father
with friends on a howitzer; *bottom:* My father.

Your Grandparents, wedding portrait

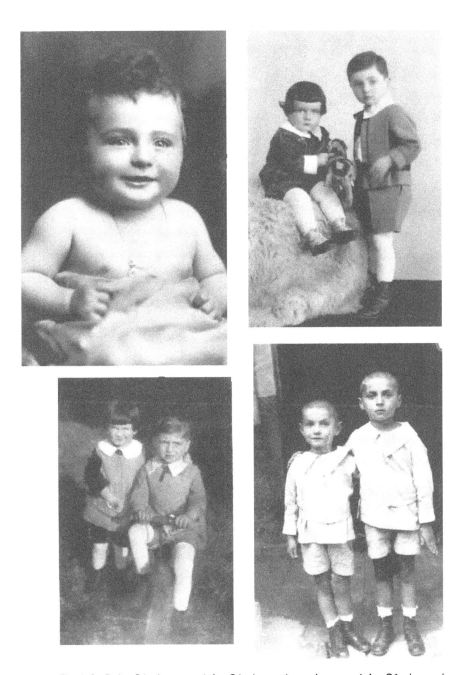

*Top left:* Baby Sándor; *top right:* Sándor and me; *bottom right:* Sándor and me (the "bald haircut" incident); *bottom left:* Sándor on tricycle and me.

My brother and me with Grandmother Kluger

*Top:* Family get-together, Pápa, 1936—Uncle George's visit.
Back row standing, left to right: Cousin János, my father, Uncle
Matthew. I am standing in front of Uncle Matthew.
Left to right, seated: Uncle Miklós, Aunt Alice, Aunt Józsa, Cousin
Imre, Grandmother Kluger, Uncle George, my mother.
Left to right, front row: Cousin Jancsi, my brother Sándor, Cousin Klári
with Baby Ágnes.
*Bottom right:* Vera Neumann—my heartthrob.
*Bottom left:* Me—third-year student at Kollégium.

*Top left:* Rozsa, Jocó, and me with Csipő Lajos; *top right:* Figure skating competition; *bottom right:* Csipő Lajos, my favorite teacher; *bottom left:* "Hockey players." Left to right: Rozsa Miklós, me, Jocó, unknown, and another friend.

*Top:* Bicycle outing—my brother, tallest, in the center (as the photographer, I seldom got into any of the pictures); *right center:* My brother (holding cigarette) with friends, 1942 or 1943; *bottom right:* My brother (one of the first pictures I lit with the lights I made. The lamp and lampshade on the radio are my own make); *left right:* Me, probably 1941–1942.

*Top left:* Jocó—another one of my early photographic masterpieces; *top right:* On a ski trip with Jocó; *bottom right:* Horvát Hajnalka and my brother on a sled with Hajnal's little brother, Bandi, standing behind; *bottom left:* On the ski mountain at Zirc with Jocó.

*Top:* Class picture, 1941 or 1942; *center:* Class picture, 1943; *bottom:* On a school excursion to Budapest with Jocó and a graduate student, our guide.

*Top:* Marching to the "Tornavizsga," 1943. The fellow with the most medals is me; *left center:* "Tornavizsga" fencing team. I am fourth from left; *bottom:* Vitéz Kovács Lajos—my fencing master, phys ed teacher, and mentor.

*Top left:* My father, at left, the last time in uniform, in labor service,
1942 or 1943; *left and right center:* Two family snapshots, 1942 or 1943;
*bottom:* My mother recuperating at home after her surgery.

Photo taken in July 1944 after being inducted into Hungarian
Labor Service at Kőszeg

# CORRESPONDENCE: POSTCARDS & LETTERS—1944

## POSTCARD #1

COMMENT: Possibly the first card from my mother
(not complete)

June 21, 1944

My dear son Bandi!

We still don't know anything, but perhaps this card will reach you, so at least you'll hear something from us. Here at home we are all well, my child, and all our thoughts are with you, hoping that you are in good health and that we could hear from you. We are hoping very hard to know about you; we received a card from Sándor on Monday, he was asking about you and asked for your address. — [...] Your good deed, sharing your things from home, was gratifying to me and your father; this is the kind of deed, my dear little son, that men don't forget. I imagine your little goods from home are gone? — [...] Here it is constantly raining, surely there also, be sure to dress so as not to get drenched and get a cold! — [...] Your question regarding the work you couldn't finish, it is still not finished; I'm not sure Klári will be able to do it. Sanyika [?] goes to work at [...] carrying out your plan, he is very proud of you! Sends kisses. Iván, Bata work in the garden and come home at night. I will now write to Sándor also. The good God be with you, my dear child, and think of us often.

Together with your father, our hugs and kisses,

your loving mother

## POSTCARD #2

COMMENT: Card from my mother
(not complete)

June 23, 1944

My dear Bandi!

I don't know if you received the postcard I wrote you this past week? We have no information from as far as I can tell, but I'm writing. We are all right, my son, and I know it reassures you to know this of us; we think of you a lot and it seems that you left us a long time ago, but both of you are on our minds every minute. Repeatedly I only ask you two take care of yourselves and your health. Regretfully, the tailor did not finish your suit; perhaps you can do without it? I wished you had your warm clothing with you. We would be very glad if we could only hear something from you, my child, but waiting patiently in hopes that you are well and have no problems.

We kiss your freckle-faced picture, your loving parents

*Obverse side:* Unreadable, possibly from someone else in the family.

## POSTCARD #3

COMMENT: First card from my father
(not complete)

June 23, 1944

My beloved son Bandi!

Your mother will probably write sometime also, but I also wish to write. You know that I accepted a position; now as I have the time, I also write. The postal service did not behave well. Little m— [...] came from you [...] since nothing came from you but from others either. I am very curious about where and what sort of [...] did you get [...] for the purpose of mail and package sending organization [...] if the opportunity presents itself, report in detail about this. I call your attention to live very carefully with your clothing as well as [...] food and money. I know that this would happen by your own decision, my son, it comforts me to be able to give you advice [...] No doubt [...] my acquaintances [...] send regards [...] and I send my friends my regards [...]

[...] Here at home we are all right, for the moment there are no changes. Uncle Miklós will write you also, Alice néni told me yesterday. [...] I would be very happy [...] would get from you, particularly the good news. Continue behaving in a manly manner, as until now.

With many kisses and hugs

your father

## LETTER #1, page 1

COMMENT: Possibly the first letter from my mother

June 1944

My dear little bug, my Bandi!

I don't know if you are still at Kőszeg, but I'll try to get this letter and this little package to you. It isn't much, but it makes me feel good to think that you are getting a few pieces of home. (One piece of Bishop Bread, cc 30 Pogácsa, one piece of salami, and some shelled walnuts.) Enjoy, my life, with your usual appetite. I'll be sending you money, will tell you how much later. — We haven't heard anything from you for a very long time and count the days, hoping to receive a few lines from you. — A lot has happened since you went away, one day this, the next day that; the new inductees will fill you in about the news in Pápa, but we are as always and don't hope for anything else from the good God but to stay together and hear from you and your brother now and then that you are well. — Do not upset yourself over us, the good God will help us. You just stand erect in honor, wherever fate puts you, and never, not even for a blink of an eye, forget what I with your father

*Continued*

Drága Bédácam Baudikám! Ugau azt sem tudom
Mónegen ragtok-e még, de mégis megpróbálom eljutni
uj hozzád ezt a levelet meg ezt a kis szomagot nem sok
az egész, de bekem mégis igen jók esik a tudat hogy pár
daraб kis kacsit kephatten (1 drb püspök kenyer körül
belül 30 pogácsa 1drb saláni kis pucolt dió) fogadd el
életem a Válad megszokott jo étvággyal. Pénzt is küldünk maga
utólag bairom mennyit — Igen hosszu az idő hogy nem
hallunk Rólatok semit és néwolyitt a napokat hogy jönne
még pár sor irás Tőletele. — Azóta sok minden törtent
mióta elmentel, egik nap-on másike nap az, majd a
bevonulók elmondják a pápai hirelket, de kulönben
ragunk egformán és nem is alkamulla jó?. Lott
most, csak egyutt maradni és niho hirt kapni
Tőletek hogy egeségesek nagytok, — Ne igasatok
magatok miáttunk, majd minket is megsegit a jó?.
Ti csak áljatok meg rendeseu becsületesen a helyete
a hona a sors állitott benneteket és soha egy pillanat
se veszejtetek el, amire én apátokkal egyutt

## LETTER #1, page 2

taught you, always stay on the straight and true road. I'm writing the same to Sándor. And one other thing! Always be loving brothers, help each other, as the situation demands, if that is the way it will be, and I know it will be that way for us that will be worth knowing more than anything else. I know that you are our true, good children and even if we won't be with you, you will behave as if we could see you, and this knowledge will give us strength for all eventualities! —

Here in the family everybody is well, everybody does their part; I cook and just now am getting used to the customs here, otherwise the communal life [?] is big, all of us try to help others as we can in harmony. — I am much saddened by the news about my sisters; to start with, Ilonka néni this past Saturday was taken away to Sárvár. We have no information about Jolán néni besides that they were taken away from Győr; she wrote ten days ago for the last time. Got a card from Marci

*Continued*

tanítólabrell ljamételi maradjatok mindig az igaz
egyenes úton. Ezt írom mert Sándoromnal is, — és
még egyet legyetek továbbra is szerető jó testvérek
segítsétek egymást amikor erre szükség lesz, ha ez
így lesz, és tudom hogy ez így lesz, nekünk ez mindennél
többet ér. — Tudom hogy igazán jó gyerekeink vagytok
és ha nem is vagyunk mellettetek, úgy viselkedtek
mintha mi itt lennénk és a tudat add nekünk
erőt sok minden elviseléséhez! —

A családban mindenki jól van, mindenki végzi
rendesen kötelességét, én főzök és már most kezdem
megszokni az itteni szokásokat, egy elthenti magáz
őszhaug — összetartás igyeknük egyik a másiknak
segíteni amiben tud. — bár a negyik testvéreimre
vagyok nagyon szomorú, kezdem houka úenielcen
őket múlt szombaton sán árro vittél Jolánékhoz
semmi hírünk, csak azt tudjuk gyorból elvettéle őket
azóta 10 napja írt utoljára, Marci nem írt egy

## LETTER #1, page 3

today, the poor boy is asking for cigarettes; we are going to try to send him some, so you can imagine, my child, my thinking of them, hoping that the good God will help the poor souls. Aside from all this, all my thoughts are with you two, we talk about you a lot. I'm sorry that your suit cannot be finished, the tailor brought it back without having touched it; do not count on this, my son. Is everything all right with you, my son? Have you done laundry yet? Continue being clean as circumstances permit it; when you get permission write everything; let us know if you received this letter and the package.

I won't write any more now because I want to write to my Sándor. The good God be with you, my little son, and think of us always,

your loving mother, with kisses

lapot, dohan cigarétát két szegény, megprobáltunk küldeni neki, hát gondolhatod fiam mit érzek végettük a
jó I. legyen veletek és segitse szegény életet. - tron kinn
minden gondolatom veletek van sokat emlegetünk Benne-
tek, a ruhát vajnos nem lehet megcsináltatni, mert ha
hozta ez is anélkül hogy hozzá nyult volna, erre nem
rajuts fiam most már. hássminden rendben van-e
fiam? mosatál man? csak tiszta légy, mindig a lehetőség
szerint, ha majd engedélyezve lesz az irás irj meg,
dent, azt is meghaptad-e az a levelet csomagol?
nincs nem is irok többet mert Sándoroknak is irok még.
A jó I. legyen veled kis fiam és gondolj ránk sokat,
szerető nokolo? itujaid

## POSTCARD #4

COMMENT: The last card from my mother

July 2, 1944

My dear child:

I write quickly as we are packing and getting ready for a trip, I don't know where. We are at peace with our fate, my son. Do not get upset over us and continue being our good child and you will see that the good God will help us. Continue maintaining contact with our Sándor and as soon as possible we'll write also. Till then, if possible, write to Uncle Miklós and ask him for whatever you might need. Keep your things in good order and do not allow them to become disorganized. Our Sándor wrote us before we left Bástya St. He is working in his profession. Write him, my little son, he would be very happy hearing from you. God be with you, my little son, our blessings will follow both of you.

With our love forever, your parents

Sunday, July 2, 1944

P. S. Since Thursday, we are in the fertilizer factory.

## POSTCARD #5

COMMENT: First and only card from Uncle Miklós
the day my parents were taken away
(not complete)

July 2, 1944

Dear Bandi,

We received your letter today and are glad to hear that you are getting on all right and are happy with your situation. It is very smart to maintain a sense of humor. Under the circumstances we are also well, though for the past couple of days I have been in bed [...] The parents of Horkay András left on a trip today without future address with the entire family. Horkay's letter did not get to them. Whatever it is you might need, write. All the best for the future, with love [...]

Uncle Miklós

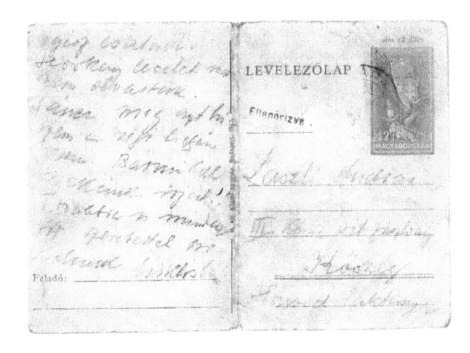

**POSTCARD #6**

COMMENT: Card from Aunt Alice to Zsibó
(not complete)

July 24, 1944

My dear Bandi,

I was just informed by Jocó that you wrote and told him we were not here. I don't understand, as I have written you two letters to Kőszeg.

Write without concern as we are at home, let us know if you need anything and if possible will gladly send it [...] I'm glad you are well, be careful of your health as it is dear, and write often in detail as it gives us joy when we get news from you two. Unfortunately there is no news of the others since they left. Uncle Miklós was operated on again three weeks ago, but, thank God, he is all right now. Jancsi misses you very much, the poor child is without companionship. Jocó is preparing to take a trip to where you are and if it would be possible to meet with you during his trip [...]

Perhaps it might be possible to send you a package, and I would be glad to send you a little thing from home I hope often. I will try to send you the photographs, but I don't know where the photo album is. Take care of yourself, my dear, as we are propped up by the possibility of your return and all of us being together again.

[...] Our hugs with lots of love, your Aunt Alice, Uncle Miklós, and Jancsi

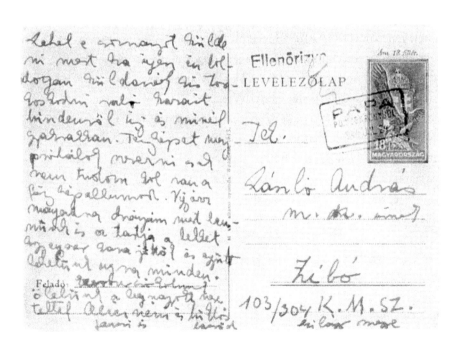

## POSTCARD #7

COMMENT: Card from Sándor to Zsibó
(not complete)

S. hely [Szombathely], 1944 VII 24 [July 24, 1944]

My dear Brother Bandi,

I have been waiting for your letter very hard as I've written you to Kőszeg, but you left there the same day. I am very sorry that I couldn't see you at the train station. I've been inquiring a lot about where you are. I have a lot to tell you. Unfortunately, I have no information about our parents; I have heard that they were at Kassa, but I don't know where they are now. I've not received any information from them; if I do, I will immediately let you know. Uncle Miklós and family are at home and I am in constant communication with them. Uncle Miklós was operated on again, but I believe he is all right. Uncle Jancsi was thoroughly forced out of his new apartment in twenty-four hours, all their things [...] but again they are in their old apartment. I received a [...] from them and from Uncle Matyi a storm coat [which I gave to a friend?]. Is your [...] satisfactory? What sort of a raincoat and [...] blanket do you have? I have two photographs of our dear parents, I'm sending one to Jocó. It is possible that Jocó will come to Szombathely to visit one of his old school friends, Horkay! I'm happy about you working in a shop, at least you can use your skills. I can't do this as we have no shop. [?] I hope that everyone from Pápa are together. My warmest regards to Dénes and all acquaintances. Rosenberg Jancsi and Pollák Sanyi send regards. Write as soon as possible, unfortunately we can only correspond with ourselves and I will also write you. I hope I accounted about everything, take good care of yourself. With kisses, your loving brother

*Written in the margin:*
Please let me know if you have a Fiegelstock Vilmos from Zalaegerszeg. [...] write. His future son-in-law is here with me.

*Note:* By this time I was at Zsibó, and though I didn't know it then, my mother and many in my family must have been dead.

## POSTCARD #8

COMMENT: Card from Aunt Alice to Zsibó
(not complete)


August 3 [?], 1944

My dear Bandi,

No news came for some days from you or from your brother, which troubles
me. Unfortunately there is no news of Laci and the others, as they are
definitely not at the previously indicated place. If I send a clothes package to
Dénes, I will pack it the same way as yours and will send a precise inventory
of everything I put in the package including the photograph [...] he will be
happy about that.

    We are well, all [...] we love best [...] to receive letters from both of you.
Aunt Margaret and Matyi are well, Uncle Matyi still goes to his office Aunt
Irene is at home; the Darvases suffered the same fate as those in Pápa, I have
no news of them whatsoever. Let me know immediately when the package
arrives in good shape.

Together with Uncle Miklós and Jancsi, I hug and kiss you,

Aunt Alice

If you need anything, write.

*Above the text:*
Today Fleisher Mihály and [...] they took his family away.

LEVELEZŐLAP

Ellenőrizve

Tel.

László András
103/304 K. M. SZ.

Zsibó

Szilágy megye.

Feladó:

**POSTCARD #9**

COMMENT: Card from Sándor to Zsibó
(not complete)

S. hely [Szombathely], 1944 Aug 8, 20h [8 p.m.]

My dear brother Bandi!

I can't describe my happiness when I received your card a half an hour ago. Perhaps the good God will grant some real news, as the news we are getting is regretfully not true and cannot be confirmed. If you have any true news, write immediately. I read your detailed account with reassuring feeling. Aunt Alice and hers are well, Uncle Miklós goes to his shop again, the news I received from them. Did you also hear from the [...]? Aunt Manci and hers six weeks ago were bombed, fortunately they weren't hurt, but since then they have only the clothes on their backs. I had some kind of a little stomach poisoning, but, thank God, I'm completely healthy. I am very happy that you've gotten very strong, eat [...] and the work will also help develop your strength, I'm doing the same thing. My greetings to Kardos Dénes, his relative Hajdu László is here. Furthermore, inquire if Feigelstock Miklós from Zegerszeg [Zalaegerszeg] is there as my best friend's future father-in-law [...] Who are with you [...] from Sárvár, my friend Kohlman Imre would like to know? Write quickly, I believe you'll be receiving a letter from Horkay Sanyi!

Take care of yourself, with hugs, kisses, your loving brother, Sándor

*Written in the margin:*
Weitner and Bachrach are supposedly in Pest somewhere.

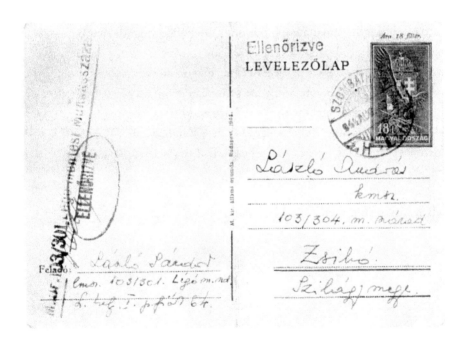

## POSTCARD #10

COMMENT: Card from Sándor to Zsibó
(not complete)

S. hely [Szombathely], 1944 VIII 27 [August 27, 1944]

My dear Bandi!

Your cards, which originated on the fourth and the seventeenth, came
in together. There is still no definite news about our dear parents. There
is a lot of bad news we hear, which is not at all certain. For instance, I
have heard that they are in the vicinity of Kassa, or that the exempted
ones will be brought back, etc. Otherwise, I am well, having forgotten
a little unpleasantness which caused a two-week-long sickness. That
is to say, I caught a small lymph poisoning, impetigo vulgaria, but by
now even the trace is vaguely visible. We are moving from our district
to another one in the same place. In case you go away from your
present billet, immediately notify me so we can maintain our contact.
I'm in continuous contact with Aunt Alice and hers; according to her,
Uncle Miklós is completely healthy. My dear Bandi, when you write
me, always mark the date of my last card. Did you receive our parents'
picture? Sándor will send it.

Many kisses, your loving brother, Sándor

## LETTER #2, page 1

COMMENT: Letter from Sándor. Written as though from a friend. Possibly smuggled to circumvent censors.

Sz. hely [Szombathely], 1944 VIII 28 [August 28, 1944], 21h [9 p.m.]

My dear friend, András!

I finally have some time to write you. I hope this will find you. I hope you'll receive the enclosed photograph as I'm sending it in accordance with my friend Sándor's wishes. I received cigarettes from Aunt Alice; it came in the nick of time and I am carefully rationing it, though it will quickly be gone. I am in a fortunate position to often receive mail from them. I am glad you are well equipped. Sándor just now had his boots repaired and resoled, and I believe he will have his long, white pants dyed. What's with Jocó? I don't believe his [...] will permit him to summer in Kolozsvár. Does he write you? Sándor and his company are working here locally. They are working in the local ghetto, inventorying the left-behind Jewish personal possessions. They tell me their food is good and plentiful; my friend looks good, having put on five kilograms. He had to send the cap yesterday [?] [...]

*Continued*

Sz. hely. 1944. VIII. 28. 21h.

Kedves Barátom András!
Végre van időm és írhatok Neked.
Remélem még ott talál levelem. Ugyanis
nevetném, ha a mellékelt fényképet
megkapnád mert, Sándort barátom
kívánságára küldöm el. Aliz nénitől
kaptam cigarettát, igen jól jött, bár nagy
beosztással élek vele, hamar elfogy.
Általában abban a szerencsés helyzet-
ben vagyok, hogy még gyakran kapok tőlük
levelet is. Örülök hogy jól vagy
felszerelve. Sándort is most fejeltette
és talpaltatta meg bakkancsát, és azt
kérem megfogja festetni a fehér
len hosszúnadrágját is.
Mi van ~~Bocóval~~. Nem hiszem, hogy
beosztása megengedi, hogy Kolozsvárra
menjen nyaralni. Írhatott Neked Toni?
Sándorék itt dolgoznak helyben. A volt
gettóban dolgoznak, a zsidóvagyonok
leltározásánál. Azt mondják, kosztjuk
is jó és bőséges, barátom jól néz ki
már vagy öt kilót hízott. A tagsági
tegnap szállott nekik kiadni.

## LETTER #2, page 2

And what are you doing, dear András? Aunt Manci's address is the old one; as you no doubt know, they were bombed out of their new house. All they had was buried under the ruins. Aside from their lives, they have only the clothes they were wearing. But thank God! Try to get Uncle Matyi's address from Aunt Manci. I don't know it exactly.

I won't write more now, I want to go to bed as it is late and last night I slept very little because of an air raid. Incidentally, I'm also in air raid rescue. Thank God, so far there was no need for this kind of assignment.

Write, the quicker, the better, along with your friends

my greetings and love

your true friend

Sándor

Hát Ti mit csináltok, kedves Sándor?
A Illési néniék címe a régi, mert való-
színű tudod a régi lakásukból kimen-
kibombáztak őket. Mindenük a romok
alatt volt, és puszta életükön kívül
csak arra maradt meg, ami éppen
rajtuk volt. De hála Isten!
Illető kiscsaládt) cimét pedig rádend
meg Illési néniéktől! Én pontosan
nem tudom.
Most már többet nem írok, le akarok
feküdni mert késő van és tegnap éjjel
keveset aludtam, a riadó miatt. Tudni-
illik nekem is légó beontásom van.
De hála Isten eddig még nem került
sor ily munkára.
Írjál minél hamarabb, leveleiddel
együtt

szeretettel üdvözöl
igaz barátod
Sándor

**LETTER #3, page 1**

COMMENT: Letter from Aunt Alice

[Late summer 1944]

My dear Bandi,

I'm glad you received the pictures. I'll send [or would send] new ones, unfortunately I have no other pictures of us. The news that they are around Kassa is in error, as they are not there, this I [...] Only God knows where they are. We are hoping to get mail or news of the poor people, but it doesn't seem to come. Sándor didn't write for some days, I don't know if he is still where he was, the last he wrote they were moving and I don't know if they stayed or went away. I just now I am writing there. I received Dénes's letter and bought the requested things from the tailor. The tenant was no longer there and he sold it to Ilona, but there is a coat which I bought and will send it tomorrow. I went to Tomás for pictures; he tells me he has no picture, that they took them with them. So I don't know what I should do, perhaps I should turn to Uncle Vili and perhaps I won't send the clothes package immediately, will send you the pictures separately and will forward it to Dénes. I hope, my Bandi, that you continue to be well and don't need anything, it is so good to know that you are well. We are fairly

*Continued*

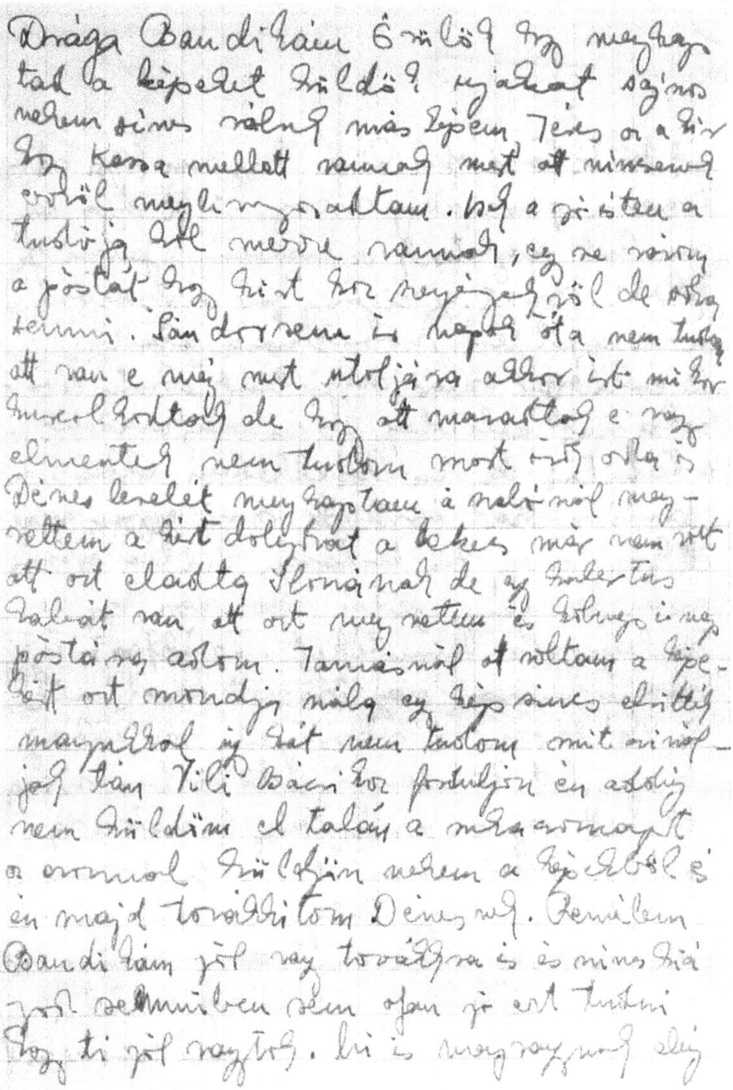

Drága Bandikám Örülök hogy megkaptad a képeket küldök újakat sajnos
nekem sincs [illegible] más képem Terus s a kis
hogy Kassa mellett vannak mert ott mindenük-
ről [illegible]. [illegible] a [illegible] a
[illegible] [illegible] merre vannak, ez se [illegible]
a postát hogy kint [illegible] [illegible] jól de [illegible]
[illegible]. Sándoréknak is [illegible] óta nem tudj-
ott van e még mert utoljára akkor írt mikor
[illegible] de hogy ott maradtak e vagy
elmentek nem tudom most írok oda is
Dénes levelét megkaptam a [illegible] megvettem a kért dolgokat a [illegible] már nem volt
ott az [illegible] [illegible] de egy [illegible]
[illegible] van ott ott megvettem és holnap is meg
postára adom. Tamásnál ott voltam a képeket ott mondja nála egy kép sincs [illegible]
magukról így hát nem tudom mit csinál-
jak kám Vili bácsi hoz [illegible] és addig
nem küldöm el talán a [illegible]
a [illegible] küldjön nekem a képekből s
én majd továbbítom Dénesnek. Remélem
Bandikám jól vagy továbbra is és minden [illegible]
[illegible] [illegible] [illegible] [illegible] jó [illegible] tudni
hogy ti jól vagytok. Mi is megvagyunk elég

## LETTER #3, page 2

well, Uncle Miklós is very fat, you won't recognize him, as he hardly moves and has a good appetite the results are obvious. Jancsi is as black as a Gypsy, goes to the Strand [...] the only [...]

The yearbook came out; I wrote to the school; supposedly, the teaching will start on the twenty-fifth, but I doubt it. Jancsi wanted to write also, but he is not home and he is a little lazy; unfortunately writing is not his virtue, though no days go by without repeatedly mentioning you. Continue to write. It brings us tremendous happiness and write if you need anything. In the meantime, the recommended package I sent was regretfully returned to my great sorrow. My greetings to Dénes, and ask that [...] immediately [...] so I would know what to do and I'll gladly take care of whatever.

I hug and kiss you,

your loving Aunt Alice

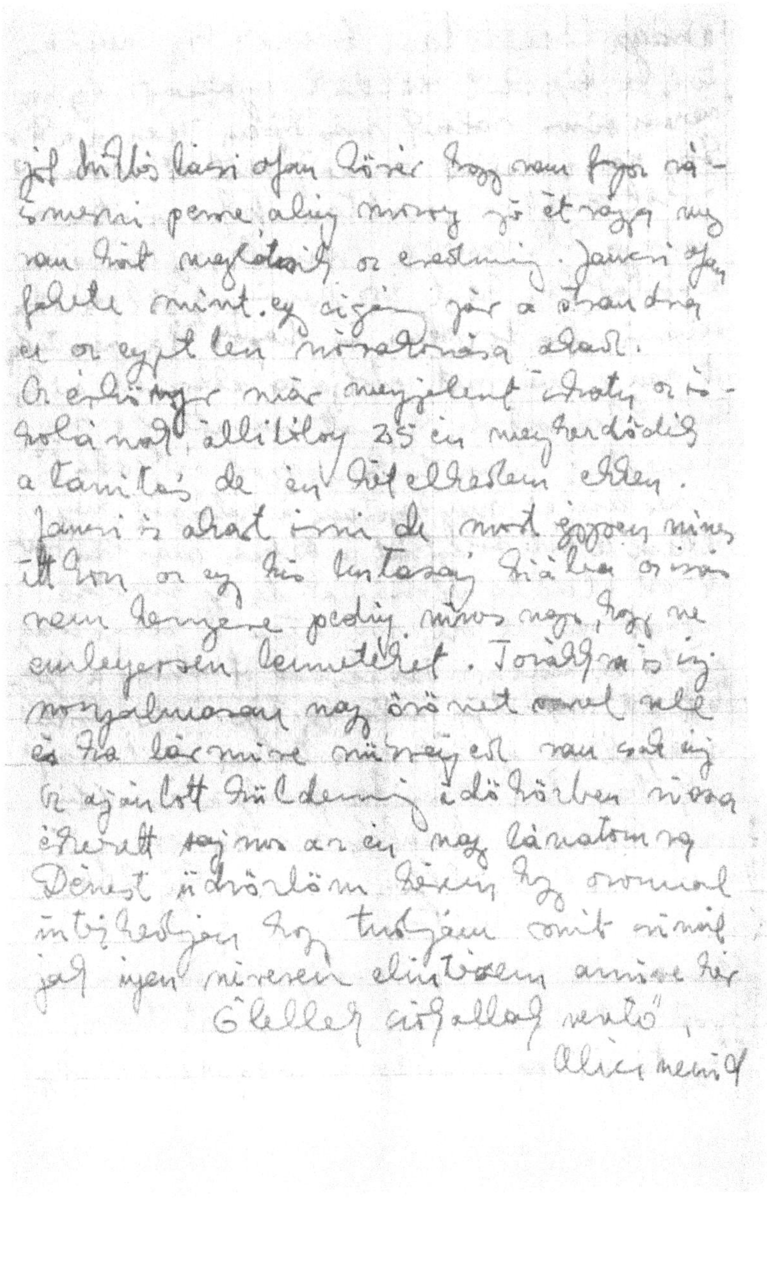

## LETTER #4, page 1

COMMENT: Letter from Aunt Alice

[Fall 1944]

My dear Bandi,

I hope you received to your hand the winter stuff, though I hope that you will be coming home in good health by then, I wish it was so. Unfortunately, your parents didn't leave anything with me and I can only send a few items. I was unable to locate wool socks, we don't have a single pair as we never needed such a thing, but if in the meantime I could find some, I'll be sending them separately. I am afraid that the pants will probably be short, but I was unable to get anything else, perhaps [...] What else would you need, write and if possible I'll send it. I hope you received the registered things, till now it wasn't returned, I'll send money and [...] in it. I'm afraid to put food [...]

*Continued*

Drága Bandikám!

Remélem kézhez kaptad a téli holmit bár azt remélem addigra egészségesen haza jöttök bár úgy lenne. Sajnos a szüleid semmit nem hagytak nálam így csak egy pár holmit tudok küldeni képtelen voltam egy gyapjú kamásnit szerezni nektek egy sínes kis tudtok ugyanis mire tovább nem volt szükség nálunk de ha időközben sok teletek rá külön elküldöm. Félek a nadrág rövid lesz sajnos mást nem tudtam szerezni akkor rágyártsd föl a lábszárvédőt így fűzött hoz-zátok. Kire volna még szükségetek írjátok meg úgy ha lehetőség van rá elküldöm. Azt remélem az ajánlott küldeményt megkaptad mert mind-ezideig nem jött vissza pengét és auto-ment fogport is küldtem benne. Nem merek ebbe a csomagba élelmiszert

## LETTER #4, page 2

in this package as I worry that you won't get it and you didn't write if you can get some foods from home, or just clothing. I hope you are in good health and you bear the labor camp stramm [sturdy, tough]. Sándor didn't write in several days, I'll also be writing him today. Sorry that we know nothing of Horkay's parents; the news, Dénes's uncle wrote, is wrong, they say they aren't there, we did write Dénes's uncle, but he didn't reply. This uncertainty is terrible, Uncle Matyi is trying to move everything to find out something without any success. Continue to write, my dear Bandi, it causes us such pleasure, and if it is possible to receive foodstuff packages, let us know immediately, and if you need anything else just ask without reservation. Uncle Miklós is all right now, though very [?] putting on weight as he can't move much. I can't convince Jancsi, he has always been a lazy writer, but always says that he sends regards and can't wait till you come home [...]

*Continued*

tunni attól félek akkor nem kapod
meg pedig ej de mineven Mildenik
valamit fordit nem irtas a levelbe
kifet-e sок mihát irtáf. Remélem eyй
fejes roy és tovább is strammal rolg
el a mineratálort. Sándor napod óta
nem irt ma nog nehi is beelef. Sajno
Horrai mülciról semmit nem hustog
or a tir amit Dénes nagláss jg irt
tejes ort mondjag ott minenel ejet
ekent irhug Dénes ház jginat és nem
is rálamolt, retteneto er a li noytalg
pay pedig hatyi hicri is mindent mey
moryst valamit meytudni röluj
és semmi nem rikünl. Ing dragg
Bandikám toválgra is ofan Brömat
ahrol vele és ha lehet élelminer
vommayet Mildeni orommal egfeito
és ha lärmi tellene esal tey batrau.
Millös lásì mär jöl van sal igen tirig
ty tveret moroghat jancrik van tnolog
navenni ty ingon lusta író volt mindig
ort mondja ardollat és alig xinja ty hava

## LETTER #4, page 3

He misses you a lot. He diligently helps out in the shop waiting on customers, but only in the morning; in the afternoon he goes to the Strand. It is true, he was very sick just now for a couple of days with inflamed tonsils, high fever, but, thank God he is well now. I put the following items in the package:

| | |
|---|---|
| 1 pc. Black Coat | 1 pr. Gloves |
| 1 Vest | 1 Spare battery |
| 1 Pants, brown | 1 Flashlight |
| 1 Knitted vest | 1 package [...] |

The coat lining is not in the best of shape, but I don't think you have to be a fashion plate there.

We kiss and hug you with

the greatest of love

Aunt Alice, Miklós, and Jancsi

LANG JENÖ, * 26. 6. 1892 — Subotica.
LANG JOSEF, * 28. 11. 1916 — Krosno.
LANG MARGARETE, * 17. 8. 1923 — Göncz.
LANG MARGIT, * 10. 1. 1903 — Gyor.
LANG MORDCHA, * 1. 6. 1921 — Krasnik.
LANG OLGA, * 4. 3. 1906 — Bratislava.
LANG PETR, * 21. 8. 1924 — Praha.
LANG SÁRI, * 12. 10. 1917 — Vác.
LANG SIMON, * 1. 6. 1910 — Szmigrud.
LANG SZOLIM, * 19. 6. 1912 — Chodel.
LANGE JAKOB, * 6. 6. 1899 — Warszawa.
LANGER ELUKIM, * 31. 12. 1912 — Bielitz.
LANGER HERSCH, * 30. 9. 1915 — Jilza.
LANGER MIECZYSLAV, * 18. 6. 1927 — Kraków.
LANGER MOSES, * 8. 4. 1914 — Štučin.
LANGER OSKAR, * 29. 3. 1924 — Wadowic.
LANGER OSKAR, * 29. 3. 1926 — Wadowic.
LANGER SALOMON, 3. 10. 1914 — Jaworzno.
LANGER VILÉM, * 10. 5. 1915 — Plzeń.
LANGERMANN JOZSA, * 23. 7. 1906 — Pusterzebel.
LANGFELD DORA, * 5. 6. 1920 — Potor.
LANGFELD LAURA, * 15. 9. 1915 — Márosvásárhely.
LANGFUSS CHAIM, * 27. 4. 1921 — Lodź.
LANGNAS MOSES, * 15. 7. 1920 — Wieruschow.
LANGNAS SCHMUL, * 1. 3. 1919 — Wieruschow.
LANGSAM ABRAHAM, * 14. 8. 1913 — Myslenice.
LANGSAM JOZI, * 1. 2. 1931 — Zamoly.
LANGSAM PINKAS, * 2. 8. 1907 — Rymanow.
LÁNYI NIKOLAUS, * 23. 2. 1909 — Budapest.
LANYI OLGA, * 12. 10. 1928 — Budapest.
LANZSMAN LEIBE, * 7. 2. 1911 — Kaunas.

LAPIDES MARTA, * 29. 12. 1922 — Radom.
LAPIDUSZ MAIER, * 10. 2. 1926 — Osmiana.
LASAR ERNÖ, * 24. 12. 1924 — Budapest.
LASAR REGINA, * 22. 9. 1925 — Wlole.
LASAROWITS ROSA, * 7. 1. 1905 — Cluj.
LASAROWITS TIBOR, * 28. 1. 1931 — Szadalmäs.
LASKAR YVETTE, * 12. 10. 1928 — Marseille.
LASOHER HERMANN, 19. 10. 1916. Schaulen.
LASLO ADAM, * 17. 12. 1892 — Budapest.
LASLO ELISABETH, * 12. 3. 1885 — Szeged.
LASMAN HELLA, * 5. 3. 1923 — Lódź.
LASORAŽKY HEINRICH, * 17. 5. 1914 — Lódź.
LASSANYI ELISABETH, * 22. 1. 1905 — Jaszopati.
LASSMAN BARUCH SZMUL, * 15. 10. 1916 — Piotrków.
LASSMANN BRONISLAVA, * 1. 9. 1917 — Lódź.
LÁSZLÓ ANDRÁS, * 12. 1. 1926 — Pápa.
LASZLOFY ELISABETH, * 26. 8. 1912 — Satoraljaujhely.
LASZCZOVER BENJAMIN, * 21. 5. 1906 — Rzeszow.
LAUDON EMIL, * 1. 10. 1921 — Szarki.
LAUFER ARNOLD, Dr., * 22. 10. 1889 — Beograd.
LAUFER ICEK, * 17. 11. 1924 — Rujec.
LAUFER ILONA, * 28. 5. 1904 — Gyongkösä.
LAUFER ISRAEL, * 11. 3. 1929 — Bustya Haza.
LAUFER KLÁRA, * 14. 10. 1900 — Budapest.
LAUFEROVÁ BETTY, * 7. 3. 1900 — Praha.
LASSANY ROSSIKA, * 13. 8. 1892 — Szolnok.
LASZLO ISTVAN, * 11. 3. 1909 — Pécs.
LÁSZLÓ LÁSZLO, * 12. 7. 1891 — Pápa.
LAUB JAKOB, * 3. 9. 1924 — Chropacov.
LAUBER ERNA, * 12. 12. 1930 — Bethlen.

*19                                          291

*From the Theresienstadt archives:* Page 291 from the book *List of Hungarians Brought on Transports of Death Who Survived* (I checked my father's and my names. The other Lászlós listed are not related.)

# PHOTOGRAPHS:
# POST WAR — 1945 – 1946

*Top left:* The elder Sinkós, Juliska néni and Jóska bácsi; *top right:* Jocó, 1945; *bottom right:* Horvát Hajnalka, 1945; *bottom left:* Juliska néni with Big Jocó, my friend's older brother, 1945.

*Top:* Visiting Mauthausen concentration camp; *second row, left:* A man of leisure, Germany 1946; *second row, right:* Swimming in the Danube, Summer 1946. The fellow at the top ready to dive is me; *third row:* On my motorbike with a friend at the displaced persons camp in Ulm, Germany, 1946. *bottom right:* Ready to leave Germany, Fall 1946.

CPSIA information can be obtained
at www.ICGtesting.com
Printed in the USA
BVHW051605210423
662800BV00014B/1070